The Myths of Greece and Rome

Richard T. Scanlan

Professor of Classics
University of Illinois

 BURGESS INTERNATIONAL GROUP INC
Bellwether Press Division

Copyright © 1986 by Burgess International Group, Inc.,
Bellwether Press Division
ISBN 0-8087-6938-3

Printed in the United States of America.
J I
Address orders to:

Burgess International Group, Inc.
7110 Ohms Lane
Edina, MN 55435
Telephone 612/831-1344
Telex 29-0458

Bellwether Press
A Division of Burgess International Group, Inc.

CONTENTS

Chapters   **Page**

1. Introduction to Myth........................   5

2. Definition of Myth..........................   9

3. Types of Myth...............................   10

4. The Mythic Mind.............................   11

5. Interpretations of Myth.....................   13

6. Cosmology...................................   17

7. Zeus and his Challengers....................   27

8. Zeus the King...............................   33

9. Zeus and Hera...............................   38

10. Poseidon...................................   43

11. Hestia.....................................   48

12. Demeter....................................   50

13. Artemis....................................   54

14. Apollo.....................................   58

15. Athena.....................................   68

16. Ares.......................................   71

17. Aphrodite..................................   74

18. Hephaestus.................................   78

19. Hermes.....................................   80

20. Hades......................................   83

21. Dionysus...................................   89

22. Orpheus....................................   96

23. Heroes and the Heroic......................   99

24. Perseus.. 104

25. Bellerophon.................................... 110

26. Heracles....................................... 115

27. Theseus.. 128

28. The Theban Saga............................... 140

29. Jason and the Argonauts...................... 146

30. A Few Love Stories........................... 156

31. Troy... 166

32. Leading Families in the Trojan War.......... 169

33. Pre-war Events................................ 180

34. The War at Troy.............................. 188

35. The Returns................................... 195

36. The Return of Odysseus...................... 201

37. Aeneas.. 208

38. Rome.. 213

39. Appendix I: Chronology...................... 219

40. Appendix II: Select Bibliography............ 220

41. Selective Index.............................. 222

1. INTRODUCTION TO MYTH

A. Meaning

B. Importance

C. Origin

D. Transmission

Meaning

The etymological meaning of "mythology" is "the study of stories."

> myth = stories
> logy = the study of

The word "mythology" is often used as a synonym for "myth," so we can say the "mythology of Greece" or the "myth of Greece", "Greek mythology" or "Greek myth."

Importance

Myths are as important in the functioning of primitive societies as technological knowledge is for us today. Consider what would happen if the minds of all of our technicians suddenly went blank, if we had no idea how to run the complicated machinery which is such an integral part of our lives. Complete chaos would result and a collapse surely of our civilization as we know it.

Myths explain the relationship of individuals to the gods, to the external world of nature, and to other persons. They take the form of dramatic stories which concentrate on those matters that interest and trouble their creators. Every mythic system -no matter how inconsistent or childish or absurd it may seem to us- offers a way of viewing reality, of making sense out of nature and human life. With the development of Christianity and science, the myths of the Greeks and the Romans slowly lost their appeal as a way of interpreting experience and came to be regarded as incredible, unreal, and superstitious. The moon as a goddess? The sun as a god? A flying horse? Nonsense! The word "myth" came to mean a story or belief that was false, and the negative connotation has continued to the present day. To say in popular usage that something is a myth condemns it as a fiction, although that is clearly not the way we intend to use the word. For us, a myth will indicate a way of perceiving and explaining reality by the society in which it was created. Given this meaning for the word, it is no small compliment to the imagination of the Greeks that their myths continue to relate to us in various and significant ways even though we are so far removed in time from their origination.

Origin

Anthropologists in their study of twentieth century primitive societies have confirmed the prevailing belief that myth-making is an essential function in every early community. Each myth seems to originate with an individual storyteller. It appears as a spontaneous, imaginative response to some important phenomenon or significant event within the society. What is the object we call the sun? Why does it change positions in the sky? And what is the sky? What is the moon? Why does it change its shape? What is thunder? Lightning? Why are the fields fertile sometimes and not at others? Why is it forbidden to enter the forest? What lies beyond the mountains? The mythmaker (perhaps someone comparable to our poets and novelists today) catches in a memorable tale the very essence of some notable experience. A great number of stories may have to be offered before one is created which satisfies the needs of the community. Two or more myths explaining the same phenomenon may even exist simultaneously for a time before one slowly disappears or blends into the other.

Anthropologists tell us that three elements are generally present in a society before the creation of myth occurs.

1. The group is aware of mortality; its members realize that there is an eventual end to human existence.

2. Individuals recognize that the community to which they belong is greater than they are. Each person is one part of a more significant whole.

3. The society develops an awareness of the natural world and begins to question its relationship to the individual's own existence.

Once the above three sensitivities are present, mythmakers are much more likely to be cultivated and their stories to be preserved.

But why do some stories succeed and others fail? Why do some continue to serve the community while others are forgotten? Joseph Campbell in one of his many books on the subject maintains that, if a myth serves the following functions within a society, it is more likely to survive.

1. A myth must produce a sense of wonder.

2. A myth must explain how the world began, i.e., it must be related to other stories which provide the society with an understandable cosmological system.

3. A myth must support the social order in which it is created. Myths do not advocate change; they support the status quo.

4. A myth must provide the individual with psychological or spiritual enrichment, i.e., with a kind of psychic uplift.

Transmission

Myths are at first transmitted orally from generation to generation. Such retelling is important in the story's development since significant changes often occur as it proceeds through time and speaks to succeeding generations. The major kinds of modification can be categorized as follows.

1. Myths are changed as new stories or elements are added. If a god or hero in the original version of the myth has one exciting adventure during a journey, that episode may suggest others to creative story tellers who transmit and elaborate the tale for their generations.

2. A coherence may be seen between two separate narratives which allows them to be joined into one. Such blending is quite common.

3. As societies develop, it happens that their more savage customs are -hopefully- abandoned and replaced by more refined or civilized behavior. Human sacrifice, for example, is often a religious rite found in early communities. As civilization replaces barbarism, an animal sacrifice will often take the place of the human. The myth which accompanied and explained the original ceremony must now be changed to accommodate the new practice. Frequently, as a result, if we wish to discover the original meaning of the myth, we must peel back the layers of cultural refinement. A difficult and speculative task!

The mythmaker, then, not only creates new stories, he adds on to existing ones, he adjusts others to altered conditions, he blends separate entities, and he recites unchanged still others which have been transmitted to him. In a time when there is no writing, the memory of the mythmaker is crucial. It is only he who is able to remember and to relate the many traditional stories which address the society's problems or explain its complicated rituals.

Now that we have seen the function and significance of myth in early societies, we can proceed to a more thorough definition of our subject.

Questions

1. What is the etymological meaning of mythology?

2. Which relationships do myths attempt to explain for each individual?

3. What developments tended to weaken a belief in the truth of ancient myths?

4. What is the popular connotation of myth today? How does it differ from the more technical meaning of the word?

5. How do myths originate?

6. What elements are usually present in a society before myth creation begins?

7. What seem to be the attributes of those myths which survive?

8. What do we mean by blending?

9. How are myths changed by cultural refinement?

10. Why is a good memory especially important for the mythmaker?

2. DEFINITION OF MYTH

"Myth" would not seem to be a difficult word to define, yet almost every person who studies the subject eventually produces his own definition. While there are common elements in the many meanings of the word, there are also dissimilarities and shifts in emphases. Let us begin our quest with a dictionary offering. I have numbered the parts.

A myth is (1) a story (2) that is usually of unknown origin and (3) at least partially traditional (4) that ostensibly relates historical events usually of such a description as (5) to serve to explain some particular belief, institution, or natural phenomenon. (Webster)

We shall next consider the definitions provided by four scholars.

Myths are certain products of the imagination of a people which take the form of stories. (H.J. Rose in **A Handbook of Greek Mythology**)

A myth is a story about gods, other supernatural beings, or heroes of a long past time. (M. Reinhold, **Past and Present**)

Myth is a cognitive structure analogous to language through which primitive people organize their experience. (J. Peradotto, **Classical Mythology**)

Myth is the symbolic form which is generated, shaped and transmitted by the creative imagination of pre- and extra-logical people as they respond to and encapsulate the data of experience. (R.J. Schork, "Classical Mythology," **The Classical Journal,** 1965)

We must, of course, like everyone else, provide our own attempt.

A myth is a traditional story about gods, other supernatural beings, or heroes which supplies a group of images, models, and explanations. The myths of a given society provide a system through which individuals can adjust to the world around them.

Questions

1. Which of the six definitions provided is broadest in its definition? Which is narrowest?

2. Which elements are common to all the definitions?

3. TYPES OF MYTH

Myths are often arranged into three classifications.

1. Pure myth or true myth or myth proper

Myths of this first species tend to be examples of primitive science or religion. They explain natural phenomena or the origin of things, and they describe how individuals should behave toward the gods.

2. Saga or legend

Myths of this variety tend to be examples of primitive history; they contain a germ or seed of historical fact and enlarge upon it with great flourish. A good example of a saga or legend is the story of the war at Troy.

3. Folk-tale or fairy-tale

Myths of the third group tend to be examples of primitive fiction. Tales of this sort are told for pleasure and amusement. Frequently the stories contain supernatural characters such as ghosts, elves, dwarfs, or demons, and they often include elements of magic, e.g., spells, potions, and objects.

Most myths do not fit neatly into a single category; they tend rather to exemplify first one and then another in various parts of the same story.

Questions

Place each of the following into one of the three categories of myth.

Why we offer a lamb once a year as a sacrifice to a god.
Using a special hat to become invisible.
Why the volcano erupts.
The mythic story of the city of Thebes.
Why the moon changes shape.
Wearing wings which allow one to fly.
When struck by this arrow, one falls in love.
How Heracles began the Olympic Games.
How Prometheus stole the fire of the gods and gave it to humans.

4. THE MYTHIC MIND

A. The attitude toward the external world

B. The nature of reality

C. The distinction between the whole and the part

D. Substantialization

E. Cause and effect

There are important differences in ways of thinking between the pre-logical or mythic mind and our own. We shall examine five major contrasts so as to be able better to understand and develop an empathy for the myths which such people create.

1. The attitude toward the external world

For the mythic mind everything outside of the self is alive. There is nothing impersonal or inanimate. Everything possesses a spirit which in turn has a personal relationship with the individual. This association is a reverent one, as the primitive person stands in awe of the powerful forces around him. Such a relationship is sometimes called "I-Thou" to portray its personal and sacred nature.

The logical mind distinguishes between animate and inanimate objects. The new relationship can be called objective or scientific. It is one which exists between subject and object, and it often creates a wide disparity between our perceptions of the world and the theories which we use to explain them. The sun, for example, appears to rise, move through the sky, and set. Our explanation says otherwise. In order to arrive at our scientific answers, we must draw back from the situation and carefully analyze it. Such study is not possible for the primitive person; he gives an immediate and intuitive response. In our move to such abstractions, we have lost as well as gained according to Martin Buber, a noted contemporary philosopher. In his book, **I and Thou,** he maintains that the price we have paid for our objective analysis is a unique awareness of our separateness from nature.

2. The nature of reality

For mythic minds the distinction between what is real and what is unreal is not as sharp as it is for us. We distinguish between the statue and the god being portrayed; for them, the representation **is** the god. We distinguish between the priest and the god whom he serves; for them, the priest is the god incarnate. We distinguish between dreams and day-to-day reality; for them, dreams are more meaningful than life's daily events.

3. The distinction between the whole and the part

For us the whole of anything is the sum of its parts. For the prelogical mind, a part can **be** the whole. What the hand does, the man does; therefore, the hand is the man. To possess a lock of hair from someone, or a piece of clothing, or, best of all, a name, was thought to give one great power over that person, and what one did to the "part," would happen to the "whole" because they are one and the same.

4. Substantialization

The mythic mind thinks in concrete (= substantial) terms, i.e., it uses stories to explain things rather than abstractions. As far as can be determined, people who live when myths are being constructed do not think abstractly but only in specific, concrete ways.

5. Cause and effect

We generally believe that there are a limited number of logical causes for any given effect. In early thought, however, anything can come from anything else. A complete change of state can just happen, if it is so ordained. The extra-logical mind would have no difficulty accepting the transformation of a woman into a tree, a young man into a flower, a hunter into a stag, or a hero into a constellation. These are simply examples of metamorphoses: changes from one form to another; marvelous to behold, but as readily accepted as an egg into a chicken or a caterpillar into a butterfly. The world is full of wonders!

While the Greek myths originated in early times when the thought characteristics described above were present, the versions in which they come down to us are from writers who lived hundreds of years later. These authors —every bit as sophisticated as those of our own time— were using the myths of their society to accomplish various literary purposes. Because the stories represented a common ground which they shared with their audience, they were able more readily to present ideas and emotions through them. We should be aware as we study them that many of the myths have been transmitted to us in a very cultivated form and not as they existed originally.

Questions

1. What are the major differences between the pre-logical and the logical mind? Any common factor among the various contrasts?

2. In what way are the Greek myths which have come down to us different from those originally created?

5. INTERPRETATIONS OF MYTH

A. Ancient theories

    1. Rationalism
    2. Etymological theory
    3. Allegorical theory
    4. Euhemerism

B. Modern theories

    1. Naturalism
    2. Ritualism
    3. Diffusionism
    4. Evolutionism
    5. Freudianism
    6. Jungian archetypes
    7. Structuralism
    8. Historical criticism

Ancient theories

Toward the end of the fifth century B.C. Greek thinkers began to develop various hypotheses to interpret the myths which they had inherited from their ancestors. Many of these narratives were over a thousand years old, and their actual source was lost in the distant past. The Greeks developed four main explanations.

1. Rationalism

According to the rationalistic theory, myths represent an early form of logical thinking: they all -no matter how incredible- have a logical base. For example, the myth of Pegasus, the flying horse, can be explained by imagining the reaction of the first Greeks to see a horse. Compared to the animals they knew, the horse must surely have seemed to fly as it skimmed the ground in a rapid gallop and leaped high obstacles. Or consider the reaction of the first Greeks to see a man riding such an animal. They could easily have thought that the two were one, and so created the centaur.

2. Etymological theory

The etymological theory states that all myths derive from and can be traced back to certain words in the language. The large bulk of stories which surround major mythological figures find their ultimate source in an imaginative use of words by an early mythmaker. Hades, for example, originally meant "unseen" but came eventually to be the name for the god of the dead. Hermes and his stories develop out of the Greek word which meant "messenger."

3. Allegorical theory

In the allegorical explanation all myths contain hidden meanings which the narrative deliberately conceals or encodes. King Midas, for example, is permitted by a god to have whatever he may desire and chooses to have all things turn to gold at his touch. After a brief period of elation, Midas soon discovers the fatal consequences of his choice: his food and drink are likewise susceptible to the golden touch. The King -now a wiser man- returns to the god and with great embarrassment asks that his special power be removed. His request is granted, and Midas is restored to his original state. The allegorists would maintain that the truths represented by the story are those concerning the evil of greed, the value of moderation, and the beauty of life as it is without unnatural embellishment.

The allegorists offered two reasons why stories were used in the first place rather than the a simple statement of the ideas they represented: they interested people who might not listen to emotionless concepts but who could be attracted by imaginative narratives, and they prevented great truths which had been discovered about life from falling into the hands of potential enemies.

4. Euhemerism

Euhemerus, a Greek who lived from 325-275 B.C., maintained that all myths arise from historical events which are merely exaggerated. Those stories which were much more embellished than others resulted in the characters being transformed not just into great heroes with magnificent accomplishments, but into gods. Such an interpretation seems harmless enough to us (and indeed to have considerable substance to it), but it created much trouble for Euhemerus who was condemned as an atheist and sent into exile.

Modern theories

Modern interpretations of myth address two basic questions in their analyses.

(1) Is there a single explanation for the origin of all myths?

(2) How do we account for the many similarities in myths of cultures greatly separated by time and space?

1. Naturalism

In this hypothesis all myths are thought to arise from an attempt to explain natural phenomena. Indeed, some adherents of this interpretation narrow the source even more by arguing that all myths arise from the worship of the sun or the moon.

2. Ritualism

According to this theory, all myths are invented to accompany and explain religious ritual; they describe the significant events which have resulted in a particular ceremony.

3. Diffusionism

The diffusionists maintain that all myths arose in a few major cultural centers and spread throughout the world.

4. Evolutionism

According to this theory, myth-making occurs at a certain stage in the evolution of the human mind. Myths are, therefore, an essential part of all developing societies, and the similarities from one culture to the next can be explained by the relatively limited number of experiences open to such communities when the myths arise.

5. Freudianism

When Sigmund Freud, the founder of modern psychology, interpreted the dreams of his patients, he found great similarities between them and the ancient myths. This discovery led to the development of his theory about the origin of myth. Freud believed that certain infantile or childhood psychic states (fantasies, desires, longings) are repressed, i.e., they are eliminated from the conscious mind, but continue to exist within the individual in some form. Sometimes these feelings emerge into consciousness under various disguises, one of which is myth. Primitive mythmakers were thus restructuring their childhood fantasies in their tales, and, since such longings are primarily sexual in nature, so too were the myths. However, while we apparently must have such stories in order to function as whole persons, the logical censor in the modern mind cuts off myth creation. How can this dilemma be resolved? Freud maintains that the creation of myth today takes place when we dream, i.e., when the mind's rational censor is turned off. When we dream, we think like primitives; dreams are myths for us, and, according to Freud, the two are indistinguishable.

6. Jungian archetypes

Carl Jung was also an eminent psychologist who, while he accepted Freud's theory about the origin of myths, did not believe that it went far enough in explaining the striking similarity between the motifs found in ancient stories and those in the dreams of his patients.

Jung postulated that each of us possesses a "collective unconscious" which we inherit genetically. It contains certain very general ideas, themes, or motifs which are passed along from one generation to the next and are retained as part of our human inheritance. It is something akin (although much more general in nature) to the various instincts we see in other species which allow, for example, birds to build a nest or ants to colonize. These motifs which form the collective unconscious are called archetypes by Jung, and they greatly influence the creation of myths.

7. Structuralism

The structural theory is a fairly recent development and is closely allied with the research of linguists. According to this theory, all human behavior -the way we eat, dress, speak, choose sexual partners, paint pictures, tell stories- is patterned into codes which have the characteristics of language. To understand the real meaning of myth, therefore, we must analyze it linguistically.

The tentative conclusion at which the structuralists have arrived is that the function of myth is to offer a solution between two polarized extremes within a society. Myths provide a synthesis between a given thesis and its antithesis. Their primary purpose is to soothe tensions.

8. Historical-critical theory

The historical-critical approach maintains that there are a multitude of factors which influence the origin and development of myths and that no single explanation will suffice. We must examine each story individually to see how it began and evolved. For some we shall find the answer, for others we shall never know how or why they came into being.

Questions

1. What common element(s) do the ancient theories of myth share?

2. Restate in your own words each of the modern interpretations of myth.

6. COSMOLOGY

A. Modern cosmology

B. Mythic cosmology

C. The first generation of gods

D. The overthrow of Uranus

E. Further creation in the early world

F. The second generation of gods

G. The Five Ages

H. The children of Cronus

I. The Titanomachy

Modern cosmology

The word "cosmology" is derived from two Greek bases which together mean "the study of the universe." Modern cosmology is a speculative science which examines the beginning of the universe, its size, its structure, and its probable end.

The most popular theory currently about how everything began is called the "Big Bang." It postulates that at first there existed only the thin gas such as we now find between galaxies (= clusters of stars). Over many eons of time, this gas condensed and formed into an enormous and very unstable blob of matter which is sometimes called "ylem" from the name given by the philospher Aristotle to the basic substance of the universe. The instability of this mass led to a gigantic explosion out of which everything in the cosmos as we know it was formed. Even today the galaxies are rapidly receding from each other because of the force of the original explosion billions of years ago.

Many questions are, of course, left unanswered. How do we account for the gases which existed prior to the explosion? Is there a first cause for everything? Is the universe finite? If so, what exists outside of it? Do multiple universes exist? Is the universe eternal? If not, how will it end? Will it be followed by another? Such questions sound more philosophic or religious than scientific because at this level the three disciplines are closely allied.

Mythic cosmology

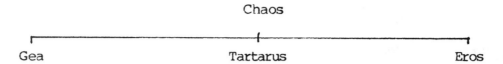

Chaos

Gea   Tartarus   Eros

The Greeks believed that everything began with Chaos, a word which we can take to mean "an enormous mass in a state of complete disorder." Out of Chaos first emerged Gea, a goddess who both represented and was the Earth. Next came Tartarus, both a god and a place under the earth for imprisoning divinities who were out of favor for one reason or another and which -much later- became the place in the Land of the Dead reserved for legendary human sinners. Finally came Eros, a god who both represented and was the physical desire leading to reproduction. His presence was necessary to continue the creative force within the world.

Further division and distinction occurred as Chaos was separated into Night and Darkness, and they, in turn, gave birth to Air and Day.

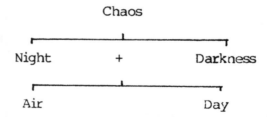

Chaos

Night   +   Darkness

Air   Day

Next Gea without the aid of a mate produced the Sky, the Mountains, and the Sea.

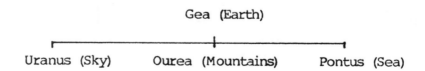

Gea (Earth)

Uranus (Sky)   Ourea (Mountains)   Pontus (Sea)

With these births the initial stage of creation was completed.

The first generation of gods

Gea next mated with her son Uranus, and produced the first race of gods over whom they became the rulers. Their children were the twelve Titans, the three Cyclopes, and the three Hundred-handed Ones.

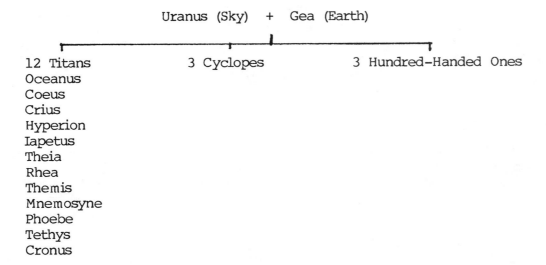

Uranus (Sky) + Gea (Earth)

12 Titans	3 Cyclopes	3 Hundred-Handed Ones
Oceanus		
Coeus		
Crius		
Hyperion		
Iapetus		
Theia		
Rhea		
Themis		
Mnemosyne		
Phoebe		
Tethys		
Cronus		

Little is known about the twelve Titans except that they were very early gods of great power who were human in form but huge in size. (We have the English words "titan" and "titanic" from their name). They are significant primarily as the parents or grandparents of later divinities.

The Cyclopes, also huge in size, had just one eye in the center of their forehead. Later in the history of the gods they became the craftsmen who made the thunderbolts of Zeus (a god who has yet to appear).

The three Hundred-handed Ones were giants who were also useful to Zeus at a later time because of the rapid fire power they provided in throwing stones.

The overthrow of Uranus

Uranus was not pleased with the monstrous appearance of his last two sets of children nor with their great strength which he feared might someday be used against him, and so he placed the Cyclopes and the Hundred-handed Ones under the earth in Tartarus. His action offended and angered his wife Gea who loved all of her offspring equally. She decided to punish her husband for the cruel and unjust punishment he had inflicted. She persuaded Cronus, the youngest of the twelve Titans, to aid her in her plot.

That night as Uranus lay with Gea, Cronus attacked his unsuspecting father with a sickle and castrated him. This violent action rendered Uranus powerless, and Cronus was able to replace him as ruler of the gods. We should note in this bloody incident that divinities are not necessarily omnipotent or eternal. They can be injured, and they can be replaced.

During the attack which Cronus made on his father, the blood of Uranus was spilled upon Gea (the earth) who became pregnant because of it and eventually gave birth to the Furies and the Giants.

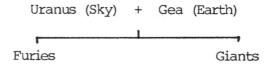

Uranus (Sky)   +   Gea (Earth)

Furies   Giants

The Furies were female spirits who punished those who had committed a wrong against blood relatives, especially against a mother or father. They were thought to be hideous creatures who would often drive their prey mad, but they were not regarded as evil, since they took vengeance only on those whose crime deserved it.

The Giants were monstrous warriors of great size whose legs ended in snakes. They would eventually fight a long war against Zeus and other gods yet to come.

Further creation in the early world

Cronus became the second ruler of the gods, and he chose his sister Rhea to be his wife. Before we describe the events directly associated with the god, we shall look at other examples of creation in this early world.

Night, a child of Chaos, gave birth to fifteen creatures such as Old Age, Sleep, Blame, Pain, Retribution, and Strife. Strife, in turn, gave birth to Fighting, Quarrels, Murders, Lies, Disputes, Hunger, Suffering and other troublesome offspring.

Gea –unfortunately– married Pontus, another of her children. This coupling, while having a beneficent side, produced many hideous monsters.

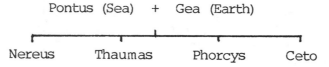

Pontus (Sea)   +   Gea (Earth)

Nereus   Thaumas   Phorcys   Ceto

Nereus, a minor god of the sea, married Doris, a daughter of the Titan, Oceanus. She gave birth to fifty daughters called the Nereids who were nymphs of the sea.

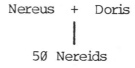

Nereus   +   Doris

50 Nereids

Thaumas married Electra, another daughter of Oceanus, and she gave birth to Iris and the Harpies.

-20-

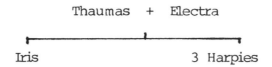

Thaumas + Electra

Iris   3 Harpies

Iris, the goddess of the rainbow, was often used by the gods as a messenger.

Iris' three sisters were called Harpies (= Snatchers) and were portrayed as large birds with the faces of women. They were generally regarded as unfriendly to humans and often carried away people as well as their possessions. Their most famous appearance occurs in the story of Jason's quest for the Golden Fleece.

Phorcys, another minor sea-god, married his sister Ceto, a sea-monster, and produced many hideous offspring.

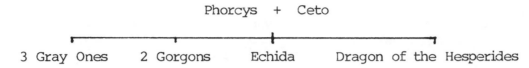

Phorcys + Ceto

3 Gray Ones   2 Gorgons   Echida   Dragon of the Hesperides

The three Gray Ones were thought of as old women. Their blindness was alleviated by a single eye which they were able somehow to share, one using it at a time; their toothlessness was abetted by a single, razor-sharp tooth which they also passed back and forth. They were generally unfriendly toward humans and prefered to be left alone.

The two Gorgons were such hideous creatures that merely to look upon them turned the viewer to stone. The most infamous of these creatures, Medusa, was not transformed into a Gorgon until much later. We shall look at her story in another context.

Echidna, partially human and partially reptile, mated with Typhon, a creature of similar mixture who was a child of Gea (Earth) and Tartarus (Underworld).

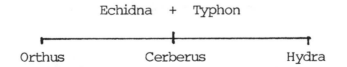

Echidna + Typhon

Orthus   Cerberus   Hydra

The most noted of this family was Cerberus, the three-headed watchdog of the Land of the Dead. Orthus was another dog of huge size also associated with the spirit world, and the Hydra was an enormous snake with nine heads who lived in the swamps near the town of Lerna. Heracles eventually confronted this monster.

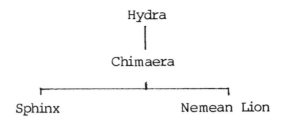

Hydra
|
Chimaera

Sphinx   Nemean Lion

The Hydra gave birth to the Chimaera, a monstrous combination of lion, goat and snake who, just to make matters worse, breathed fire. The Chimaera, in turn, produced the Sphinx who was usually portrayed as having the head of a woman and the body of a lion with wings. The most famous occurrence of the monster in Greek myth is in the Oedipus story. Another offspring of the Chimaera was a huge lion which lived near the town of Nemea. This beast will form another of the many challenges for the hero, Heracles.

At the same time as these various monsters were being born, many benign nature divinities were created, each representing a further elaboration of the physical universe.

The Titan Oceanus, who was associated with the river which flows around the edge of the circular and flat world, married his sister, Tethys, and the two produced a huge number of rivers, streams and springs, all of which are portrayed as sons and daughters, animate rather than inanimate creations.

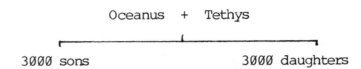

Oceanus + Tethys

3000 sons   3000 daughters

The number 3000 is merely a way to indicate a great abundance of children.

The Titan Hyperion, who was the first god of the sun, married his sister, Theia, and the two produced Helios, another sun-god, Selene, goddess of the moon, and Eos, goddess of the dawn.

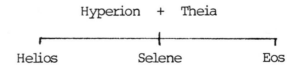

Hyperion + Theia

Helios   Selene   Eos

Eos, in her turn, became the mother of all of the winds and the stars.

Many other creatures who represent various aspects of the natural world in addition to the few that we have mentioned come into being during this early time.

The second generation of gods

After Cronus, one of the original twelve Titans, had attacked Uranus, his father, and rendered him powerless, he chose his sister, the Titaness Rhea, as his wife. The two of them ruled over the second generation of gods, just as Uranus and Gea had the first. Cronus was often pictured with a sickle or a scythe -his weapon in the lethal attack- and was considered to be an agricultural god. Rhea, his wife, was thought to be a goddess of the earth as her mother was before her.

The Five Ages

The reign of Cronus was called a Golden Age because mankind lived in perfect happiness. This fortunate race of beings eventually died out and was replaced by a second generation less perfect than the first. The time of their existence was called the Silver Age. Zeus, now ruler of the gods, became dissatisfied with this race of humans and replaced them with a third generation; however, the people who lived then were so warlike that they all killed each other. Their period of time was called the Bronze Age.

Zeus next created a race of great warriors who destroyed monsters and fought in huge battles. This fourth generation was called the Heroic Age. But these brave men also perished.

In the fifth generation, the Age of Iron, the time contemporary with the writer who offers us this chronology (Hesiod in the **Works and Days**), Zeus created a race of people who became the most imperfect of all. They live only by their own labor; pain and suffering are an essential part of life, and old age and death await those who survive. This period will, as the others before it, reach its end. What will come after -if anything- only the gods know.

As you can and will see, the story of the Five Ages of the human race fits uneasily with other versions of the beginning and development of the human race. Mythic explanations are not necessarily precisely consistent one with the other since they have come down to us from different places and different times. We should remember that superficial inconsistencies are of little concern as long as the mythic system is believed in and thought to have integrity.

We should note that the story of the Ages of Mankind reveals the idea of perfection in the past, a golden beginning from which eveything declines, each period worse than the one before it, until we finally come to our own time, the worst of all. In this story, we seem to be living on borrowed time until the gods will finally lose patience and destroy us. What will follow is impossible to foresee. A more corrupt period is difficult to imagine, so perhaps the gods will simply abandon the idea of humanity. In any case, it is clear that the entire idea of the Ages is antithetical to the idea of progress, to the perception that the human race has been moving from barbarism and savagery to a time of perfection in the future. This, as you know, is the theme of our age with its industrial revolution and its many scientific discoveries and technological inventions. Each day will be better and better, we say; our children will have more advantages than we. Only recently has this idea come into question.

The same idea of progress is inherent in the development of the gods whom we have been describing. The early gods are primitive and savage and their children are often monsters. As we move toward the rule of Zeus, we find gods who represent the highest values in our civilization. The two interpretations of the past thus seem fundamentally at odds with each other. But not necessarily, if we stretch things a bit. Gods, after all, can improve and become more civilized while humankind worsens and becomes less so.

The children of Cronus

Cronus and his wife Rhea produced six children, three daughters and three sons.

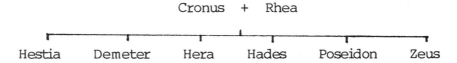

Cronus + Rhea

Hestia   Demeter   Hera   Hades   Poseidon   Zeus

Each of these offspring will be a part of the third generation of gods who are called the Olympians, and we shall describe their attributes in that context. Now we shall relate the traumatic experience which awaited each of them just after birth.

Cronus had received a prophecy that he would be overthrown by one of his own children, so as soon as Rhea gave birth, Cronus swallowed the infant. In this way he hoped to be able to prevent the prophecy from being fulfilled. Rhea was understandably irritated at her husband's cruelty –note the parallel with Gea– and decided to take action against him. When, on the island of Crete, she gave birth to Zeus, the last of her children, instead of bringing the newly born infant to her husband, she substituted a rock which Cronus swallowed without thinking or looking. Through this strategy Zeus was able to grow to maturity undisturbed on Crete.

When Zeus came to manhood, he returned to the mainland where, with the help of his grandmother, Gea, he was able to force his father, Cronus, to vomit forth not only his brothers and sisters, but even the rock (which was eventually given a prominent position of display at the shrine of Delphi even into historical times.)

The Titanomachy

Zeus was determined to overthrow Cronus just as Cronus had replaced Uranus earlier. He and his siblings declared war on their father, citing his cruel actions against them as the cause. The many Titans who then existed were forced to choose sides. This war of the gods was called the Titanomachy, and was finally decided in Zeus' favor after he released the Cyclops -who made his lightning and thunderbolts- and the Hundred-handed Ones who overwhelmed Cronus and his allies with their rapid throwing ability. (These creatures had apparently not been freed by Cronus earlier). Most of the defeated Titans were placed in Tartarus, but some had special assignments, as we shall see.

Cronus is sometimes equated with a personification of time because of the similarity of his name with the Greek word for time, **chronos.** He was equated by the Romans with their god, Saturn, a primitive agricultural deity. An important festival was held in his honor each December during which there was much feasting and exchanging of gifts. This god also gave his name to Saturday and to the sixth planet in our solar system, as Uranus gave his to the seventh.

Sources

The best single source for the stories of creation and the early gods is Hesiod's **Theogony.**

Questions

1. What is the most popular theory among modern cosmologists as to how the universe began?

2. Who was Gea?

3. Who was Tartarus?

4. Who was Eros?

5. Who were the rulers of the first generation of gods?

6. Who were the Titans?

7. Who were the Cyclopes?

8. Describe the overthrow of Uranus. Who was responsible? How was the action accomplished? Why did it take place?

9. Explain origin and function of the Furies.

10. Who were the Nereids?

11. Who were the Harpies?

12. Who was Iris?

13. Who were the Gray Ones?

14. Who were the Gorgons?

15. Who was Cerberus?

16. Describe the Hydra and name its eventual conqueror.

17. Describe the Chimaera.

18. Describe the Sphinx. With which hero will it be associated?

19. Which god produced most of the rivers, streams and springs?

20. Who was Hyperion?

21. Who was Helios?

22. Who was Selene?

23. Who was Eos?

24. Who were the rulers of the second generation of gods?

25. Describe The Five Ages of the human race. How does this account seem to conflict with another more prevalent explanation of the past which is found in Greek myth?

26. What did Cronus do to his children? Why?

27. How did Rhea trick her husband? Why?

28. Where did Zeus grow to manhood?

29. What was the Titanomachy? Who were the leaders on both sides? Who won? What happened to the losers?

30. What was the Roman name for Cronus?

7. ZEUS AND HIS CHALLENGERS

A. Zeus and Prometheus

    1. Background
    2. Human creation
    3. Sacrifices
    4. The theft of fire
    5. Pandora
    6. The flood
    7. Punishment

B. Zeus and the Giants

C. Zeus and Typhon

D. Zeus and the Aloads

E. Zeus the King

Zeus and Prometheus

1. Background

Zeus did not immediately replace his father Cronus as leader of the gods. The civil war of the Titans, as we have seen, took place over a very long time. And there were other challenges as well to his authority of which the most famous was that posed by Prometheus.

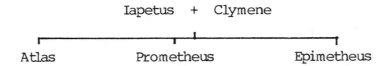

Iapetus + Clymene

Atlas   Prometheus   Epimetheus

Iapetus was one of the original twelve Titans born to Uranus and Gea. He married Clymene, one of the daughters of his brother, Oceanus. Three of their children are important for our purposes: Atlas, Prometheus, and Epimetheus.

Atlas fought against Zeus during the Titanomachy and, as a punishment, was condemned to support the sky on his mighty shoulders. It was the strength of this Titan which kept the sky from crushing the earth.

Prometheus, whose name means "Foresight", and his brother Epimetheus, "Hindsight", were allowed to move about freely since they had supported Zeus in the war.

2. Human creation

Prometheus was regarded as a god of civilization who was often shown as opposing the apparent tyranny of Zeus, the new ruler. Many accomplishments which benefited the human race are attributed to him by various writers in antiquity. By some he is described as the creator of mankind. He and his brother, Epimetheus, were given the task by Zeus to populate the earth. Epimetheus became so excited by the job that he gave away such gifts as swiftness, powerful claws, wings, and warm coats to the creatures he had fashioned. Nothing worthy seemed to remain for Prometheus to use. So from clay he formed a race of beings in the image of the gods themselves. Zeus was angered by Prometheus' action because he felt that mankind too much resembled the gods and might some day try to rival them. In these early stories Zeus did not hold the human race in high regard, and Prometheus became their champion.

3. Sacrifices

Zeus demanded constant sacrifices from the newly created race of humans despite the fact that they had barely enough food for survival. They appealed to their creator for help, and Prometheus could not ignore their pleas. He killed an animal and placed the bones and gristle under a few good pieces. He then did the reverse to another pile, placing bad scraps on top and good underneath. Prometheus next summoned Zeus and asked him to choose which of the two offerings he would prefer in all future sacrifices. The great ruler of the gods was deceived: he chose the portion which appeared to contain the best meat. Thus it was that the human race from then on had only to offer the worst parts of the animals to the gods and were allowed to keep the best for themselves.

4. The theft of fire

Because fire was reserved for the gods, humans were not able to keep warm or cook their food. Prometheus, in what is perhaps his most famous action, stole fire from the gods and gave it to mankind. This great gift -which symbolizes a transition from barbarism to civilization- was another of the ways in which Prometheus helped the creatures he had created.

5. Pandora

Angered by the theft of divine fire, Zeus decided upon a special punishment for the human race. He created a mortal woman whom he called Pandora ("All Gifts") and gave her to Epimetheus as a wife. Some say that this was the first woman created and that Prometheus had designed only a race of men. In any case, Prometheus had warned his brother to beware of Zeus and not to accept any gifts from the god, but Epimetheus forgot.

Pandora brought with her a box which Zeus had given her as a wedding gift. When she opened the present to see what wonders the god had placed there, Zeus' plan became clear: the many evils which would forever plague human beings escaped. Prometheus was able to close the box before the last of the evils -the ability to see the future- escaped. In this way the god was able to preserve the precious gift of hope for the human race.

6. The flood

On another occasion Zeus became so upset with the actions of the human race that he decided to destroy it completely with a flood. Prometheus anticipated Zeus' plan and secretly arranged to have two humans -known for their piety- survive the disaster: Deucalion, Prometheus' son by a mortal woman, and Pyrrha, the wife of Deucalion and the daughter of Epimetheus and Pandora. Once the waters had receded, the two of them repopulated the earth by following Prometheus' advice to throw stones over their shoulders. Each stone was miraculously transformed into a person.

7. Punishment

The patience of Zeus regarding Prometheus and his favoritism toward the human race was finally exhausted. He ordered the Titan to be chained to a rock in the Caucasus Mountains where he hung for thousands of years. Each day the eagle of Zeus would come to rip open the body of the god, and each night the wounds would heal in preparation for a new attack in the morning. Finally, Heracles, the heroic son of Zeus, killed the eagle with his mighty bow and set the Titan free. Some say that Zeus permitted this to happen in order to bring additional glory to his famous son. Others say that he allowed it in order to discover a secret which Prometheus had been concealing. Still others maintain that Zeus had matured and had become a benevolent and compassionate god.

The myth of Prometheus has been a vital one throughout the long history of our civilization. The early Christians compared the sufferings of Prometheus for the benefit of the human race to those of Christ. In more modern times, Prometheus has become a symbol of revolt against any kind of tyranny. The works of literature which celebrate this great god are innumerable.

We should observe that Zeus was considered to be a god who grew and matured. He learned from Prometheus. His original opposition to the human race changed to an attitude of compassion and understanding, and he eventually replaced Prometheus as mankind's greatest benefactor.

Zeus and the Giants

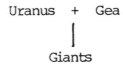

Uranus + Gea
|
Giants

When Cronus castrated his father, the blood of Uranus spilled on the earth. From this action Gea became pregnant and bore the Giants, twelve (although the number varies) creatures huge in size and human in form to the waist but whose legs ended in snakes.

The Giants claimed prior rights to the rulership of the gods, but Zeus, of course, was unwilling to recognize such an assertion by these hideous creatures. A war resulted which was called the Gigantomachy, a struggle often confused by both ancient and modern writers with the Titanomachy. Hostilities lasted a very long time, and Zeus had to employ the assistance of all of the gods in his domain as well as that of his mortal son, Heracles, in order to achieve an eventual victory.

Zeus and Typhon

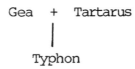

Gea + Tartarus
|
Typhon

The horrible monster Typhon was the child of Gea, goddess of the earth, and Tartarus, the god of the lowest place in the Underworld. Gea, angry at the destruction of the Giants, conceived an even more dangerous opponent for Zeus. Typhon had the body of a dragon and a hundred burning snake heads which spoke together in a screaming babble. This monster believed that he should be the ruler of the gods. Zeus fought Typhon in a long and difficult combat, until he finally buried the monster under Mt. Etna, a volcano located in Sicily. Whenever there was an eruption, it was thought to be Typhon with his burning heads attempting futilely to escape. Some say that the monster was imprisoned in Tartarus where, in its useless efforts to get free, it became the source of the violent winds which we call typhoons.

Zeus and the Aloads

The Aload brothers, Otus and Ephialtes, were sons of the sea-god, Poseidon. By the age of nine they were already ten feet wide and fifty feet in height, and they were still growing. This brash pair decided that they -because of their size- should rule the gods.

With their mighty strength they piled Mt. Ossa on top of Mt. Olympus and Mt. Pelion on top of Mt. Ossa in an attempt to challenge the gods in their abode in the sky. They were both killed for their sacrilege. Some say that it was the god Apollo who shot them with his bow and who ended this final threat to Zeus' authority.

Zeus the king

Thus we see that Zeus emerged as the victor in each challenge to his power. He proved his right to be the ruler of the new race of gods and to replace his father, as Cronus had replaced Uranus.

We should note again that Zeus developed as a god. He was not in his youth what he became in his maturity. The god increased in strength, authority, wisdom, justice, compassion and benevolence. We should also observe that, while Zeus was the supreme ruler of the third -and last- generation of gods, he was the creator neither of the world nor of life nor of the human race.

Sources

Various segments from the myths of the gods may be found chiefly in the works mentioned in the bibliography. There is, unfortunately, no single work which has survived from antiquity that presents all of the stories. We ourselves must organize a coherent version as best we can from the literature which remains.

Questions

1. Who was Atlas? What was his punishment? Why was he punished?

2. Who created the human race? Why did this process anger Zeus?

3. How was Prometheus connected with animal sacrifices? How did he anger Zeus in this regard?

4. What was Prometheus' most famous action? What does it symbolize?

5. Who was Pandora? Why was she created? How was she connected with Prometheus?

6. Why did Zeus cause the flood? Who survived it? Who was responsible for their survival? Why were they allowed to survive? How was the earth repopulated?

7. What was Prometheus' punishment? Who set him free? Why did Zeus permit the freeing of Prometheus?

8. Who were the Giants? What was their claim? What was the Gigantomachy?

9. Who was Typhon? What two natural phenomena are connected with his story?

10. Who were the Aload brothers? What caused their desire to overthrow Zeus? What actions show their strength? What was the result of their actions?

11. What do all of the stories about Zeus' challengers accomplish?

8. ZEUS THE KING

A. The sky-god

B. Division of authority

C. Mt. Olympus and the twelve Olympians

D. The marriages of Zeus

    1. Zeus and Metis
    2. Zeus and Themis
    3. Zeus and Eurynome
    4. Zeus and Demeter
    5. Zeus and Mnemosyne
    6. Zeus and Leto
    7. Zeus and Hera

E. Zeus the king

The sky-god

Zeus was the acknowledged leader of the new generation of gods because he had, first, rescued his brothers and sisters from their imprisonment by Cronus, and, secondly, organized and led the successful revolt against his father in the Titanomachy.

Zeus is consistently identified as a sky-god, and it is possible that his worship was brought into Greece with invaders called the Achaeans about 1900 B.C. The name is probably derived from an Indo-European god of very early times and means "sky" or "heaven." Many of his attributes and titles are related to his function as god of the sky, e.g., Rainer, Thunderer, Cloud Gatherer, Lightning God, Sender of Fair Winds. The phrase Zeus Pater (= Zeus the Father) is probably derived from the Sanskrit "Dyaeus Pitar," and is directly related to "Jupiter," the Roman name for the god.

Division of authority

After Zeus had defeated Cronus and his allies, he and his brothers, Poseidon and Hades, determined their spheres of authority in the new regime by drawing lots. Zeus won the sky, Poseidon the sea, and Hades the Underworld. The surface of the earth and Mt. Olympus were neutral territories.

Mt. Olympus and the twelve Olympians

The earliest belief was that Zeus and the eleven other major gods associated with him lived on Mt. Olympus. This belief persisted even when the more sophisticated concept of the sky as the dwelling place of the gods became prevalent.

Mt. Olympus is located in northern Greece and is about 10,000 feet in altitude. It is generally covered by clouds, but when it is clear, one can make out a formation at the top that was considered to be the throne of Zeus.

Although the number twelve became associated with the major Olympian gods, they were accompanied by innumerable minor divinities and demigods. Such a polytheistic system was characteristic of Mediterranean cultures in ancient times.

The marriages of Zeus

Now that Zeus had successfully met the various challenges to his authority, i.e., Prometheus, the Giants, Typhon, and the Aloads, he entered into a number of marriages which would help to civilize and otherwise benefit the human race. These marriages do not represent a belief in polygamy as such, but are rather a way of demonstrating in narrative form the pervasive influence of Zeus.

1. Zeus and Metis

Zeus' first marriage was with Metis, the goddess of wisdom and a daughter of the Titan, Oceanus. After Metis had become pregnant, Zeus received an ominous prophecy from his grandparents, Uranus and Gea: the child born of Metis would in turn produce a son who would overthrow him. Zeus was determined to prevent the prophecy from being fulfilled, and so, when the time came for Metis to give birth, he swallowed the goddess. Soon after this marvelous feat, he developed a tremendous headache, and one of the gods —some say Prometheus, others Hephaestus— obligingly opened his skull with an ax to relieve the pressure. From his head leaped the goddess Athena. Zeus had successfully avoided the prophecy: there was no child of Metis; he himself had given birth. The wisdom which the god had gained by swallowing Metis remained not only with him but was also transmitted to his daughter, Athena.

2. Zeus and Themis

Themis was one of the original twelve Titans. She was goddess of justice. Some say that she was also an earth goddess and that she replaced her mother, Gea, as a prophetess at the shrine of Delphi where she herself was in turn replaced by Apollo. The marriage of Zeus and Themis would thus be that of sky and earth.

The first set of children from this marriage were the Seasons, initially three in number but eventually four. They often accompanied the gods associated with fertility, e.g., Demeter, Persephone, and Dionysus. They were also the gatekeepers at Mt. Olympus where they rolled back the clouds.

The second set of children were the three Fates, called Moerae (= Parts, Shares) by the Greeks and Fata (= Things Spoken) or Parcae (= Bringers Forth) by the Romans. The Fates were the divine beings who determined the course of human events. They were the personification of destiny. In some cases they carried out the will of the gods, in others, the gods -even Zeus- had to obey them.

The Fates were often portrayed as three old women who are weaving. One holds the thread, one weaves the pattern, and the last one cuts the thread. They were named Lachesis (= Assigner of Lots), Clotho (= Spinner), and Atropos (= Irreversible).

3. Zeus and Eurynome

The marriage of Zeus and Eurynome, another of the daughters of Oceanus, produced the three Graces. These young women were the goddesses of beauty, happiness, and festivity. They were usually portrayed as three dancing women who were either naked or lightly clothed. They were present on all happy occasions.

4. Zeus and Demeter

Zeus next married his sister, Demeter, who gave birth to a beautiful daughter called Persephone (Proserpina for the Romans). As we shall see later in more detail, she was, like her mother, associated with the fertility of the earth. She also became the wife of Hades and queen in the Land of the Dead.

5. Zeus and Mnemosyne

Zeus made love to Mnemosyne, one of the original twelve Titans, for nine nights, and she eventually gave birth to the nine Muses. The Muses were female divinities who inspired creative artists, thinkers, and performers. Although there is considerable variation both in their names and in their spheres of authority, a more or less standard list follows.

Clio	history
Euterpe	music
Thalia	comedy
Melpomene	tragedy
Terpsichore	dance
Erato	lyric poetry
Polyhymnia	songs
Urania	astronomy
Calliope	epic poetry

The Muses were especially associated with Mt. Helicon and Mt. Parnassus as their sacred places. The latter location is also connected with Apollo who in his function as god of poetry became the leader of the Muses. When they were not present in one of their holy districts or were not busy bringing inspiration to humans, the Muses could be found entertaining the gods with their songs and dances.

6. Zeus and Leto

Zeus next married Leto, a second generation Titaness, a daughter of Coeus and Phoebe. She was known as Latona to the Romans. Leto gave birth to the twins, Artemis, goddess of wild nature, and her brother, Apollo, god of rationality. We shall see more of them later.

7. Zeus and Hera

Zeus' final marriage was with his sister, Hera, and it was she who became the queen of the third generation of gods, replacing Rhea.

There were three children of Zeus and Hera. Their beautiful daughter, Hebe, became the cupbearer of the gods at their banquets and kept their goblets full of the immortal nectar.

Their son, Ares, was the god of war, and another daughter, Eileithyia, was the goddess of childbirth. Eileithyia was relegated to a minor position in myth because Hera assumed her function as the chief goddess associated with birth.

Some say that Hephaestus, the craftsman of the gods, was also the child of Zeus and Hera. Others say that Hera, angry that Zeus produced Athena by himself, conceived Hephaestus without any aid from her husband.

While Hera was considered the last official wife of Zeus, the god continued to have extramarital love affairs both with goddesses and with mortal women. In the first instance, it was to produce additional divinities, in the second, to produce great heroes who would rid the world of various evils. These romances were regarded with anger and hurt by Hera, and she was often portrayed as a wronged wife. However, aside from this one aspect, the married life of the couple was a happy one.

Zeus the King

As we have seen, Zeus matured as a god, just as the society which created him evolved. He became righteous. just, merciful, benevolent, and omnipotent. No one could challenge his right and ability to rule, although various gods might at times disagree with him. He was always a mysterious and enigmatic force whose influence permeated the universe. Only the god Apollo was as complex as this creation of Greek myth and religion.

Questions

1. Which areas of authority were awarded to Zeus, Poseidon, and Hades? How were they determined?

2. What were the two beliefs about the dwelling place of the gods?

3. Define polytheism and monotheism. Which system was typical of the Greeks?

4. Define polygamy and monogamy. Which is typical of the Greeks?

5. What was the prophecy connected with Metis? How did Zeus thwart it? Who was the child of this marriage? How does one of her attributes reflect her mother?

6. Describe Themis.

7. Who were the Seasons?

8. Describe the Fates and explain their function.

9. Who were the Graces and what was their function?

10. Describe Persephone.

11. Who were the Muses? What was their function? With which geographic locations were they often associated? Who was their leader?

12. Who were the children of Zeus and Leto?

13. Who were the children of Zeus and Hera? Describe their functions. What was an alternate story concerning the conception of Hephaestus?

14. Why did Zeus continue to have love affairs with goddesses and mortal women?

15. How does a belief in Zeus' maturation seem to conflict with the myth of the Five Ages?

9. ZEUS AND HERA

A. Zeus and the Olympians

B. Hera

    1. Io
    2. Argus
    3. Ixion

Zeus and the Olympians

Because Mt. Olympus was considered to be one of their homes, the major gods who were associated with Zeus were called the Olympians. The number twelve soon came to be associated with these divinities; one of the most sacred oaths in ancient times was to swear "By the twelve."

I. The Twelve Olympians

Greek	Roman	Function
Zeus	Jupiter	Ruler of gods and humans; sky-god
Hera	Juno	Wife of Zeus; marriage; birth
Poseidon	Neptune	Sea
Demeter	Ceres	Agriculture; grain; fertility
Hestia	Vesta	Hearth fire
Apollo	Apollo	Prophecy; sun; music; medicine
Artemis	Diana	Nature; wild animals
Athena	Minerva	Wisdom; war; weaving
Ares	Mars	War
Aphrodite	Venus	Physical love; beauty
Hephaestus	Vulcan	Fire; craftsman for the gods
Hermes	Mercury	Messenger; guide; commerce; thieves

II. Other Gods of Olympus

Dionysus	Bacchus	Wine; fertility
Eros	Cupid, Amor	Physical love
Iris	Iris	Rainbow; messenger
Hebe		Cupbearer of the gods
Three Graces		Festivity; happiness; celebration
Nine Muses		Inspiration
The Seasons		Gate Guards of Mt. Olympus

III. Gods of the Waters

Poseidon	Neptune	Major god of the sea
Triton		Son of Poseidon; sea-god
Oceanus		God of river around edge of earth
Pontus		An early sea-god
Nereus		Minor sea-god
Nereids		Salt-water nymphs
Naiads		Fresh-water nymphs
Proteus		Minor sea-god

                    IV. Gods of the earth
Pan   Faunus   Wild nature; shepherds
Nymphs   Minor female divinities
Satyrs   Male fertility beings; usually goat-men
Centaurs   Male fertility beings; usually horse-men

                    V. Gods of the Underworld
Hades   Pluto, Dis   Ruler of the Underworld
Persephone   Proserpina   Wife of Hades; fertility

Hades, although a brother of Zeus, was not considered one of the twelve major Olympians, since he spent his time in the Land of the Dead under the earth.

Hestia, while a goddess of very early times, had few myths associated with her and was often replaced on the list by Dionysus, a late-appearing god of fertilty.

The two names on the list which we have not yet mentioned are Aphrodite and Hermes. Aphrodite, as we shall see, is sometimes considered a daughter of Zeus and at others a child of Uranus, while Hermes was the son of Zeus and Maia, a daughter of Atlas.

Zeus was the leader of these gods and of many other divinities who existed at the same time. He was a god of the sky and, by extension, of the weather. He protected the family and the city. It was he who blessed kings and allowed them to rule over their communities. He enforced the law of hospitality under which the host must respect his guest and the guest the host. Zeus was, in fact, the guardian of all laws and customs.

Hera

The wife of Zeus was Hera who reigned as queen of the Olympians. Her name was originally a title which meant "Our Lady" or "Great Lady." While at her beginning she was probably an earth goddess like Gea and Rhea before her, she became associated chiefly with marriage and childbirth.

The marriage of Zeus and Hera was celebrated annually in the month of January. It was a very sacred event and meant as a prototype for human matrimony.

The Roman name for the goddess was Juno from which is derived the name for the month of June.

Because Zeus tended to have many female lovers through whom he enlarged the number of gods and heroes, Hera was often portrayed as a wife who was troubled by her husband's apparent infidelities. Since she could not directly punish the Ruler of the Gods for his love affairs, she often took vengeance on his mistresses or indeed even on the children produced from these romances. Such action on Hera's part gives us insight into the early Greek concept of crime and punishment. While we might today call the woman involved in such a relationship an innocent victim of Zeus' passion (it would be impossible for a mere mortal to resist so powerful a god), Hera obviously operated out of the belief that having participated in the deed was sufficient; there were no extenuating circumstances. Likewise, in her punishment of the apparently innocent children who result from such amorousness, we can observe the idea that guilt is inherited, that children can be punished for the sins of their parents. This latter concept provides one explanation for the troubling problem as to why the apparently innocent must suffer in a world supposedly ruled by just gods.

1. Io

We shall look at one story out of many which portray Hera as a jealous wife.

Zeus fell in love with Io, an attractive mortal woman. He attempted to conceal his romance from Hera by approaching the maiden in the form of a dark cloud. But Hera was not deceived: she saw the single cloud in an otherwise clear sky and swooped down from Olympus in an attempt to prove Zeus' infidelity. Her husband saw her drawing near and quickly transformed Io into a cow. He then assured his wife that he was merely observing agricultural life on earth.

2. Argus

Hera did not believe Zeus. She summoned Argus, who, since he had one hundred eyes, was famous for his constant vigilance. The task which Hera gave to him was to see to it that the cow was not transformed into a woman and thus become available to her husband.

Zeus' passion for Io had not diminished, but Argus kept him from his objective. The Ruler of the Gods sent for his son, Hermes, and asked that he remove the troublesome guard.

Hermes flew quickly to earth, for a request of his father was always a command. The god had great musical talent. Almost immediately after his birth he had invented the lyre, an instrument which became very popular, a kind of electric guitar of antiquity. Now he approached Argus in disguise and began to sing a soothing lullaby. Argus discovered to his dismay that he could not keep his eyes from closing while listening to the tranquil melody of the mysterious stranger. One by one the eyelids drooped until -for the first time- all one hundred eyes were closed and the ever-watchful guard slept. Hermes quickly drew his sword and killed the unfortunate man.

While Hermes had obeyed his father and disposed of Argus, he did not wish to make a permanent enemy of Hera, so he carefully removed the eyes of the dead watchman -each a different hue- and gave them as a pacifying gift to the goddess. Hera placed them in the tail of her favorite bird, the peacock, which from that time to this has possessed a tail of many colors.

Warned in this way by Hermes, Hera once again attempted to prevent Zeus from approaching Io. The goddess sent flies to sting the cow and force her from Greece. The unfortunate young woman in her animal shape was driven down the eastern coast of the Mediterranean until she finally came to Egypt where Zeus was eventually able to satisfy his passion, despite Hera's efforts. Io gave birth to a son, Epaphus, whom many Greek heroes and peoples would claim as an ancestor.

In another instance Hera killed Dionysus, a son of Zeus by the woman Semele whose violent death she also caused. In her great anger Hera tore apart the infant Dionysus, but he was reassembled and restored to life by Zeus.

Even Heracles, the greatest of the Greek heroes, was not immune to Hera's animosity. He suffered much throughout his life only because he was the child of Zeus and a mortal woman.

It may seem inconguous to us that this Queen of the Gods, this goddess of marriage and childbirth, should also be portrayed as a jealous and vindictive wife. Yet contradictory aspects are typical of most Greek gods; they are complex, multi-faceted creations, and, like human beings, not always consistent in their behavior.

3. Ixion

Because of his accomplishments, the great hero, Ixion, was once invited to dine with the gods on Mt. Olympus. When he saw Hera, he instantly fell in love with her and tried brazenly to seduce her. Hera informed Zeus of this inappropriate behavior, and the Ruler of the Gods prepared a suitable punishment. He formed a cloud into a likeness of Hera and placed it in her bed. Hera then invited Ixion to her room, where Zeus -as planned- broke in upon them. He threw Ixion into Tartarus, the place of punishment in the Underworld, where he was forever rotated on a wheel of fire.

The cloud which had been formed into Hera's likeness eventually gave birth to Centaurus, a creature which was both man and horse. Centaurus in turn was the founder of the race of centaurs who are generally portrayed as horses whose shoulders merge into the upper bodies of men. They were a savage tribe who lived in a mountainous area of Greece. They enjoyed drinking wine and pursuing women and nymphs. They represent the undisciplined fertility of wild nature. Chiron, the only centaur who was civilized and educated, was noted as a teacher of heroes.

-41-

Questions

1. Why were the gods of Zeus' time called the Olympians?

2. List the twelve major Olympians with their Greek and Roman names and their individual functions.

3. What does Hera's name mean? What is her Roman name?

4. Of what was Hera the goddess?

5. Whom did Hera often punish for her husband's apparent infidelities?

6. Who was Io? What was her connection with Zeus? How did Hera punish her?

7. Who was Argus?

8. What was Hermes' role in Zeus' romance with Io?

9. List two other individuals who were punished by Hera because their mothers had love affairs with Zeus.

10. Who was Ixion? What was his crime? What was his punishment? What does the story reveal about Hera?

11. Who was Centaurus?

12. Who were the Centaurs?

10. POSEIDON

A. Characteristics

B. Other sea-gods

C. Competition with Athena

D. Poseidon and Demeter

E. Marriage

F. The Aloads

G. Polyphemus

H. Antaeus

I. Medusa

J. Scylla and Charybdis

K. Sunium

Characteristics

Poseidon was primarily a god of the sea, but he was also associated with earthquakes and horses. His Roman equivalent was called Neptune.

Poseidon was a child of Cronus and Rhea, and, like his brother Hades and his sisters, Demeter, Vesta, and Hera, he was swallowed by his father. Once freed, he joined his brother Zeus in the Titanomachy. Some say that -after the victory- Poseidon made the bronze doors which imprisoned his father in Tartarus.

The god, like the sea, was unpredictable and easily aroused to anger. He is frequently pictured with a trident, a three-pronged spear which was used by fishermen. He lived sometimes with the other gods on Mt. Olympus, sometimes at the bottom of the sea or sometimes in various dwellings near or in the water. He often traveled over the surface of the waves in a chariot pulled by horses and accompanied by various creatures associated with the sea.

Poseidon created the first horse by striking a rock with his trident, and he occasionally took the form of his creation. Like Zeus, he also at times took the form of a bull, an animal associated with fertility.

The god was probably connected with earthquakes because of the way in which the shore trembles when large waves break. He was given the title "Earthshaker."

The name "Poseidon" can be taken to mean "Husband of Da" and probably comes from early times when the god was the spouse of an earth goddess who is unknown to us.

As we have seen, once Zeus was victorious in the Titanomachy, he and his brothers drew lots to determine which areas each should rule. It was in this way that Poseidon became associated with the sea.

Other sea-gods

Since the Greeks were a seafaring people, and, since no place in the country is far from the water, it is understandable why sea-gods play such an important part in their myths.

Pontus was the first god of the sea. He was born along with Uranus (Sky) and Ourea (Mountains) from Gea (Earth) at a very early time.

Oceanus, one of the twelve Titans who were the children of Uranus and Gea, became the next sea divinity. He eventually came to represent the river which was thought to flow around the perimeter of the the circular and flat earth. He had numerous sons and daughters all of whom were associated with fresh or salt-water.

Although Nereus, a child of Pontus and Gea, was a sea-god who preceded Poseidon, he remained as a minor divinity during the time of the Olympian. Nereus was often identified as the "Old Man of the Sea." He had a prophetic gift and the ability to change into whatever form he wished, a power he used whenever men attempted to compel him to reveal future events. As we have seen, he married Doris, a daughter of Oceanus, and they became the parents of the fifty Nereids who were nymphs of the sea.

It is appropriate at this point to describe what was meant by the title "nymph." A nymph was a minor female divinity usually associated with a particular place, object, or natural phenomenon. Nereids, for example, were connected with salt-water, Naiads with fresh-water, Dryads with trees. Nymphs were usually restricted in movement to the area surrounding whatever it was with which they were associated. They were always young, beautiful, and frequently amorous.

Proteus was still another minor sea-god coexisting with Poseidon. He too was called the "Old Man of the Sea," had prophetic powers, and the ability to change shape. Because of the latter characteristic, he has given us the word "protean" which means "changeable." Proteus lived near the mouth of the Nile River in Egypt. His parentage is unclear. Some say that he was an ancient god who was demoted, others that he was a son of Poseidon, still others claim that he was originally an Egyptian divinity.

Competition with Athena

There are many stories in which Poseidon competes with other gods in order to become the ruling deity in a particular area. Some say that these myths reflect a much earlier time when Poseidon was the supreme god in Greece. The most famous of these episodes involved a competition between Poseidon and Athena for control of Attica, an area which includes Athens and its adjacent territory.

To demonstrate his power, Poseidon struck a rock on the Acropolis (a sacred hill in Athens) with his trident, and caused a fountain of salt-water to gush forth. Athena in her turn caused an olive tree to grow nearby. The gods who served as judges were more impressed by the goddess' contribution to Athenian welfare and gave the territory to her. Poseidon angrily flooded a nearby plain, but he was placated by the Athenians who wisely continued to worship both divinities, although they considered Athena their patron.

Poseidon and Demeter

On another occasion, Poseidon fell in love with his sister, Demeter. She resisted him and even changed herself into a horse in order to escape. But to no avail. Poseidon changed himself into a stallion and caught her. The child of this union was an immortal horse called Arion, a name which means "Very Swift."

Marriage

Poseidon married Amphitrite, one of the Nereids. Their son was Triton, whose function was to calm the waves -at his father's command- by blowing on a conch shell. "Triton" is also frequently used as a name for any minor male divinity of the sea.

Poseidon -like Zeus- continued to have love affairs after his marriage. His children by these romances were sometimes monsters, but even when they were human, they were usually savage, ill-tempered, and very powerful.

The Aloads

As we have seen, Poseidon was the father of the two Aload brothers, Otus and Ephialtes, who because of their great size and strength thought that they could overthrow Zeus. But they were too impatient, made their move too soon, and failed.

Polyphemus

Poseidon was also the father of the one-eyed giant, Polyphemus the Cyclops. This cannibal nearly killed the famous hero, Odysseus.

Antaeus

Antaeus was another of Poseidon's sons. He was an infamous wrestler who would challenge anyone passing through his country to a match to the death. Since Antaeus was invincible as long as he was in contact with the earth, he always won. It was Heracles who finally discovered his secret and killed the bully during their match.

Medusa

Poseidon made love to the beautiful maiden, Medusa, in a temple of Athena. For such a violation of her sanctuary, Athena, a virgin goddess, transformed the unfortunate woman into a hideous Gorgon. Anyone who looked upon her face was instantly turned to stone. Medusa eventually gave birth to the winged horse, Pegasus, the offspring of this tragic love affair.

Scylla and Charybdis

The two most feared sea-monsters were also connected with Poseidon. Scylla was a beautiful sea-nymph with whom the god fell in love. When Amphitrite discovered the romance, she transformed Scylla into a sea-monster who was a woman to the waist but from there on became a mass of writhing snakes at the end of each of which was the head of a ravenous dog.

Scylla lived on one side of a narrow strait between Sicily and Italy. If sailors came too close to her lair, one of the dog-headed snakes would seize them from the deck of their ship. If, to avoid Scylla, they sailed too close to the opposite shore, they would be caught in the clutches of Charybdis, a whirlpool which would pull the ship and its crew to a watery death at the bottom of the sea. The phrase in English today, "to be between Scylla and Charybdis" means to be caught between two equally dangerous choices.

Sunium

Perhaps the most famous temple of Poseidon is that located at Sunium in southern Attica overlooking from a high cliff the beautiful blue expanse of the Mediterranean. For countless years as they sailed past this temple on the outward voyage, mariners would have prayed to Poseidon for safety at sea, and again, as they returned, would have offered thanksgiving to the god. It is at Sunium that we bid farewell to Poseidon.

-46-

Questions

1. Who are the parents of Poseidon? What was his area of authority? What is a characteristic symbol of the god?

2. To what aspect of Poseidon does the title "Earthshaker" refer?

3. Who was the first god of the sea?

4. Of what was Oceanus the god?

5. Who was Nereus?

6. Who were the Nereids?

7. Explain the meaning of "nymph" in classical mythology.

8. Who was Proteus? In what ways is he similar to Nereus?

9. Describe the contest between Poseidon and Athena.

10. Who was Arion?

11. Who was Amphitrite?

12. Who was Triton and what was his function?

13. What characteristics are shared by the Aloads, Polyphemus, and Antaeus?

14. By whom and why is Medusa punished? What is her punishment?

15. Describe Scylla and Charybdis.

11. HESTIA

A. Characteristics

B. Vesta

C. The Vestal Virgins

Characteristics

Hestia was the goddess of the family hearth and its fire. By extension she came to be regarded as guardian of the home, the family, the local community, and the state as a whole.

There are few myths connected with Hestia. She was the eldest daughter of Cronus and Rhea. She chose to remain a virgin throughout her life, rejecting offers by both Poseidon and Apollo.

Vesta

The Roman equivalent for the goddess was called Vesta. Her most famous temple was located in the Roman Forum, an area which contained many public buildings and which formed the symbolic center of the vast Roman empire. As with all temples of the goddess, the one in the Forum was circular. This design was employed to suggest the antiquity of her worship, since circular structures were used before the rectangular shape became customary. Within the building was an altar which symbolized the hearth of the entire state and on which burned the flame of the goddess. There was an opening in the roof to allow the smoke to escape.

The Vestal Virgins

The rites of Vesta were performed by priestesses who were called Vestal Virgins, each of whom took a vow of virginity in honor of the goddess they served.

Girls between the ages of six and ten were selected to become Vestals. The parents, of course, would make the decision, but it was such a great honor that the invitation was seldom rejected.

A girl so chosen would serve the goddess for thirty years. She would spend ten years learning the rituals, ten years performing them, and a final ten years teaching them to others. At the end of this period, a woman could leave the order, or she could remain in the service of the goddess in a semi-retired capacity. Most chose to remain.

The worship of Vesta has a very early origin among the Romans. As we shall see, the legend about the foundation of Rome contains a reference to an already existing group of Vestal Virgins. The order continued until it was eventually closed down by the Christians in A.D. 394.

The priestesses were held in high esteem by the Romans: they occupied seats of honor at major public events and could pardon criminals if they so chose. They were also permitted the rare privilege of burial within the city.

Punishment was severe for any priestess who broke the vow of virginity, since it was believed that such an action would bring the wrath of Vesta upon the state as a whole. A priestess who broke her vow was buried alive, and her lover was flogged to death. There were few instances of such infractions during the long and dignified history of these holy women.

Questions

1. Who was Hestia?

2. Who was Vesta? Where was her major temple located? What was its unusual architectural feature?

3. Describe the religious order of the Vestal Virgins.

4. For approximately how long did the religious order of the Vestal Virgins exist?

5. What were some of the indications of the high esteem in which the Vestal Virgins were regarded? What was the punishment for a priestess who broke her vow of virginity?

12. DEMETER

A. Background

B. The abduction of Persephone

C. The Eleusinian Mysteries

D. Characteristics of Mystery Religions

Background

Demeter was the goddess of grain and of the earth's fertility in general. She represents for the Olympians what Gea and Rhea were for their generations of gods. Her Roman equivalent was Ceres from whose name we have the word "cereal."

Demeter was a daughter of Cronus and Rhea. Her marriage with Zeus produced Persephone, sometimes called Kore (= Maiden), who grew to become a lovely young woman. The Roman name for this goddess was Proserpina.

Demeter and Persephone represented essentially the same thing: the fertility of the earth. When a distinction was made, Persephone represented the seed and Demeter the blossoming grain.

The abduction of Persephone

It happened that Hades saw the charming Persephone, fell at once in love with her, and wished to make her his wife. He consulted Zeus, the father of the goddess, who warned him that Demeter would never permit her daughter to marry a god who lived in the dark regions beneath the earth. He suggested that Hades simply carry the maiden off to his kingdom. The Ruler of the Underworld followed his brother's advice. One day, as Persephone was out in the fields, a great fissure suddenly opened in the earth and Hades burst forth. Before the goddess realized what was happening, he seized her and carried her off to the Land of the Dead.

As soon as Demeter realized that her daughter was missing, she began to search for her everywhere on the earth, but all in vain. Finally, she consulted Helios, the god of the sun, who saw everything. Helios told her what had happened to Persephone and tried unsuccessfully to convince her that marriage to such a powerful god was a great honor.

Demeter could not be comforted. She took human form and wandered the earth in sorrow. Despite her condition, she attracted the lustful attention of Poseidon. She rejected his advances and even transformed herself into a mare to escape him, but Poseidon took the form of a stallion and caught her. The result of this mating was, as we have seen, the immortal horse, Arion, who became famous for his great speed.

The attack of Poseidon only compounded the grief which Demeter already felt. She completely abandoned her duties as goddess, and the human race, as a result, began to starve because of the continued failure of the crops. Zeus and the other gods became alarmed that mankind might perish. They begged the goddess to restore fertility to the earth. When she refused, Zeus approached his brother Hades and asked him to return Persephone to her mother. The god agreed to do so, but before she left he secretly offered the young woman a pomegranate to eat, since any god who tasted the food of Hades had to spend a portion of each year in the Underworld.

Zeus now had to negotiate a compromise between Hades and Demeter. He arranged that Persephone should spend one-third of each year in the Underworld with her husband and the rest of the time on earth with her mother. When the goddess was with Hades, the earth was barren; when she returned to her mother, the fields were planted and began to bloom. The return of the daughter to the mother was celebrated each year with a fertility festival called the Thesmophoria during which the entire story of Demeter and Persephone was reenacted. It was a very significant feast since the welfare of the community depended on the success of the crops.

As we can see, the myth of Demeter and Persephone is closely connected with the cyclic pattern of the seasons: birth, death, rebirth. When Persephone joins her husband, her absence is death; when she rejoins her mother, she is reborn. The fields die each year with the harvest only to be revitalized with the planting of the new seed. Such a close connection with the human mysteries of life and death made these two goddesses especially appealing.

The Eleusinian Mysteries

When Demeter was wandering the earth in sorrow over her missing daughter, the people of Eleusis, a small town a few miles west of Athens, were especially kind to her. The goddess rewarded the citizens for their solicitude by revealing to their king the secrets of life and death which she had come to know so well because of the fate of her daughter. The ruler of Eleusis became her priest, and the secrets of the goddess were passed orally from the priest of one generation to that of the next.

The rites of Demeter at Eleusis were celebrated each September and were called the Eleusinian Mysteries. They have a very long history, beginning as early, perhaps, as 1600 B.C. and continuing until they were terminated by the Christians about A.D. 600. The rituals, which were open only to initiates, began each year at Athens and then moved by sacred procession to the temple of the goddess at Eleusis where they concluded. What took place in the temple was secret, and severe penalties were imposed for discussing the rituals publically. The general subject was birth, death, and rebirth, and the rites provided participants with the belief that life continued in some meaningful way after death. We know from ancient testimony that the Mysteries were most impressive, but we know very little about the specific content. Nothing has been found in writing; the secrets of Demeter have been well kept.

The person at Eleusis to whom Demeter first revealed her mysteries was named Triptolemus; he was said by some to be the son of King Eleusis, the founder of the city. Triptolemus was portrayed as a young man who was instrumental in the spread of agriculture throughout the world. It was he who invented the wheel and the plow and who taught people how to plant their fields. The young prince was eventually thought of as a god and became closely associated in a divine trinity with Demeter and Persephone.

Characteristics of Mystery Religions

While the Eleusinian Mysteries were the most prestigious, there were many other similar beliefs in the ancient world, and we shall note a few features which they all shared.

1. Mystery religions were generally restricted to those who were selected to become initiates. Such a restriction was in sharp contrast to public worship of the gods which was open to all. Thus, Demeter could be worshipped publicly in any of her temples, and in the special way at Eleusis where one must be chosen to participate.

2. Initiation was most often an annual event.

3. The rituals were secret.

4. There was a strong emotional content to the rites.

5. The subject matter was closely connected with death and rebirth.

6. The mystery religions were not mutually exclusive even though different gods were involved in each.

Questions

1. Describe Demeter's areas of authority.

2. Who was Persephone? Of what was she the goddess?

3. How was Hades connected with Persephone and Demeter?

4. Who was Arion?

5. What compromise did Zeus achieve between Demeter and Hades? How is the agreement related to the annual fertility cycle?

6. What were the Eleusinian mysteries?

7. Who was Triptolemus?

8. What are the major characteristics of mystery religions?

13. ARTEMIS

A. The Olympians

B. Birth of Artemis

C. Tityus

D. Niobe

E. Characteristics of Artemis

F. Callisto

G. Orion

H. Actaeon

I. Endymion

The Olympians

With Demeter we have discussed all of the first generation of the Olympian gods, i.e., the children of Cronus. Hades as Lord of the Underworld was not considered one of those who lived on Mt. Olympus. With Artemis we begin the second generation of gods, all of whom were considered to be not only under Zeus' authority but to be his children as well. They are named Artemis, Apollo, Athena, Ares, Aphrodite, Hephaestus, and Hermes.

Birth of Artemis

As we have seen, the sixth of the seven marriages of Zeus was with Leto, a Titaness, the daughter of Coeus and Phoebe. Leto gave birth to Artemis on the slopes of Mt. Cynthus located on the small island of Delos. Artemis was, as a result, often called Cynthia or Delia. Immediately after her birth, the goddess helped her mother to deliver Apollo, her twin brother.

The two children of Leto were often shown with a bow and arrows which they could use for ordinary hunting or to send disease and death among humans and animals.

Tityus

Shortly after they were born, the twins killed Tityus, a giant who had earlier attempted to rape their mother. Tityus was one of the few sinners punished in Tartarus where he was stretched on the floor while vultures forever chewed on his body.

Niobe

Artemis and Apollo avenged their mother in still another famous instance. Niobe, queen in the city of Thebes, had seven sons and seven daughters of whom she was very proud. And it was this pride which led to her downfall. She boasted that she had not only more but better children than Leto. The goddess was greatly insulted by such brashness in a mere mortal, and she decided upon a severe penalty: she ordered Artemis and Apollo to kill all of Niobe's children. There was no escape once this command had been given; the twins without hesitation carried out the decree of their mother. All of the children of Niobe fell to their arrows. Too late she realized what she had done. Niobe was overwhelmed with grief at the tragedy which she had brought onto her family. The gods eventually took pity on the inconsolable woman and changed her into a rock, the most unfeeling of all objects. But even in this form, Niobe wept, and her tears continued to pour forth.

Characteristics of Artemis

Artemis, whom the Romans called Diana, was the goddess of wild nature and of the animals who live there. She was often portrayed as a huntress with a bow and arrow, but she also carefully protected the animals in her domain. Like the open country itself, she was unpredictable: she could be benevolent and merciful but also harsh and deadly. She was also associated with childbirth as were Hera and Eileithyia, even though virginity was a most important characteristic of the goddess. She valued her own chastity highly, as she did that of the nymphs who accompanied her. Her religious worship usually required virgin priestesses as well.

As Artemis developed, she eventually acquired the attributes of the goddess of the moon, perhaps as a parallel to her brother, Apollo, who was god of the sun. When she took the form of this goddess, she was addressed either as "Selene" or "Luna," both of which mean "moon," or as "Phoebe" which means "bright."

Artemis also absorbed the characteristics of Hecate, goddess of night, darkness, witchcraft, black magic, and the haunted crossroads. Hecate, who was a fearsome divinity, was often portrayed as having three heads (sometimes those of animals as well as human) on one female body.

Each of the three personalities -Artemis, Selene, Hecate- were completely separate from each other, yet at the same time they were aspects of the same divinity. What the goddess might do as Selene, e.g., to have a love affair with a mortal, she would never do as Artemis or Hecate. The goddess represented a form of ancient trinity, three gods in one, separate yet the same. It was a mystery to be believed rather than understood.

Callisto

There are many stories which portray the importance of virginity to Artemis.

Callisto was one of the nymphs who accompanied the goddess as she roamed through the countryside. Zeus became enamoured of her and forced his affections on the innocent young woman who became pregnant. When Artemis discovered the nymph's condition, she immediately punished her by transforming her into a bear. Zeus tried to compensate his former love by changing her into a constellation called the Great Bear (Ursa Major) which we can still see today. Some say that he also transformed the child of Callisto into the Little Bear (Ursa Minor) so that the son could be close to his mother in the sky. These constellations are better known as the Big and Little Dipper today.

Orion

Orion acquired great fame as a hunter and spent much of his time chasing his prey in the woods. Because of his skill, Artemis even invited him to join on some of her hunts, but the goddess should have been more cautious. Orion had another kind of reputation as well. He had earlier tried to force his affections on the Pleiades, the seven daughters of Pleione who was the wife of Atlas. Zeus had answered the prayers of the maidens as they fled the savage hunter by transforming them into a constellation which still today bears their name. So it was inevitable that when Orion saw the beauty of Artemis' nymphs, he would fall in love with one of them. When she rejected him because of her commitment to maidenhood, Orion decided to force her to comply. Artemis soon realized what was happening and sent a huge scorpion to kill the hunter, but Zeus felt that he deserved better because of his great accomplishments, so he transformed the young man into a constellation (Orion) which even today pursues the Pleiades across the sky. Artemis was not impressed: she changed the scorpion into a constellation (Scorpio) which in turn pursues Orion.

Actaeon

Actaeon of Thebes was another famous hunter. One day as he wandered through the woods, he inadvertently came upon Artemis and her nymphs who were bathing after an arduous hunt. The goddess became angry that Actaeon —even though quite innocently— had seen her nakedness. She immediately transformed the youth into a stag, and he was torn apart by his own hunting dogs.

Endymion

Endymion was a handsome young shepherd with whom Artemis in her aspect as Selene, goddess of the moon, fell in love. She spent more and more time with her handsome lover and gave less and less attention to her lunar duties. Zeus observed the erratic behavior of the moon and soon discovered the cause. Much to Selene's sorrow, the ruler of the gods approached Endymion on Mt. Latmus and gave him a choice of fates: death in any way Endymion preferred, or eternal sleep along with eternal youth. Endymion chose the latter and was immediately put into a trance. Each night Selene would pass over her perpetually sleeping lover and look down on him in helpless sorrow.

Questions

1. Where was Artemis born? Who were her parents? Who was her brother? Explain the names Cynthia and Delia.

2. Who was Tityus? How and why was he punished?

3. Who was Niobe? How and why was she punished?

4. Of what was Artemis the goddess?

5. Who was Selene? Explain the names Luna and Phoebe.

6. Describe Hecate.

7. How does Artemis represent a form of ancient trinity?

8. Who was Callisto? What was her eventual fate? What does her story tell us about Artemis?

9. Who was Orion? What was his eventual fate? What does his story tell us about Artemis?

10. Explain how the Pleiades and Scorpio are connected with Artemis.

11. Who was Actaeon? What does his story tell us about Artemis?

12. Who was Endymion? Why would his story not be connected with Artemis directly? What is the significance of the choice which Zeus presents to Endymion?

14. APOLLO

A. Characteristics

B. Delos

C. Delphi

D. Sibyl

E. Cassandra

F. Castalia

G. Daphne

H. Pythian Games

I. Sun gods

J. Orestes

K. Apollo and music

    1. Pan and Midas
    2. Marsyas

L. Asclepius

Characteristics

Apollo was a god as complex and mysterious as Zeus, if not more so. Some say that he represents the most noble creation of Greek civilization. He was the god of reason and moderation, the giver of laws and thus the rewarder of right action and the punisher of wrong. He was, along with his sister, a god of archery, and could with his arrows send disease or cure to humans; in this capacity he became the god associated with medicine. He was the god of the sun as Artemis was of the moon. He was also god of music and poetry, and, in what is perhaps his best known attribute, of prophecy. It seems likely from the many areas associated with him that Apollo was a compression of many gods into one, although his actual origin is still uncertain.

Delos

As we have seen, the parents of Apollo were Zeus and Leto, and his twin sister was Artemis. The god was born on the small island of Delos which until the time of his birth had been a floating bit of land with no fixed roots. A temple with a sacred road approaching it was built at the place where the god had his beginning, and he was often called "Delian" because of his birthplace. The site became one of the most frequently visited in antiquity.

Delphi

Shortly after his birth -it did not take the god long to grow to manhood- Apollo left his island birthplace and came to the shrine of Delphi on the slopes of Mt. Parnassus in central Greece. The site had long been associated with prophecy: Gea had foretold the future there, then her daughter Themis, and finally Phoebe, a sister of Themis. Apollo wished now to make the sanctuary his own. It was, however, guarded by a fierce dragon called Pytho. Apollo killed the monster with his arrows and took possession of the sacred place. From this accomplishment, he is often given the title "Pythian."

Delphi was surely one of the most beautiful and impressive locales in antiquity, and even today the ruins high up on the slope of Mt. Parnassus convey some of its former grandeur. The most famous building on the site, the temple of the god himself, had carved into its wall two famous precepts associated with Apollo: "Know Thyself" and "Nothing in Excess." It also contained two famous stones: that which Rhea gave to Cronus in place of Zeus and which he later vomited forth along with his children, and that which was said to mark the center of the world. The story goes that Zeus wished to find the middle of the earth's surface and to do so he released eagles from opposite edges. They met at Delphi, and the place was marked with the "omphalus" or navel stone.

The sanctuary, as connected with Apollo, probably goes back to about 750 B.C. Tradition has it that it was closed by the Christians about A.D. 360.

Prophecy at Delphi was spoken by a priestess called the Pythia, so named from the monster which Apollo had killed. The priestess would sit on a three-legged chair in a specific room within the temple of the god. The room would be filled with the smoke of burning laurel leaves, hemp, and barley. The priestess also chewed on bay leaves and drank from the nearby Castalian spring whose waters were supposed to produce prophetic insights. She would eventually enter a trance-like state -completely possessed by the god who would speak through her- and produced sounds which would seem like babble to an outsider. Her utterances were copied down by priests who interpreted and translated them before they were finally presented to the petitioner. The prophecy was called the "oracle" of Apollo, and, by extension, the same word was used to refer to the physical site of the shrine as well.

The technique of prophecy whereby the speaker enters an ecstatic or inspired state is called the mantic tradition. It was the only type of prophecy used at Delphi. There were, however, other ways of foretelling the future. One could observe the flights of birds, or the movement of the stars, or one could examine the placement of internal organs within a sacrificial animal. Special training was required in order to be an interpreter of any of these prophetic signs.

In addition to the religious aspect of prophecy, there was also the fact that the priests at Delphi were very well informed about current political situations. They would obtain information from suppliants of the god who came from all parts of the Mediterranean world, from contacts they had in various countries, and from an immense correspondence. Information came to Delphi through a vast and varied network somewhat comparable to intelligence gathering agencies today.

The Pythia was often able to present a simple "yes" or "no" response to a petitioner, but sometimes the question was of such a nature that no clear-cut answer was possible. Once, for example, when King Croesus wished to know if he should attack the Persian Empire, the response of Apollo was that if he did so, a mighty empire would fall. Croesus did not question the oracle further to see whose empire it would be; he assumed it was that of the Persians. He declared war and soon discovered to his sorrow what the Pythia had meant. For responses such as these, Apollo was given the title "Loxias" which means "Ambiguous One."

Grateful petitioners would leave offerings of various kinds for Apollo. These were kept in buildings which resembled small temples and were called treasuries. Some twenty cities constructed such treasuries which lined both sides of the Sacred Road leading up the mountain to the temple. Delphi became one of the wealthiest sanctuaries in antiquity.

We should remember that, while some came to Delphi in a crass and unbelieving state of mind, seeking merely to use the information of the priests, most approached the sanctuary in a spirit of reverence and awe and fully believed that the god spoke to them through his chosen representative.

Sibyl

Apollo is not associated with one particular goddess or mortal woman. As we might expect from such a complicated divinity, his myths involve many different females with whom, for some reason, he is often unsuccessful.

Apollo fell in love with a beautiful woman by the name of Sibyl who rejected all of the god's advances. In desperation, he promised her whatever she wished, if she would only love him. Sibyl picked up a handful of sand and asked for a year of life for each grain she held. The request was granted, but she continued to scorn and now to mock the infatuated god. Apollo felt that he had been betrayed; his love turned to anger and resentment. While he could not withdraw the favor he had granted, he changed it to such an extent that the original blessing became a curse. Sibyl would indeed live one year for each grain of sand, but she would continue to age. As the endless years passed, her ancient body shriveled to such a small size that she was placed in a container which was hung from the ceiling of a temple of Apollo and would blow back and forth in the wind. People would come to look in wonder at this sad sight and to listen for the whispered voice of ancient Sibyl repeating just one phrase: "I want to die."

The name of Sibyl became a title for prophetic priestesses of Apollo at shrines other than the one at Delphi where the designation "Pythia" was used. A Roman writer (Varro) listed ten Sibyls active in different sanctuaries in his time.

The most famous Sibyl lived at the temple of Apollo in Cumae, a site a few miles north of Naples in Italy. It was the Cumaean Sibyl who acted as a guide for the hero Aeneas when he entered the Underworld. It was also she who, in the 10,000 years of her life, compiled the nine Sibylline Books which foretold Rome's destiny. She offered these books for a certain amount of money to the Roman king, Tarquin the Proud, and when he refused to pay her price, she destroyed three and offered the king the remaining six at the original cost. Tarquin again refused, and the Sibyl destroyed three more of the volumes and offered the three remaining at the same price. Tarquin finally capitulated and paid for the three what he would have originally paid for all of them, and through his stubbornness lost forever the information in the books which the Sibyl had destroyed.

Cassandra

In another episode, Apollo fell in love with Cassandra, the beautiful princess of Troy. When she rejected him, he offered her the gift of prophecy to win her affection. To no avail; Cassandra continued to flee from the god's embraces. Angered at the mortal woman's audacity to reject the love of a god, Apollo changed the favor he had granted to a curse: Cassandra would be able indeed to foresee the future, but no one would believe her prophetic utterances. She would know that what she prophesied would come to pass, but no one would heed her words. She predicted, for example, the destruction of Troy by the Greeks, but she was ignored; she even predicted her own death, but her listeners disregarded her until it was too late.

Castalia

In another episode, Apollo fell in love with the nymph Castalia and pursued her. She hid from the god in a cave on Mt. Parnassus from which a stream of water flowed from that time on. Some say that the nymph was transformed into the fountain and that the water inspired those who drank it to see the future. The Castalian spring can still be seen today.

Daphne

Once Apollo was consumed by love for the beautiful Daphne who rejected him and fled from his embraces. But the god could not be denied, he pursued the young woman and quickly overtook her. The gods took pity on the helpless maiden and intervened. They transformed Daphne into the first laurel tree. Apollo was once more frustrated in his passion, but he considered the tree sacred and, from that time on, laurel wreathes were awarded to the victors in the Pythian Games held at Delphi.

Pythian Games

In addition to the structures we have already mentioned at Delphi, the Sacred Road, the Treasuries, the Temple of Apollo, one can also see -farther up the mountain- a theater and a stadium, both of which were chiefly connected with the Pythian Games.

The Pythian Games were second in importance only to those held at Olympia. They took place at Delphi every four years in the year prior to the Olympic contests. There were various athletic events held in the stadium, but there were also music and poetry contests which took place in the theater.

Sun gods

Since the sun observes everything which occurs beneath it, the fact that Apollo was god of the sun was closely connected with his being prophetic. The belief was that the sun-god drove a chariot across the sky from the ocean at the eastern edge of the world to the one at the western end. He would then put his chariot in a boat which would carry him on the water along the perimeter of the earth back to the east for the next day's journey.

As we have seen, there were other sun-gods prior to Apollo. Hyperion, one of the original twelve Titans was the first. His son was Helios who became the second. Helios in turn had a son called Phaethon.

When Phaethon was still a young man, someone questioned his claim that he was the son of Helios. Phaethon determined to verify his birth by asking his father directly. He journeyed to the eastern edge of the world where Helios confirmed the fact and, as proof, promised to give his son anything he requested. When Phaethon asked to drive the chariot of the sun, Helios tried to dissuade him, saying that he was too young for such a task. To no avail; Phaethon demanded that his father keep his word. Reluctantly Helios allowed him to mount the chariot and set off. The powerful horses at once recognized unfamiliar hands on the reins. They wandered far off their course. They galloped high into the sky, and men froze to death on earth; they swooped too low and the sun's heat created the desert in Africa and burned to black the skin of the inhabitants. Zeus observed these catastrophes and decided that he could not allow such disorder to continue. He struck Phaethon with a thunderbolt and ordered Helios back into his chariot.

There were two ways in which the Greeks regarded the three generations of sun-gods. In one belief, each deity replaced the previous one; in another interpretation, each god represented a different aspect of the sun, and, by the time of Apollo, they all —except Phaethon— existed concurrently.

Because of his function as god of the sun, Apollo was often called "Phoebus" which means "Bright" or "Shining."

Orestes

As lawgiver and god of right and wrong, Apollo was more advanced than earlier gods in the complexity of the moral standards which he represented. Previously, it was only the deed itself which mattered. With Apollo came the concept of extenuating circumstances and the motive behind the action. For example, in a famous story, Apollo defended Orestes, a young man who, according to the tribal code, had to avenge his father's death by killing his slayers. One of the murderers happened to be his own mother. In killing her, Orestes was attacked by the Furies because he had shed the blood of a parent. According to the ancient code of morality, Orestes would have been driven to madness and death by these Avengers, but Apollo, in the first jury trial ever held, defended Orestes' actions and pointed out the conflicting obligations under which the young man found himself. The jury decided that Orestes was innocent.

Apollo and music

Apollo was also the god of music. He was often pictured with a lyre, a stringed musical instrument which was something like a small harp. Hermes had invented the lyre and gave it to Apollo.

As god of music, Apollo was often shown with the nine Muses where he was given the title "Musagetes" which means "Leader of the Muses." As we have seen, one of the homes of these spirits of inspiration was Apollo's sanctuary on Mt. Parnassus.

1. Pan and Midas

Apollo was sometimes challenged to contests of musical skill. Such stories perhaps reflect the contests of the Pythian Games.

The god was once invited by Pan, a minor divinity of shepherds and wild nature, to compete in a music contest. King Midas was selected as judge, and the match took place. It was clear to everyone that Apollo had won (although it would have been wise to choose him regardless, since he was the more powerful god), but Midas chose Pan as the victor. Apollo -and Pan- were dumbfounded. Surely only someone who listened with the ears of an ass would have chosen the lesser god, so that was the penalty which Apollo gave to Midas for his foolishness: the ears of an ass. How could Midas, a king, keep the respect of his subjects when they saw his embarrassing transformation? He quickly had a hat made which covered the long, pointed, and hairy ears. Only his barber knew, and, under pain of death, he had to remain silent. But the haircutter could restrain himself only so long. One day, after he had cut the king's hair, he rushed out into the woods, dug a hole in the ground, and shouted into it: "Midas has the ears of an ass!" Then he covered the hole and rushed back to town. Reeds grew on the spot, the wind blew through them, and they whispered the secret: "Midas has the ears of an ass!" First one person in the kingdom heard it, then another, until eventually Midas' secret was known to all.

2. Marsyas

In another story the satyr (= goat-man) Marsyas found a flute which had been invented by the goddess Athena and became an expert with it. He too challenged Apollo. This time the Muses were the judges, and the contestants decided that the winner could do whatever he wished to the loser. The contest was held, and the Muses chose Apollo as the victor. To punish Marsyas for his brashness and pride in challenging a god, Apollo flayed him. The blood of the satyr became the River Marsyas in Asia Minor.

Asclepius

As Apollo was sometimes shown with a lyre to represent him as god of music, he was often portrayed with a bow and arrows to represent his connection with medicine. His arrows could inflict disease and death, or they could bring a cure.

Apollo once had a successful romance with a mortal woman by the name of Coronis. Because of his past experiences with women, Apollo remained suspicious of her even though she became pregnant with their child. He had a white raven watch her, and the bird did indeed find her to be unfaithful to the god. When Apollo heard the report of the raven, he angrily changed the color of the bird from white to black which it has remained to this very day. Apollo then killed Coronis for her infidelity, but saved their child, whom he called Asclepius. He gave his infant son to the centaur Chiron to raise. Chiron, the most famous teacher in Greek myth, and the only civilized centaur, taught Asclepius all of his knowledge of medicine which was added to what the child learned from his divine father. Asclepius soon became a renowned physician. His skill was so great that it was rumored he could even bring his patients back from the dead. Since snakes were thought to connect the Underworld with the Land of the Living, a snake soon became associated with Asclepius as his symbol.

Because of his great medical skill, Asclepius was made immortal by the gods. His temples were similar to hospitals and his priests to doctors.

The most famous of Asclepius' shrines was located at Epidaurus. People came from throughout the Mediterranean world to be treated at this clinic.

The usual methods of treatment were to have the patient sleep in the temple of the god and then to have the priests interpret the dreams of the sick person. It was believed that, through the dreams, Asclepius would provide information necessary for the cure. Other techniques employed were dieting, exercise, and the use of various kinds of herbs and drugs. Epidaurus had a stadium for workouts and a theater in which patients could watch dramatic performances which would allow them to vent their own emotions vicariously. All of these techniques represent an early use of holistic medicine. Evidence that these temples of Asclepius were effective can be found in their heavy use.

Asclepius had two sons who were physicians with the Greek army at Troy. He also had several daughters whose names were just medical abstractions, e.g., Hygieia (Health) and Panacea (Cure-all).

The Hippocratic Oath (named after another physican from ancient times who lived about 460 - 377 B.C.) which doctors swear upon entering their profession begins as follows: "I swear by Apollo the physician, by Asclepius, by Hygieia, and by Panacea that I will carry out according to my ability and judgment this oath and indenture."

Asclepius was known as Aesculapius to the Romans. His temple was located on an island in the Tiber River in the center of Rome. It was said that the god was brought to the city during a terrible plague in 293 B.C. on advice found in the Sibylline Books.

The Romans had no god equivalent to Apollo. They simply adopted him as their own and kept his Greek name.

Questions

1. List the many attributes of Apollo. What connections seem to exist among the various areas of authority?

2. Why is Apollo often called "Delian"?

3. Explain the title "Pythian."

4. Who practiced prophecy at Delphi before Apollo? What does this tradition tell us about the shrine?

5. Which mountain is associated with Delphi?

6. What two stones were on display at Delphi?

7. For how long was the shrine at Delphi active?

8. Describe the procedure used by the Pythia at Delphi.

9. Describe other techniques used for foretelling the future in addition to those used at Delphi.

10. In addition to divine inspiration, what other sources of information did the priests of Delphi have to help them make accurate predictions?

11. How did the shrine at Delphi support itself financially?

12. Explain the title "Loxias."

13. To what does the word "oracle" refer?

14. Why was Sibyl punished? What was her punishment? What is the meaning of this short myth?

15. To whom did the title "Sibyl" refer? To whom did the title "Pythia" refer?

16. What were the Sibylline Books? What is the significance of the story concerning their loss?

17. Who was Cassandra? Why was she punished? How was she punished? What is the meaning of the myth?

18. How is the story of Castalia connected with Apollo?

19. What custom does the story of Daphne explain? How?

20. What were the Pythian Games? Where did the name "Pythian" originate?

21. Name three sun-gods in addition to Apollo.

22. What is Phaethon's story? What is its meaning?

23. Explain the title "Phoebus."

24. What was the story of Orestes and what does it represent about Apollo?

25. Explain the title "Musagetes."

26. What does the story of the musical contest with Pan show us about Apollo?

27. How does the story of Apollo and Marsyas contrast with that of Apollo and Pan?

28. Who was the child of Apollo and Coronis? Why was he famous?

29. What was Epidaurus? Describe the techniques used there.

30. What is the Hippocratic Oath? How is it connected with Asclepius?

31. Who was Aesculapius? Where was his major temple located?

15. ATHENA

A. Characteristics

B. Birth

C. Parthenon

D. Panathenaic Festival

E. Goddess of war

F. Goddess of wisdom

G. Arachne

Characteristics

Athena was the virgin goddess of domestic arts and crafts, of wisdom, and of war. She was the patroness of Athens and the protector of cities in general. She was known to the Romans as Minerva.

Birth

As we have seen, after Metis, an early goddess of wisdom, had become pregnant by Zeus, it was foretold that her child would produce a son who would overthrown him. To keep the prophecy from being fulfilled, Zeus swallowed her just as she was about to give birth, and their child, Athena, burst forth from his head. By thus becoming both mother and father, Zeus successfully avoided the ominous consequences.

Parthenon

We have also seen how the goddess successfully competed against Poseidon in order to become the patron deity of the Athenians. When she was not on Mt. Olympus with the other gods, Athena could often be found on the acropolis (i.e., the "high city," a hill of about 200 feet above street level) in Athens. It is there that we find what was perhaps the most famous temple in the ancient world, the Parthenon. This magnificent structure, which was built in Athena's honor, contained an ivory and gold statue of the goddess created by the artist, Phidias. The name of the temple comes from a title of the goddess which means "virgin."

Panathenaic Festival

The Athenians conducted the Panathenaic Festival annually in honor of their patroness. A view of some of the activities surrounding the procession which which took place during the celebration can be found on the marble reliefs preserved from the Parthenon.

Goddess of war

Athena was also thought of as a guardian of cities in general and as a goddess of war. These two aspects were combined, since she made use of her warlike abilities in defense of any city which successfully acquired her services. In this capacity, the goddess was often represented as wearing a helmet and carrying a shield and a spear, but unlike Ares who represented the frenzy of battle, Athena was associated with the defensive battle which employs clever and intelligent tactics and saves the city. This is not to minimize her warlike characteristics which she used at various times. Some even say that, when she leaped forth from the head of her father at birth, she did so with a loud war cry and was wearing her military attire. On another occasion, when she was assisting Zeus in the Gigantomachy, she not only killed one of the giants, Pallas, but flayed him, and then used his skin on her shield. Some writers say that this is why the goddess is often called Pallas Athena, although others maintain that Pallas means "maiden."

Goddess of wisdom

While Athena is said to be associated with wisdom, it is really cleverness and cunning which she admired, combined with courage. She would often assist heroes in their tasks when she found that they possessed such qualities. Men like Perseus, Bellerophon, Heracles, Cadmus, and Jason owed much to her support.

Arachne

As the goddess who was associated with cities, Athena was thought of as a promoter of civilization and was thus identified with whatever might be necessary to maintain and promote civilized life, especially the domestic arts and crafts. In this capacity, she was particularly associated with weaving.

There is a story that a young woman by the name of Arachne who was a very talented weaver challenged Athena to compete with her. The goddess visited her disguised as an old woman and advised Arachne to apologize to Athena and to limit her competition to mortals. The young woman rejected the advice and insisted that her work could surpass that of the goddess.

The contest began. Athena wove a magnificent picture of her contest with Poseidon for the loyalty of Athens. Arachne, foolishly compounding her boldness, portrayed scenes of the secret loves of the gods. When Athena examined the woman's work, she could find no fault with the technique, but she became very angry because of the insolence involved in the choice of subject. She forced Arachne to hang herself, and then, at the last moment, released the knot and transformed the foolish woman into a spider which from that time on has been condemned to weave its web.

In this brief story we find not only an explanation for the origin of arachnids, but a clear warning to those who dare to challenge the gods.

Questions

1. Describe the miraculous nature of Athena's birth. In what way can the action of Zeus in swallowing Metis be taken as symbolic or metaphorical?

2. What was the Parthenon? Where was it located?

3. In what way did Athena usually employ her military ability?

4. What were the offenses of Arachne? What personality trait do they reveal? How was she punished? In what way does the story reveal the fairness of Athena?

16. ARES

A. Characteristics

B. Mars

C. Warrior

D. Lover

E. The Areopagus and Campus Martius

Characteristics

Ares, a son of Zeus and Hera, was the god of war. He represented the uncontrolled frenzy of battle and all of the destruction and horrors of war. He was not a popular god among the Greeks, for, while they valued courage, strength, and ability, they were very suspicious of the mindless spirit of devastation. Even Zeus, his own father, disliked the quarrelsome manner of the god. Most of Ares' cult centers were outside of Greece, and he may have been of foreign origin, even though he is found among the twelve Olympians from a very early time.

Mars

The Romans called their god of war Mars, and they held him in such high regard that he was considered second only to Jupiter (i.e., Zeus) in importance. Much more emphasis was placed upon the god as protector of the city and the state than upon his bloodlust. Mars was believed to be the father of Romulus and Remus, the founders of Rome itself. The Romans named the first month of their year Martius in honor of the god (it was considered to be the season for the renewal of battles after the winter), and the name has come down to us as March.

Warrior

Despite the fact that he was a war god, Ares was not always effective in battle. During the Trojan War, Diomedes, a Greek leader, fought Ares and wounded him. In the same war Athena brought him down with a huge stone. As a part of earlier adventures, Otus and Ephialtes, the two giants who attempted to overthrow Zeus by piling mountains on top of one another, captured and imprisoned Ares, and the great Heracles is said to have defeated him on a number of occasions.

Lover

While Ares did not marry, he had many children by numerous women. His offspring were -like their father- often savage and destructive; we shall see some of them later in the hero tales. The Amazons, a fierce race of women warriors, also claimed to be descended from the god.

Ares' most famous romance was with the goddess of love, Aphrodite. Since she was already married to Hephaestus, their affair had to be conducted secretly. Despite this inconvenience, they had four children.

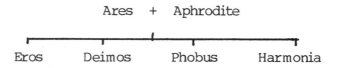

Ares + Aphrodite

Eros   Deimos   Phobus   Harmonia

Eros -whose Roman name was Cupid- represented love and physical desire. He was a double for his mother in much the same way as Persephone was for Demeter.

Deimos (Panic) and Phobus (Fear) are simply personifications of feelings often associated with battle. They frequently drove their father's chariot into combat.

The one daughter from the union was Harmonia, who apparently inherited more from her mother than her father since her name means "concord" or "agreement." Ares gave her in marriage to Cadmus, founder of the city of Thebes.

The love affair between Ares and Aphrodite ended when Helios, the god of the sun (who sees all that happens), informed Hephaestus. The craftsman of the gods made a special net which he placed above his wife's bed; he then announced that he had to leave Olympus for a time. When Ares delightedly took advantage of his absence, the net fell and tightly bound the two. Hephaestus and the other gods entered to enjoy the lovers' embarrassment. Ares was ordered to make restitution for his offenses and to end the illicit romance.

The Areopagus and the Campus Martius

Two significant geographical sites are associated with the god. The Areopagus, which means the "Hill of Ares," is a rocky outcropping next to the Acropolis in Athens. Some say that the Amazons named it after the god when they camped on the site during their war with the Athenians; others say that Ares himself was put on trial there for murder and gave his name to the site. The Athenians used the Areopagus as a meeting place for governmental bodies and for homicide trials.

Another famous site associated with the god of war was the Campus Martius (= the "Field of Mars") in Rome. For centuries the Romans conducted their elections in this open area near the Forum.

Questions

1. How does Ares differ from Mars?

2. Describe Ares as a warrior.

3. With whom did Ares have his most famous romance?

4. Who was the most famous child of this love affair?

5. How did Hephaestus trap Ares?

6. What was the Areopagus? What took place there?

7. What was the Campus Martius?

17. APHRODITE

A. Characteristics

B. Birth

C. Love affairs

D. Favorites and enemies

E. Eros

F. Cupid and Psyche

Characteristics

Aphrodite was the goddess of physical love and passionate desire. Her Roman equivalent was Venus.

Birth

Some say that Aphrodite was the daughter of Zeus and Dione, a daughter of Oceanus. Others claim that her origin was much more ancient and that she was born from the mating of "aphros" which means "foam of the sea" with the severed genitals of Uranus which Cronus had thrown into the nearby water after his attack on his father.

She was -in either version- associated with the sea at birth and with the islands Cythera (south of mainland Greece) and Cyprus. She was given titles related to the two locations, e.g., Cytherea, Cypris, Cyprus-born.

In actuality Aphrodite was probably a goddess who came to Greece from the Middle East where she was called Ishtar or Astarte and was associated with the fertility of the earth.

Love affairs

Aphrodite was married to Hephaestus, but, being who she was, she had love affairs with other gods as well. As we have seen, her most famous liaison was with Ares.

She was forced by Zeus to submit to Hermes. The child which resulted was named Hermaphrodite, a compound of their names. He grew to be a handsome young man with whom a nymph, Salmacis, fell in love. He rejected her advances until one day, as he was bathing in a spring, she leaped upon him and prayed to the gods that they would never be separated. Her pleas were answered; their two bodies were fused into one. From that time on, a creature which combines both male and female characteristics has been called a hermaphrodite.

Some say that Aphrodite also had love affairs with the gods Dionysus and Poseidon.

The goddess did not restrict her attentions just to other deities; she had love affairs with mortals as well. Perhaps her most famous mortal romance was that with the hunter, Adonis. Despite the goddess' love for this handsome young man, he was nevertheless killed by a boar during one of his hunts. Like Aphrodite herself, Adonis was probably derived from a Middle Eastern fertility god whose death marked the harvesting of the crops and whose rebirth in the spring restored life to the fields.

Aphrodite also had a love affair with Anchises who was associated with the city of Troy. Aphrodite made the hero promise never to reveal their romance, but, despite the warning, he could not restrain himself from boasting about his famous partner. Zeus punished him by striking the unfortunate man with a lightning bolt which permanently crippled him. The child born of this romance was Aeneas who not only distinguished himself in battle during the Trojan War, but was also chosen by the gods to bring the survivors to Italy where eventually a new Troy would rise in the form of Rome.

Favorites and enemies

Aphrodite often demonstrated favoritism toward young men who worshipped her. Because he had chosen her as the most beautiful of the goddesses, she helped Paris, a prince of Troy, to seduce Helen the most attractive woman in the world. She answered the prayers of Pygmalion by bringing to life the statue of an ideal woman which he had carved. She aided Hippomenes to defeat Atalanta in a footrace and thus to win her as his bride. She caused Medea to fall in love with Jason and to help him obtain the Golden Fleece.

Aphrodite was also harsh with those who rejected her. When the young man, Hippolytus, refused to worship her in favor of Artemis, Aphrodite caused his violent death in a chariot crash, and after the women on the island of Lemnos refused to venerate her properly, she forced their husbands to reject them completely and to take foreign wives.

Eros

Eros was one of the children of Aphrodite and Ares. He represented physical love as did his mother. He was often represented as a playful young child with wings. To be struck by one of his gold-tipped arrows would cause even one of the gods to fall in love.

In this form he was often called Cupid or Amor by the Romans. While there was only one Eros or Cupid, he was sometimes spoken of in the plural (to indicate, perhaps, his wide-spread influence) and portrayed in that way by the artists.

Eros (Cupid) was also presented as a handsome young man as well as a chubby little infant, and, when he so appeared, his most famous story was the one involving the lovely Psyche.

Cupid and Psyche

Psyche was so beautiful that she aroused the jealousy of Venus (Aphrodite) who believed that the men of Psyche's village were worshipping a mortal woman more than herself. She commanded her son to punish the maiden.

An oracle indicated that Psyche must be isolated in uninhabited country where she would be forced to wed an evil spirit. Her father reluctantly complied, and the unfortunate woman was placed in a lonely cottage in the middle of a great forest. Each night she found her humble abode transformed magically into an enchanted palace where invisible hands served her. When she retired, she was soothed by a man's voice who told her that he was her husband; he made her promise never to look upon him, and before dawn he would leave her. Psyche felt no fear even though her husband behaved in such a mysterious manner. Her visitor was in actuality Cupid himself, who had fallen in love with the young woman whom he had been commanded by his mother to punish. To conceal both his love and his disobedience of his mother's orders, he visited his beloved under cover of darkness and without revealing his identity.

Psyche grew lonely for her family, and so, after much pleading, Cupid finally allowed her sisters to visit her. When she revealed to them what was happening to her, the sisters, partially in envy, partially in fear, warned her that her husband might in actuality be the monster which the oracle had foretold. They urged her to look upon her lover while he slept, and to kill him if necessary.

Because Psyche was young and credulous, she followed the advice of her sisters. That very night, after her husband had fallen asleep, she cautiously took the lamp and knife she had set nearby and brought them to the bed. The flickering light revealed the handsome young god, but, in her excitement, Psyche's hand trembled, and she inadvertently spilled drops of oil from her lamp onto the body of her sleeping lover. Cupid awoke with a start and immediately recognized what Psyche had done. He looked at the young woman with feelings of sadness and disappointment, while Psyche -ashamed- tried to hide from his gaze. "You promised," he said. "And love cannot exist without trust." With those few words he left the grieving maiden.

Psyche was overcome with sorrow and shame. She would do anything to bring Cupid back. Now it happened about this time that Venus discovered her son's disobedience. Not only had he not punished Psyche, he had even taken her secretly as his wife. The goddess at first became very angry and criticized her son harshly, but, when she came to realize how much he really loved the woman despite the fact that she had broken her promise to him, and how the remorseful Psyche was willing to do anything to be reunited with him, Venus set a series of formidable tasks for the young wife to accomplish before she could look upon her husband again. To Venus' surprise, Psyche —with the help of various sympathetic gods— successfully completed all of the challenges. Cupid, who had long since forgiven Psyche, was now permitted to rejoin his devoted wife. He begged the Ruler of the Gods to make her his immortal bride, and his request was granted. Even Venus forgave them and welcomed them to Mt. Olympus.

Questions

1. What are the two stories concerning the origin of Aphrodite?

2. What is a hermaphrodite and how did the word originate?

3. What does the word "adonis" mean in English usage today? How is the current meaning related to its mythological source?

4. In what way is the love affair between Aphrodite and Anchises connected with Roman myth?

5. How would you describe Aphrodite's treatment of those who worshipped her and those who ignored her? Give examples.

6. Who were the parents of Eros? What were his characteristics?

7. What lessons does the story of Cupid and Psyche teach?

8. Cupid represents physical love and the word "psyche" means "soul." What additional symbolism can be obtained from the story when we are aware of these meanings?

18. HEPHAESTUS

A. Characteristics

B. Birth

C. Marriage

Characteristics

Hephaestus was the master craftsman and metalworker of the gods. His forge was always a place of much activity as he designed and produced ingenious and artistic creations. His masterpieces included the palaces of the gods, Zeus' throne and scepter, the chariot of Helios, the arrows of Apollo and Artemis, the sickle of Demeter, and weapons for Athena. He also created the armor for great heroes such as Achilles and Aeneas. The Roman name for the god was Vulcan.

Hephaestus probably came to Greece from the east where he was associated with volcanoes. It was thought that he had his workplace under such mountains and that the smoke and flames came from his forge. Some believe that Hephaestus replaced Prometheus as a god of fire.

Birth

It was widely believed that Hera became angry with Zeus because he had given birth to Athena from his head and without her cooperation, and so she decided to perform a comparable miracle by conceiving and giving birth to Hephaestus without any help from her husband. There was another tradition, however, which said that Hephaestus was the son of both divinities.

While Hephaestus was still a youngster, he once attempted to intervene in a quarrel between Zeus and Hera. Angered by such audaciousness, Zeus hurled the boy from the heavenly palace. He fell for one full day before he struck the earth, and, although he survived the fall, he was lame from that time on.

Marriage

As we have seen, Hephaestus was the husband of Aphrodite from whom he had to endure many infidelities, although he was eventually able to trap and embarrass his wife with her most infamous lover, Ares.

Hephaestus himself was not associated with any other women except for a brief desire for Athena which was frustrated by the goddess. He was a craftsman and chiefly of significance in his workshop.

Questions

1. Given the tasks of Hephaestus in ancient myth, what would be his profession today?

2. What are the two variants concerning Hephaestus' conception?

3. What does the treatment of Hephaestus by Zeus suggest about the family life of the gods?

4. With which goddess is Hephaestus chiefly associated?

19. HERMES

A. Characteristics

B. Birth

C. Hermaphrodite

D. Pan

Characteristics

While Hermes was the youngest of the gods, he had very primitive origins. He was a messenger of Zeus, the herald of the gods, the guide for travelers, the leader of spirits to the Underworld, giver of fertility, and the patron for orators, writers, businessmen, thieves and athletes. His Roman name was Mercury.

It is difficult to tie these various attributes to one divinity, but Hermes' origin can probably be seen in the word "herma" or "hermaion" which means "stone heap." Such piles of stones often became landmarks for travelers, especially in areas where there was no clear path. The spirit which was thought to live in such heaps became associated with guiding journeyers to their destination. Each passer-by would add his stone to the pile for good luck. Since such a mound would often mark a grave, Hermes was also thought of as a god who could guide the dead to their home in the spirit world, and, since in this capacity, he entered and left the Underworld, he became associated with the birth-death cycle of the crops and thus with fertility in general.

A larger stone was often placed in the center of the piles which over the years became more formalized and was carved into a pillar about four feet high with the only representations on it being the head of the god and his genitals. Such posts -ubiquitous in the ancient world- were called herms and were thought to bring fertility and good fortune.

Since Hermes was a guide to travelers, it was natural that he should be the messenger of Zeus and the herald of the gods. As such, he was often pictured with a broad-rimmed traveler's hat -sometimes with wings on it- and with winged shoes or sandals. He carried the caduceus, a staff entwined with snakes which was used in antiquity to indicate that its bearer was a herald and could not be harmed without severe penalties. Hermes' caduceus was said to have wings and to possess magic powers.

Since as messenger and herald he would have to be an effective and persuasive speaker, Hermes became the god of orators and writers, and, since businessmen and thieves of necessity did much traveling and often conducted their affairs in the crossroads, he became their protector as well. There is another connection for the god with thieves. From birth Hermes was always a clever, sly, and cunning god. He delighted in being a trickster and would cheat and lie where necessary. Such behavior was just another side of the god's personality, and it coexisted with his more positive features. Hermes was a great-grandfather to Odysseus, and, as we shall see, he passed along some of his craftiness to that great hero of the Trojan War.

The connection with athletes is a little more tenuous, but it is probably because the god was associated with good fortune, and contestants need all the luck available as they compete against each other. His quickness and grace in movement may have been another link.

Birth

Zeus was Hermes' father, and Maia, a daughter of Atlas, his mother. The infant was so precocious that within hours of his birth he leaped from his cradle and invented the lyre, a stringed instrument of great popularity in antiquity. He next stole some of Apollo's cattle, just to see if he could deceive the god, and then crawled back into his cradle to resume his role as innocent babe. But Apollo was not deluded. As compensation, Hermes gave the god the lyre which he had invented. Apollo was so pleased with the new instrument that he allowed Hermes to keep his cattle, and the two gods became the best of friends.

Hermes was often chosen by Zeus to be his companion when he visited earth in disguise, but his most frequent appearances were as divine messenger and herald. He was always benevolent toward the human race, especially toward travelers, and, because of this characteristic, he was often called Hermes the Helper.

Hermaphrodite

While Hermes never had a wife, he was associated with many mortal women. His one love affair with a goddess was with Aphrodite, and, as we have already seen, their unfortunate child was Hermaphrodite.

Pan

Pan was the most famous child of Hermes. He was a god of wild nature, of mountains, of flocks, and of shepherds. From birth the god combined human physical features with those of a goat. He was in behavior much like the animal with which he was so closely allied: he moved about quickly, was short-tempered and lustful. The god had the power by means of a shout to produce in an enemy a sudden and unreasoning state of terror which was called "panic" from his name.

It is said that once when Pan was pursuing a nymph by the name of Syrinx, the gods took pity on her and transformed her into a cluster of reeds. Pan picked some of different lengths, bound them together, and created beautiful music by blowing into them. He called his new musical instrument the syrinx. It became very popular with shepherds who played it as they watched their flocks.

The Roman name for Pan was Faunus who was also thought to be an early Italian king. These spirits of wild nature were often pluralized into pans and fauns, a process similar to what we have already seen with Triton and Cupid.

With Hermes we conclude our discussion of the twelve major Olympian gods.

Questions

1. What characteristics of Hermes probably derive from his connection with stone heaps?

2. What was a "herm"?

3. What was the caduceus used to indicate?

4. Who were the parents of Hermes?

5. With what musical instrument is Hermes associated?

6. Who was Pan? With what musical instrument is he associated?

20. HADES

A. Background

B. The Land of the Dead

C. Thanatos and Hermes

D. Charon and the River Styx

E. Cerberus

F. The Plain of Asphodel

G. The Three Judges

H. Elysium

I. Tartarus

J. Developing concepts

K. The rivers of the Underworld

Background

Hades was the god who ruled the Land of the Dead. His name means, appropriately enough, "Unseen One." The Greeks hesitated to speak the name of this fearful divinity, so they often called him Pluto which means "rich" or "wealthy" and refers both to the great number of spirits under his authority and to the fact that all crops grow from beneath the earth, the location of his kingdom. The Romans borrowed the name Pluto from the Greeks, but they also called the god Dis which likewise means "rich" and Orcus which means "death."

The Land of the Dead was called the Underworld, or the House of Hades, or sometimes -by transference- just Hades.

The god, as we have seen, was one of the children of Cronus and Rhea who was swallowed by his father and rescued by his brother Zeus. When he, Zeus, and Poseidon drew lots for areas of authority, the Land of the Dead fell to Hades.

The god lived among his subjects; he was seldom seen on earth or in Olympus. He was a grim, inexorable, but just ruler in his domain and should not be thought of as a devil or an evil spirit. He saw to it that no one escaped, although there were a few occasions when he permitted great heroes to enter and leave his territory while they were still alive. He had absolute power in his dominion and was often called "Zeus of the Underworld."

His wife was Persephone, and, while she came to the Land of the Dead unwillingly and spent only one-third of the year there, she did not seem to resent her time with her husband and indeed acquired similar characteristics as a just ruler.

The Land of the Dead

The Land of the dead was thought to have a physical location. At first it was believed to be far in the west, beyond the River Ocean which encircled the perimeter of the earth. Later, it was considered to be under the earth, although -as with the gods dwelling on Mt. Olympus or in the remote sky- both views continued to exist. Many towns claimed to have entrances to the Lower Realm. The one most famous in literature was the cave of the Sibyl on the shore of Lake Avernus near Naples in Italy. It was this entrance which Aeneas used when he entered the Underworld while still alive.

The Greeks used both cremation and inhumation for their dead. Funerals for the nobility were often accompanied not only by the killing of animals but also by human sacrifice of slaves to accompany their master into the other world or by the slaying of enemy captives, if the death took place in battle. Athletic contests were sometimes held to honor the dead person.

Thanatos and Hermes

There were other deities in addition to Hades who were associated with the dead and who helped in bridging the passage from one world to the next.

Thanatos (Death) was the god whose task was apparently to release the spirit of the person from the corpse. He usually accomplished this duty by cutting a lock of hair or sometimes by just carrying the person off. He was somewhat comparable to our Grim Reaper. Hermes then guided the spirits of the dead to the Underworld.

Charon and the River Styx

The Underworld can best be thought of as a circular area, in shape like the earth above it. As the upper land was surrounded by the River Ocean, the Underworld was encircled by the River Styx.

It was to the shore of the Styx that the spirits first arrived. If their funeral rites had been properly performed, then they were permitted to cross the river into the Land of the Dead itself. If burial rituals had not been duly observed, the spirits were condemned to remain for one hundred years on what was called the "Far Bank" of the Styx. Such a penalty was very severe, since each spirit longed to be in its proper place. These unhappy souls would often return to the land of the living and cause harm to those who had neglected the rituals.

Passage across the River Styx was only possible in the boat of the god Charon. This stern god, usually portrayed as a bearded old man, would only accept those who were dead and properly buried, and, some say, who were able to pay for their crossing with a coin.

Cerberus

Once Charon's boat had reached the shore of the Underworld itself, the spirits saw the fearsome Cerberus, a huge three-headed watchdog. It was his task to see that only the dead entered this domain and that no one left.

The Plain of Asphodel

The destination for most spirits was called the Plain of Asphodel. It was a dark, dank, and gloomy place without joy or sorrow. With very rare exceptions, there was no relationship between one's life on earth and reward or punishment in the afterlife. Existence in the Plain of Asphodel was not a pleasant prospect, yet it was thought to be what awaited almost everyone.

The Three Judges

There was a path which ran from the Styx through the Plain of Asphodel and then divided into two, much like the letter Y. The palace of Hades and Persephone was thought to be close to this intersection.

The Three Judges were also located at the division in the path. These three men were Minos, King of Crete, his brother Rhadamanthys, and Aeacus, a Greek. All three were effective and just rulers while they lived. They were originally believed to be judges in the sense in which that word is used in the Bible, i.e., each ruled over a certain part of the Underworld and would settle various disputes within his territory. Later, after the concept of reward and punishment had been introduced into the afterlife, the judges determined whether a spirit should be sent to heaven (Elysium) along one path or to hell (Tartarus) on the other.

Elysium

One of the paths, then, led to Elysium, the closest the ancient view of the afterlife came to providing a heaven. It was here under a separate sun and a separate sky that heroes judged to be truly great by the gods were able to do those things as spirits which delighted them when they were alive.

The location of Elysium (also known as the Elysian Fields or as The Blessed Isles or The Islands of the Blessed) varies. It was often considered to be physically adjacent to the Underworld and part of it (the destination of one of the divided paths). It was sometimes placed beyond the River Ocean in the West, and sometimes it was thought to exist in the sky.

For the common man there was little hope of reaching Elysium, but, perhaps as a recompense, neither was there danger that he might end in Tartarus, the end of the second path.

Tartarus

Tartarus was believed to be located in a deep chasm dropping beneath the surface of the Underworld. It was surrounded by a bronze wall and was covered by a triple thickness of night. It was the "black hole" of the Underworld. Originally thought of as a prison for rebel gods (e.g., some of the defeated Titans), it came in time to house a few legendary human sinners.

We have already seen two of those men who were given eternal punishment by the gods. Ixion, for attempting to seduce Hera, was condemned forever to spin on a wheel of fire. Tityus, for attempting to rape Leto, was continually torn at by vultures.

Tantalus, because he attempted to trick the gods into dining on human flesh, was condemned always to be hungry and always to thirst. A fruit tree hung its tempting branches over his head, but just as he attempted to seize one, a breeze would blow the branch out of his reach. A pool of water was at his feet, but as he attempted to gather some in his hands, it would soak into the earth. It is easy to see why we get the English word "tantalize" from this man's name.

Sisyphus was a trickster of both gods and men. When Zeus realized that Sisyphus had managed through deception to obtain a second life, he condemned him to Tartarus where he was made to push a huge rock up a steep hill. When he finally reached the top, the rock would roll down again to the base, and Sisyphus was forced to follow it and begin his task once more. To this repetitive action he was forever condemned.

Salmoneus was a brother of Sisyphus, and for his presumption in thinking that he was the equal of Zeus, he was killed by a lightning bolt and hurled into Tartarus.

The Danaids, daughters of King Danaus, were in Tartarus because, after marrying on the same day, they had followed their father's order and had killed their husbands on the wedding night. Their punishment was endlessly to attempt to fill sieve-like jars with water.

Aside, then, from these few individuals in Tartarus and a few great heroes in Elysium, everyone else would spend their eternity on the Plain of Asphodel.

Developing concepts

There were, as we have suggested, other beliefs. As a greater moral sensitivity developed, judgment with resulting reward or punishment became the standard form of the afterlife. Elysium became a heaven which was open to all, and Tartarus became a place of punishment for sinners. However, even in early times the mystery religions emphasized the importance of good actions in this life which led to rewards in the next. Reincarnation was an important part of some beliefs, and it was usually combined with the idea of higher or lower existences based on the moral character of one's current life. The object of such a belief would be to continue to perfect one's self in progressive existences until finally one would be morally worthy of entry into Elysium.

The rivers of the Underworld

The River Lethe in the Underworld was connected with the concept of reincarnation. Once a spirit had drunk of its waters, all memories of a previous existence were removed, and the spirit could assume a new body and a new life. Lethe was often called the River of Forgetfulness.

There were other rivers in the Underworld whose functions were not so clearly defined. The Acheron was by some writers considered to be the river which encircled the Underworld; it served the function of the Styx. The Phlegethon was a river of flames and was by some associated with the punishment of the wicked. The Cocytus was apparently just a part of the general geography.

Questions

1. What are the other names for the god Hades?

2. How did the Land of the Dead come under the jurisdiction of Hades?

3. Who was the wife of Hades? With what goddess is she closely associated?

4. Where was the Land of the Dead thought to be located?

5. Who was Thanatos and what was his function?

6. How was Hermes connected with the dead?

7. Describe the geography of the Underworld.

8. Why were some spirits forced to remain on the Far Bank of the Styx?

9. Who was Charon and what was his function?

10. Who was Cerberus and what was his function?

11. Describe the Plain of Asphodel. What was its function?

12. Where was the palace of Hades located?

13. Who were the Judges and what was their function?

14. What was Elysium? Who existed there? Where was it located?

15. Describe Tartarus. Where was it located? What was its function?

16. Describe the sins and punishments of
    Ixion
    Tityus
    Tantalus
    Sisyphus
    the Danaids

17. In what ways did the concepts associated with the Underworld change and develop?

18. With what concept was the River Lethe associated? Explain the beliefs associated with this concept.

19. List the other rivers of the Underworld and describe their function.

21. DIONYSUS

A. Characteristics

B. Worshippers

C. Bacchus

D. Birth

E. Childhood

F. Travels

    1. Midas
    2. The pirates
    3. Thrace and King Lycurgus
    4. Thebes and King Pentheus
    5. Ariadne

G. Conclusion

Characteristics

Dionysus was the god of wine and by extension the attributes connected with it. Since wine can produce drunkenness, Dionysus was associated with that as well. An intoxicated person was considered to be under the influence of the god; he is in a state of ecstacy, i.e., he is "out of his self." Since a drunken person behaves in a way that is unlike his normal actions and that is often eccentric, the god became connected with irrationality and madness. He also represented emotion, especially when it was excessive, as opposed to reason and self-control.

Dionysus was from the beginning associated with the fertility of the grape vine and gradually this function expanded to include fertility in general (crop, animal, human). He was in this regard something like a male equivalent to Demeter.

The god was associated with the country rather than the city. Dressed in the skins of wild animals, he was portrayed sometimes as a young man, sometimes as bearded and older. He could and often did assume the shape of any animal. On various occasions he became a bull, goat, tiger, lion, panther, leopard, dolphin, and a snake; he sometimes became the grain or the tree or the fruit or the vine itself. Widely varied appearance was characteristic of this god who represented the fertility of everything.

Frequently portrayed symbols of Dionysus were (1) a staff twined with a grape vine and ivy leaves and with a pine cone placed at the top, (2) a wreath of ivy or grape vines, and (3) a wine cup.

Worshippers

As the god moved through the countryside, he was accompanied by a varied group who were all linked with fertility. There were the maenads or bacchae (ecstatic women worshippers of the god), nymphs, satyrs (goat-men), sileni (old satyrs), and centaurs.

Satyrs represented lustful fertility. They combined various features of goats and men and were in a constant state of sexual excitment. Their favorite activities were drinking wine and pursuing nymphs and maenads.

Sileni were satyrs who had grown old. They enjoyed the same endeavors as their younger and friskier counterparts, but they often had to settle for drunkenness when their more nimble female prey eluded them. As with the centaurs who had Chiron as a noted teacher, so with the Sileni, there was Silenus who had been entrusted with the education of the young Dionysus, and who, as though he were a kindly old grandfather, watched over the satyrs.

The bacchae or maenads who accompanied Dionysus were an actual reflection of the religious worship of the god. The ritual which was called "orgia" (= "orgy" or "unrestrained actions") was an attempt to worship the god by establishing a communion with him and —briefly— to become Dionysus himself.

At certain times of the year (usually in the spring planting season) groups of women would go into the hills —as the spirit moved them— to perform the rites of the god. They would first attempt to encourage Dionysus to come to them by drinking sacred wine, by playing music on reed pipes with drums and cymbals, and by frenzied dancing.

The women, often dressed like the god himself in animal skins, would carry the staff of Dionysus (called the thyrsus), would wear ivy and grape wreaths, and might also hold snakes or entwine them around their bodies.

In these ways the maenads would attempt to achieve an ecstatic state so that Dionysus would appear to them in some form. A wild hunt would begin. When the bacchae came upon an animal, they believed it to be the god. They would catch it, tear it to pieces, and consume the raw flesh. It was the moment of communion; the god entered into each of his devotees. For a brief instant the huge chasm which separated deity from mortal was bridged, and the two became one. After this rite, the frenzy of the worshippers would diminish, and the maenads would return to their villages.

The Greeks were concerned about the wild nature of these rites honoring Dionysus. They eventually regulated and institutionalized them; however, the power of the god was recognized and respected, and the worshippers were permitted their rituals every second year under state supervision.

From the practices of the maenads or bacchae, the word orgy has come to mean "wild party" in English. The words "bacchanal" or "bacchanalia" are synonyms for orgy and are also derived from the unrestrained rituals.

Bacchus

Dionysus was also called Bacchus by the Greeks, and this name was taken by the Romans for their equivalent of the god whom they sometimes called Liber as well. The Roman view of Bacchus was much more limited than the Greek; they chiefly emphasized his association with wine and portrayed him as a fat, jolly old man.

Birth

There were many stories told about the birth of Dionysus. The one most commonly believed was that he was the son of Zeus and Semele, a daughter of Cadmus who was the founder of Thebes.

An angry and jealous Hera disguised herself as an old woman and raised doubts in Semele's mind that her lover was truly a god. When Zeus next visited her, an insistent Semele made him promise to grant her any wish. The infatuated god agreed, and Semele asked that she be able to see him in all of his glory. Zeus knew that her request meant certain death, since no mortal could withstand the fiery brightness of the divine aura; nonetheless, after all attempts to dissuade Semele had failed, he was forced to fulfill his promise. Although the unfortunate woman was consumed in flames, Zeus rescued the infant Dionysus from her womb and -unbelievable- placed the baby in his thigh until it was ready to be born.

Some say that it was the aura of Zeus which made Dionysus divine, since the offspring of a god and a mortal is ordinarily a human; others say it was the fact that Dionysus was born from the thigh of Zeus who thus acted as both father and mother. In any case, many of the myths of the god describe the strong resistance to the spread of his cult both because of his questionable divinity and because of the orgiastic nature of his rituals. The stories describe the rewards for those who accept the god and the penalties for those who do not. The punishments are closely related to the Dionysiac worship itself: they involve madness which is similar to the ecstatic frenzy of the maenads, and the tearing apart of the victim who becomes a human sacrifice to the god he had rejected.

Childhood

The infant Dionysus was given to Ino, Semele's sister to raise, but Hera's jealousy had not abated. Despite this kind action by Ino, Hera drove her mad and forced her to commit suicide.

Zeus feared for Dionysus because of the jealous rage of his wife, and he attempted to conceal the infant from her. He brought him to the wild country in Asia and gave him to the elderly satyr, Silenus, to educate. Silenus taught the young god about the cultivation of the grape vine specifically and about the fertility of all things in general. Some say that, despite Zeus' efforts at concealment, Hera still found the child and tore him apart, scattering the pieces of the body across the land, and that Zeus carefully reassembled each piece and restored the child to life. Some think that it was this action which gave divinity to Dionysus.

Travels

When he became a young man, Dionysus began his travels about the world spreading the knowledge which Silenus had given him and attempting to win converts to his worship. It was thought that Hera interfered again and that at times during his journeys the god was driven mad by her. He visited various places in Asia Minor, in the Middle East, in Egypt, and even went as far as India before returning.

1. Midas

As he traveled through Phrygia (modern Turkey), a country known for its orgiastic religious rites (and, according to many, the ultimate source for Dionysiac worship), he encountered King Midas in what is perhaps the most famous story connected with the god.

We have already seen Midas as a judge in the music contest between Apollo and Pan where he won the ears of an ass for his foolish choice. Now the king pleased Dionysus by restoring to him a drunken silenus who had become lost, and so the god granted him whatever he might wish. Midas, already a wealthy man, chose to have everything turn to gold at his touch. It was done. The king was at first very happy with his new talent, but he soon came to realize the foolishness of his choice. When he tried to eat or to drink, the substances turned to gold. He realized in horror that he would soon die of hunger and thirst unless the power he had been given were removed. Midas returned to the god and begged him to bestow a second wish which was to take away the capability of the first. The god granted his request, and Midas -perhaps now a wiser man- was saved.

2. The pirates

Somewhere in his travels, Dionysus was kidnapped by pirates who thought he was a wealthy young aristocrat and hoped to obtain ransom for him. The god transformed the masts of their ship into vines and himself into many different shapes until he eventually became a roaring lion. The pirates, stunned by all of the miracles, jumped into the sea where Dionysus changed them into the first dolphins.

3. Thrace and King Lycurgus

Dionysus traveled from Asia into Europe and came to the country of Thrace, north of Greece. There he was violently opposed by King Lycurgus. After his many warnings were ignored, the god caused the crops to fail and drove Lycurgus mad. The king killed his son, maimed himself, and was eventually torn to pieces by his own people.

4. Thebes and King Pentheus

Dionysus next came to Thebes, the native town of his mother. But even here the people, led by King Pentheus, rejected him. After many warnings were once again given which Pentheus ignored, the god drove the king mad and caused him to be torn apart by a group of frenzied maenads led by his own mother. The people of Thebes finally recognized –too late to prevent disaster– the power of Dionysus.

Likewise, in the towns of Argos and Orchomenus, worship was denied to Dionysus, this time by the daughters of the king. The god drove them mad, and the unfortunate women killed their own children by tearing them to pieces.

Many towns and countries, on the other hand, quietly accepted the god and his cult. In Athens, for example, the worship of Dionysus took the form of a dramatic festival at which tragedies and comedies were performed.

5. Ariadne

All of Greece eventually accepted the god, and he left to spread his worship elsewhere. He came to the island of Naxos where he found Ariadne, the beautiful daughter of King Minos of Crete. After helping Theseus to kill the dreaded Minotaur, the young woman had been cruelly abandoned by the hero. Dionysus fell in love with the lonely and deserted maiden, and she returned his affections. They married, and the gods granted her the gift of immortality. Dionysus then mounted to Olympus where, some say, Hestia withdrew so that he could take her place among the mighty twelve.

Conclusion

Friedrich Nietzsche in his famous work, **The Birth of Tragedy,** maintains that Dionysus and Apollo represent two polarities in human existence: the unrestrained, emotional, and irrational aspect on the one side, and the self-controlled, intellectual, and rational on the other. The Greeks had both gods share the shrine at Delphi where Dionysus was supreme during the three winter months each year when Apollo was away. The joint use of a famous sanctuary suggests a belief that the two gods -and the forces they represent- are present in each person and must be harmoniously and effectively blended one with the other.

Questions

1. With what human characteristics is Dionysus associated? With which Greek god would he most strongly contrast? With which goddess is he most closely allied in function? In what ways?

2. What were the various forms assumed by the god? How is such widely varied appearance connected with fertility?

3. Who were the satyrs? Describe their function.

4. Who were the Sileni? How were they associated with Dionysus?

5. Who was Silenus?

6. Who were the centaurs? How were they connected with Dionysus?

7. Describe the worship of the bacchae.

8. Give the meaning of "orgy," "bacchanal" and "bacchanalia." Show how the words derive from the worship of Dionysus.

9. How did the Roman Bacchus differ from the Greek Dionysus?

10. Who were the parents of Dionysus?

11. How did Hera cause the death of Semele?

12. What are the three explanations for the divinity of Dionysus? Why was there some question about such divinity? What were the frequent penalties for those who rejected Dionysus as a god?

13. How is the story of the rendering of Dionysus by Hera related to the god's rituals?

14. List all of the ways in which Hera acts as an enemy toward Dionysus.

15. What moral does the story of Midas contain? Why do you think such a story is associated with Dionysus?

16. Why do you think the story of the pirates and the dolphins is associated with Dionysus?

17. How and why was Lycurgus punished?

18. How and why was Pentheus punished?

19. What form did the worship of Dionysus chiefly take in Athens?

20. Who is Ariadne and how is she connected with Dionysus?

21. What is Nietzsche's theory about Dionysus and Apollo?

22. Why do you think the Greeks had Dionysus and Apollo share the sanctuary at Delphi?

22. ORPHEUS

A. Musician

B. Eurydice

C. Death

D. Orphism

Musician

We have up until this point emphasized the gods; we shall now look at our first hero myth, that of Orpheus.

Orpheus is the most famous musician in myth. Some say that he acquired his great skill at composing, singing and playing because Apollo was his father or the Muse Calliope his mother. People would come great distances just to hear him perform. It was said that even wild animals were tamed by his songs. Orpheus preferred the country to the city. He lived in the wilds, and he sang his songs there.

Eurydice

Orpheus eventually fell in love with and married the nymph, Eurydice. On their wedding day the young woman was bitten by a poisonous snake and died. Orpheus was heartbroken; however, he determined to use his great musical talent to bring her back from the Underworld.

He fearlessly entered the Land of the Dead and charmed the inhabitants with his sad and beautiful laments. Charon was so softened that he allowed Orpheus to enter his boat. Cerberus forgot his duties as watchdog. The condemned in Tartarus halted in their endless labors to listen, and even Hades and Persephone were moved to tears at the sorrowful songs of the heartbroken young man. The grim and usually unmovable god agreed to Orpheus' request. The singer would be permitted to lead Eurydice back to the Land of the Living. There was just one proviso: she must walk behind her husband, and he must not look back until they reached the Upper World.

Orpheus was overjoyed with his success. He led Eurydice's spirit from the dark Plain of Asphodel, past Cerberus, across the Styx in the boat of Charon, through the restless spirits on the Far Bank, and up to the mouth of the cave which he had entered. As he neared the end of his perilous journey, rather than rejoicing at the miracle of his accomplishment, Orpheus was filled with doubts. Was Eurydice truly behind him? He had heard no sound. She had not spoken, nor had he seen her. Were the gods mocking him? Finally, he could restrain himself no longer; he looked back. Eurydice was there; the gods had spoken in truth. But now, even as he watched, her helpless spirit receded ever farther back into the darkness of the Underworld. When he tried to follow her, the way was barred.

Death

Orpheus, now more heartbroken than ever over a tragedy compounded, returned to his native land of Thrace. He soon met his death by being torn apart by a raging band of maenads. Some say that he was killed because he would not sing for them or that he would not choose one of them as a wife to replace Eurydice. Others say that he refused to worship Dionysus and that this was his punishment. The Muses gathered the scattered pieces of the singer's body and buried them at his home near Mt. Olympus.

Orphism

The philosophic-religious cult of Orphism was supposedly based on the myth of Orpheus who was regarded as its founder. It chiefly emphasized two aspects of the hero's story: his music and his ability to conquer even death through that music (he entered and emerged from the Underworld while still living).

Devotees of Orphism believed in reincarnation. After death, one's spirit drank of the River Lethe, forgot its previous existence, and entered life again, until, after three successive lives of virtue, one gained Elysium, a place, as we have seen, of perfect happiness. Such a belief, unlike the popular notions of the time, established a clear connection between actions in this life and reward in the next. An evil life resulted in prolonging the cycle of human existence and in delaying entrance into Elysium. Not only did Orpheus provide a model of someone who had conquered death, but his songs also contained truths about those fundamental mysteries and were guides to the life of virtue which would eventually lead to eternal happiness.

Questions

1. What were the talents of Orpheus?

2. Who was Eurydice? How is she an important part of the story of Orpheus?

3. How did Orpheus persuade Hades to release Eurydice? What was the one ritual which had to be observed?

4. Why was Orpheus unsuccessful in his quest?

5. How did Orpheus meet his death?

6. In what important way did the Orphic cult regard Orpheus' quest as successful?

7. How did the Orphic cult relate virtuous action in this life to reward in the next?

8. How was Orpheus' music connected with the beliefs of Orphism?

23. HEROES AND THE HEROIC

A. Origin of hero myths

B. Definition of a hero

C. Characteristics of the heroic view of life

D. The pattern in heroic stories

E. A psychological view of hero myths

Origin of hero myths

Heroic myths are widespread and well known throughout the world. The Greeks even gave them a special place in their historical cycle:

> The Age of Gold
> The Age of Silver
> The Age of Bronze
> The Age of Heroes
> The Age of Iron

The hero tales of the Greeks were probably developed and elaborated during the time designated by archaeology as the Late Bronze Age, (also called the Mycenaean Period), from approximately 1600 to 1100 B.C. The civilization on the Greek mainland was quite sophisticated during that time as revealed by such towns as Mycenae, Tiryns, Pylos, Thebes, Corinth, Athens, Sparta, Argos, and others. Much remains to be learned about this early society which germinated not only the hero myths but many other important characteristics of the classical Greek period which would occur hundreds of years later.

There is probably a factual kernel to a good many of the hero stories which we possess, but we need more historical data in order to separate reality from imagination. The great events of the times may well be reflected:

> the conquest of Crete,
> the sack of Thebes,
> the journey to Colchis,
> the hunt for the Calydonian boar,
> and the war at Troy.

There are, on the other hand, many scholars who are very dubious about the historicity of any of the hero myths and who believe that the heroes were at one time thought to be gods or divine kings and that the stories are literary versions of the rites which such "god-kings" had to perform; hero myths, they believe, are all derived from religious ritual.

Still others believe that the hero tales are just the imaginative inventions of good story tellers, embellished by each generation; they are wholly fictional creations existing in the minds of the various bards and then becoming part of the inherited tradition.

Definition of a hero

But what is a hero? C.M. Bowra in his book **The Greek Experience** says that the Greeks defined such a person in a rather specialized way:

> he was a man who had a god or goddess as a parent or who lived when such people existed.

Characteristics of the heroic view of life

Professor Bowra goes on to discuss the nature of the heroic outlook on life. We shall summarize and list those features pertinent to our purposes.

1. The hero knows that he has superior qualities, and he uses them to win the praise of his fellow men.

2. The hero makes the most of his extraordinary talents in order to surpass other men.

3. The hero seeks dangerous tasks because by accomplishing them he shows his superior qualities.

4. A personal sense of honor is most important for the hero: any challenge to it calls for a quick and usually violent response; any task which increases it is immediately undertaken.

5. "Fame" and "good reputation" are the rewards of honor and are avidly sought by the hero.

6. The hero is conscious of his own mortality; he is keenly aware that death removes all opportunity for obtaining greater fame.

How do heroes differ from gods? Only in one way: they are mortal, the gods immortal. The hero may be as virtuous, as courageous, as talented as a given god and perhaps more so (although it is best for him not to boast of it), but he must die, while the gods live forever.

The pattern in hero stories

Many writers on myth have observed that hero stories from cultures throughout the world which are separated both by time (ancient and modern) and by space (Egypt, say, and Central America) tend, despite the great variety of actions and events found in individual stories, to reveal similar themes or motifs which in turn often form a general design. This aspect of myth is thoroughly discussed by Joseph Campbell in his book, **The Hero with a Thousand Faces.** We shall now examine the pattern found in the Greek heroic tales.

The first common feature occurring within many hero myths is that of a miraculous or unusual conception. Divine parentage is a good example of this characteristic, made even more astounding by the many forms which the deity may assume. It is usually a god who bestows his affection on a mortal woman, seldom a goddess on the man. An unusual birth may substitute for or accompany the divine conception.

The second element in the pattern of heroic myths is the hiding or abandonment of the infant-hero. The baby, threatened by hostile forces human or divine, is hidden by those concerned with his welfare.

Sometimes the opposite takes place: the infant hero is abandoned, i.e., left in the wilderness somewhere on the assumption that he will die from exposure or be eaten by wild beasts, usually because his parents have received some dire prophecy about their offspring, and they wish to avert it. The abandonment always fails in its purpose, and the infant is rescued by kind-hearted slaves, shepherds, beasts, or mythological creatures of the forest, and, of course, the ominous event which had been forecast eventually comes to pass.

The third feature of the sequence is that of the hero's withdrawal for a period of time from public life in order to prepare for the arduous tasks which lie ahead. Serious responsibilities have been placed upon him by the gods (he has been conceived with a purpose), and the hero must be ready to meet those obligations. During this period of preparation, he often receives intensive training to make him more fit for the coming tasks.

The hero is frequently identified as someone special either by some indication of divine favor or by the performance of an initiatory task for which no one else is competent. Such identification can occur soon after birth, or much later, just before he is about to undertake his major task.

As the fifth feature in the general pattern, the hero accomplishes that mission for which he has been created by the gods. Each has his major task, but, as the tales were told, they were embellished, until it often happened that many labors became associated with any given hero.

The sixth characteristic in our pattern could well be listed as a variant of the task or quest: namely, the hero attempts, often successfully, to enter and leave the Land of the Dead while still alive. To some extent this action symbolizes the hero's wish to conquer death and become an equal to the gods, but it is generally portrayed as simply another mission which does not rival the major task in significance. Sometimes those who visit the Underworld are later deified, so that the visitation is more or less a predictive act, for others, the descent to the spirit world is just another difficult task which indicates greatness but does not grant divinity.

The seventh feature is the death of the hero. Because he is seemingly invincible, the hero's downfall must usually be brought about by stealth or treachery of some kind. The events leading to the end are frequently caused either deliberately or accidentally by a woman, so that the "weak" conquer the "strong", and defeat comes from a source least suspect. There is often the idea of the scapegoat connected with the hero's death: he must suffer for the community's benefit. Whatever tasks he has accomplished throughout his life have helped us all, and now, in his death, he performs the supreme sacrifice.

The last characteristic of the pattern is that of the transformation of the hero into a god. Such deification occurs in only a few of the myths; it becomes a measure of the worthiest among the worthy. Thus, Heracles, Aeneas, and Romulus become gods while others become "almost-gods", e.g., Orpheus and Oedipus, and still others are allowed to enter Elysium, e.g., Anchises. For the Graeco-Roman hero the accomplishment of the mortal task seems sufficient; divinity is an afterthought, anti-climactic, and indeed sometimes refused when offered, as when Odysseus rejects Calypso.

A psychological view of hero myths

Modern psychology has examined the phenomenon of hero myths in great detail, and it finds the continuing relevance of such stories to be in their significance both for individuals who are trying to discover and assert their personalities and for the entire society which has an equal need to establish its collective identity. Such myths are especially meaningful, say many psychologists, when the conscious mind needs assistance in some task it cannot accomplish without drawing on the sources of strength which lie in the unconscious, e.g., at times of initiation in our culture, times of change from youth to adolescence, from adolesence to maturity, from maturity to middle age, and from middle age to old age. The essential function which the hero myth performs is to symbolize the development of the individual's awareness of his own strengths and weaknesses so that he will be equipped for the various tasks which life presents.

Questions

1. When did the Greek hero myths probably originate? *1600-1100 B.C.*

2. What are the three theories about the origin of hero myths?

3. In what ways does the definition of a hero given in the text immediately elevate his status among other men? What would be an acceptable characterization of a modern hero? How would such a description differ from that of the mythic hero?

4. Are there any values which modern heroes might share as a group with one another?

5. Can a shared pattern be found in the lives of modern heroes?

6. What is the major purpose of hero stories according to modern psychologists?

24. PERSEUS

A. The harsh prediction

B. The bronze tower

C. The abandonment

D. Rescue

E. The quest

F. The Gray Ones

G. Medusa

H. Atlas

I. Andromeda

J. The return

The harsh prediction

Acrisius was ruler in the town of Argos. He had a beautiful daughter by the name of Danae but no son to whom he might leave his kingdom. So Acrisius decided to consult an oracle to see what the future might hold for him. Oh, unfortunate decision! The priests spoke harsh words: "You shall have no son, and the son of your daughter will kill you!"

The bronze tower

Although Acrisius was terrified, he determined to avoid his fate. A king, after all, has great power: he could insure that Danae would never conceive this son who might kill him. The cruel father imprisoned his daughter in a bronze tower (some say an underground room) with narrow windows -too small for anyone to enter or leave by- and allowed access to this chamber only to those maids who provided their mistress with the necessities of life itself. Danae, saddened by the cruel action of her father, spent the long hours looking wistfully out at the world from which she was so completely isolated.

Despite the confines of her prison, the woman's rare beauty caught the eye of watchful Zeus who visited her in the form of golden rain -amazing to tell- which gently drifted through the narrow windows in the bronze tower and suffused the entire room with a golden light irresistible in its fascination.

The abandonment

Sometime afterwards Danae gave birth to a son whom she called Perseus. Acrisius was both amazed and angered that his flawless plan had somehow been circumvented. He didn't believe his daughter's story about Zeus and the golden rain, and he realized full well what a danger his grandson represented; yet he was reluctant to kill outright either his daughter or her child. "I will let the sea do it for me," he thought, "and thereby remove all guilt from myself."

Acrisius sealed Danae and the infant Perseus in a wooden chest which he set afloat and which the tide soon carried out to sea. He hoped that the waves would do what he could not. But once again the gods, apparently, wished otherwise.

Rescue

The chest instead of sinking to the bottom floated to the small island of Seriphus in the western Cyclades where it was found on the beach by a shepherd named Dictys. He rescued Perseus and his mother from the box and brought them to his home where Danae told her sad story. The kindly shepherd and his wife agreed to provide shelter and seclusion for mother and child and to treat Perseus as though he were their own son. It was under the watchful eye of Dictys, then, that Perseus grew to manhood, constantly astounding his foster-father with his great strength and seemingly innate athletic skills.

The quest

Dictys had a cruel brother, Polydectes, who was king of Seriphus. It had taken Polydectes many years to discover the presence of Danae -he was busy with other things, as kings often are- but once he did, he immediately fell in love with her and wanted her. His feelings of affection were not returned by the beautiful woman, and Perseus, now fully grown, seemed to block him from more effectively pursuing what he wanted. So Polydectes determined to rid himself of the young man by sending him on a quest, an impossible mission from which he would surely never return: he challenged Perseus to bring back the head of Medusa, one of the Gorgons, three females of such terrible appearance that one look at their faces turned men to stone. These monstrous women were winged, had scales on their bodies like reptiles, and had snakes for hair. Medusa was the only mortal one of the three. She had once been a beautiful woman, but she had angered Athena by having a love affair with Poseidon in the temple of the goddess and so was transformed into her present state. Despite the great danger involved, Perseus immediately accepted the challenge and set off on his quest.

The gods came to the aid of the young hero. Athena allowed Perseus to use her mirror-like shield so that he could look at the reflection of Medusa rather than the monster herself and thus not be turned to stone. The goddess also showed him how to distinguish which of the Gorgons was Medusa, the only one who could be killed. Hades, god of the dead, provided Perseus with a cap which made him invisible and with a leather bag in which he could carry the head of Medusa back to Polydectes. Hermes, the messenger of the gods, provided Perseus with a curved, sickle-like sword which he was to use to sever the head of the monster and with winged sandals which enabled the hero to fly. Surely Perseus was blessed by the gods as no other had been.

The Gray Ones

Hermes now guided Perseus to the distant cave of the three Gray Ones who were sisters of the Gorgons and who knew the location of their hidden lair. These women were gray from birth and had among them one tooth and one eye which they shared in regular rotation so that at any given moment only one of them could see and one could bite. They were notoriously anti-social and quite dangerous since the tooth was razor-sharp and could easily sever a hand or an arm of anyone coming too close. Perseus used the cap of invisibility and surprised the old women. He quickly seized the tooth and the eye and would not return them until the Gray Ones told him the location of the Gorgons. The sisters were frightened by the voice which seemed to come from thin air and immediately provided the information requested.

Medusa

Using his winged sandals, Perseus flew to the cave of the Gorgons. Its location is a matter of dispute: some say it was situated in the far north, others that it was on the Atlantic coast of North Africa. Wherever, it was there that our hero found the three Gorgons, Stheno, Euryale, and Medusa, all asleep. Gazing into the brightly polished shield, and wearing the cap of invisibility, Perseus carefully and ever so slowly approached them. And then he moved as swiftly as a flash of lightning! With a single stroke of the curved sword he decapitated Medusa and placed her head in the leather bag. Even as he acted, he was startled by a miracle which occurred before his very eyes: from the headless body of the monster —astounding to see— was born the winged horse, Pegasus. Our hero could afford only a moment's delay to witness this bizarre phenomenon, for he was still in great danger. He turned away and flew off, successfully eluding the other Gorgons who were disorganized by his surprise attack and did not know how to fight an unseen enemy.

Atlas

On his return Perseus flew along the coast of North Africa where he encountered Atlas, the Titan who had been assigned by Zeus the onerous task of supporting the sky on his mighty shoulders. Atlas, startled by the unfamiliar sight of someone in the sky, loudly threatened our hero as he passed by. Perseus was angered by such an unprovoked attack and responded by exposing the Titan to the head of Medusa which, of course, transformed the mammoth god into stone. Some say that this accounts for the Atlas mountain range in North Africa.

Andromeda

As he continued his flight, Perseus saw a terrible sight far below him: a beautiful woman chained to a rock along the shore, an apparent sacrifice to a horrendous sea-monster which was rapidly approaching her. He soon discovered that she was the Princess Andromeda, daughter of King Cepheus and Queen Cassiopia. She had been condemned by Poseidon, god of the sea, to be offered as a human sacrifice because her mother had boasted that Andromeda was more beautiful than any of the Nereids, the nymphs of the sea.

Perseus fell instantly in love with the beautiful Andromeda and quickly arranged with her parents that, if he should kill the sea-serpent which threatened her, he might marry their daughter. They agreed, and Perseus effectively dispatched the dragon using an aerial attack and the head of Medusa. The monster became just another rock along the coast.

As the marriage ceremony began, one of Andromeda's former suitors, a man called Phineus, made his appearance and claimed that he had prior rights as a potential husband for Andromeda since he had courted her for many years. Perseus argued that he was more deserving since Phineus had abandoned Andromeda to her fate, while he, Perseus, had rescued her. He was supported in his assertion by Andromeda's parents, Cepheus and Cassiopia. Phineus, wild and tempestuous, brought in many armed supporters and determined to win by force what he could not win by logic. Perseus was one man against many, and so, once again, he drew the head of Medusa from the bag and transformed Phineus and all of his companions into stone.

The return

Perseus and his wife Andromeda returned to the island of Seriphus where Polydectes was still unsuccessful in his pursuit of Danae who had been forced to take refuge in the sanctuary of a temple. Perseus, recognizing for the first time the true nature of the king, and realizing that he too was in great danger from the evil

Polydectes, again drew upon the power of Medusa and turned the king to stone. He then made his old guardian, Dictys, the new king of Seriphus. To show his gratitude to Athena for her aid, Perseus presented the goddess with the head of Medusa which she wore sometimes on her breastplate and sometimes on her shield. All of the implements which the gods had given to help him, Perseus returned with thanks.

After events settled down on the island of Seriphus, Perseus returned to his grandfather's kingdom of Argos. He hoped to bring about a reconciliation with Acrisius, but the old man, still fearful of the prophecy, had fled to a nearby country called Thessaly when he had heard that his grandson was alive and returning to Argos. But he could not escape his fate. It happened that sometime later Perseus was participating in an athletic contest in Thessaly. His discus struck a rock and was diverted into the crowd where it decapitated an old man. Who else but King Acrisius? Thus the prophecy which began our tale and led to so many of its actions was finally fulfilled.

Stricken with guilt for having killed a member of his own family, Perseus exchanged the kingdom of Argos for that of nearby Tiryns where he became the new ruler. He settled down with Andromeda and became a successful and popular king. He fathered famous children and was an ancestor of the great hero, Heracles. One of his sons, Perses, was the founder of the Persian people. Perseus and Andromeda were rewarded at the end of their lives by being transformed into constellations which you can still see in the sky.

Sources

The best ancient version of the myth is found in Ovid's **Metamorphoses,** Books 4 and 5.

Questions

1. Which parts of the heroic myth pattern does this story reveal?

2. How does the myth demonstrate a prophecy fulfilled? What do truthful prophecies imply about the nature of the world?

3. What does the myth teach us about fate?

4. How is the motif of family conflict important in this story? What does this feature add?

5. How does the myth demonstrate that evil is punished and good rewarded?

6. Show how the principal object of evil is transformed into an object of good.

7. In what ways does divine intervention influence human action? How is human freedom of choice still significant?

8. Show how magic is an important part of this myth.

9. In this story the hero acquires an object which gives him great power over others. What other stories can you describe which have this same feature?

10. This is one of the first examples we have of a hero rescuing a fair maiden. Think of the thousands upon thousands of copies! Describe any five from literature or films.

25. BELLEROPHON

A. Origin

B. Exile

C. The false accusation

D. The Chimaera and Pegasus

E. The Solymi

F. The Amazons

G. Reconciliation

H. Disaster

Origin

Bellerophon was born and grew up in the city of Corinth. Sisyphus, his grandfather, who founded the city, was famous for his craftiness. Among other things he managed to obtain a second life after Zeus had sent him to the Underworld. For this offense he was condemned to the eternal punishment of pushing a huge boulder to the top of a steep hill and then, as the stone inevitably rolled back down, to follow it and begin his onerous task anew.

There is some confusion as to the identity of Bellerophon's father. Some say it was Glaucus, King of Corinth, who was infamous for feeding his horses on human flesh to make them savage and quick and who met an appropriate end when his chariot tipped over and his own horses consumed him. Others say that Glaucus was only his foster-father and that his real parent was Poseidon, the god of the sea, a divinity especially important to the people of Corinth.

Exile

With such a background, it is not surprising that Bellerophon himself had difficulties when he was a young man. In an argument he accidentally killed a man (some say he killed his brother as well) and thus had to leave Corinth. Exile was often a form of punishment given in those days to members of the upper class when they had committed some serious offense.

The false accusation

In his wanderings our hero came to the court of King Proetus of Tiryns. The king took in the youthful aristocrat and treated him with the hospitality that was the custom. The wife of the king, Antia, a young and passionate woman, fell hopelessly in love with him and, after vainly trying to control herself, openly expressed her feelings. He rejected her. Scorned and ashamed, her love turned to hate. She went to her husband and accused Bellerophon of the very emotions and actions of which she herself was guilty. This motif -wife falls in love with young hero, he rejects her, she accuses him to her husband- occurs a good many times in myth. It is given the name "Potiphar's wife" after the story in the Bible where the wife of the Egyptian lord, Potiphar, attempts to seduce the young Hebrew, Joseph, is rejected, and accuses him to her husband.

King Proetus had no reason to doubt his wife, since Bellerophon, after all, had come with a bad reputation from Corinth; he wanted to kill the young man for his attempted seduction but was afraid to do so because he would violate the law of hospitality and incur the wrath of Zeus. So, as a questionable compromise, he sent him to King Iobates of Lycia, his son-in-law, along with a sealed note asking the king to do away with him. Ever since then the phrase "letter of Bellerophon" has come to mean a missive which intends harm to its bearer.

The Chimaera and Pegasus

King Iobates gladly received his new guest, but when he opened the letter, he found himself in the same position as Proetus. He could not kill Bellerophon without breaking the sacred law of hospitality. To solve his problem, Iobates decided to ask the young hero to perform a dangerous task which would surely result in his death but which would remove the king from blame. He proposed that Bellerophon attempt to kill the Chimaera, a monster which was part-lion, part-goat, and part-snake, which breathed fire like a dragon, and whose hide was apparently impervious to weapons. This creature had been devastating the countryside of Lycia, and the king and his people would be forever in the debt of anyone who could destroy it. The supremely hazardous nature of the mission only made our hero more anxious to undertake it. He accepted the task without hesitation.

Bellerophon wisely decided to consult an oracle of Apollo before beginning his task.

"Seek the aid of the winged horse, Pegasus, offspring of the dread Medusa," came the words of the god, " and pray for the assistance of Athena in capturing the horse."

The hero went immediately to a nearby temple of Athena and slept there. He had a dream in which he captured and tamed Pegasus through the aid of a golden bridle. When he awoke, he found the very harness beside him. Some say that this was the first time a bridle had been seen in Greece and that Bellerophon with Athena's aid introduced it.

It was known that Pegasus often drank at the fountain called Pirene in Corinth. The young adventurer made the long journey back to his native city, awaited the horse at the fountain, surprised him, bridled him, and finally tamed him.

Now that Bellerophon was able to ride Pegasus, the flight to Lycia was made quickly. He was also more easily able to scout the location of the Chimaera and to confuse the beast by attacking from above. Pegasus would swoop down and away before the Chimaera had an opportunity to react, and Bellerophon would throw one of his spears with such strength that it penetrated the tough hide of the animal. The blood poured from the many wounds until eventually all strength and life was gone. Our hero was victorious in this the greatest of his labors!

The Solymi

King Iobates had mixed feelings about Bellerophon's accomplishment. He was unhappy that the hero had escaped with his life, and yet he was very grateful that the monster had been slain. However, to please his father-in-law, King Proetus, who demanded the death of Bellerophon, Iobates proposed another task: subdue the Solymi, a savage tribe of desert warriors who were always a threat to the borders of his kingdom. The young man, of course, accepted. With Pegasus he was able to mount an airborne attack on the Solymi who were so frightened by the sight that they surrended without a weapon being used and agreed to pay tribute to King Iobates.

The Amazons

Iobates was gratified by the taxes which the Solymi now sent him. He was truly beginning to like Bellerophon, yet he still felt an obligation to Proetus. With mixed feelings, he presented the Amazons as the next challenge.

"Since you have been so successful in subduing the Solymi," he said, "perhaps you will be able to defeat the Amazons whom even the Solymi fear. They are women, but savage and cruel, and skilled in all of the arts of war. They have never been defeated and they cause cold fear to run through the hearts of men whenever their name is mentioned! Armies have been sent against them and have never been heard of again! Do you think that you, one man, will be able to defeat them?"

Bellerophon, his confidence growing with each accomplishment, accepted the task.

The Amazons had heard of this unusual warrior who flew through the sky, and so, when he arrived in their country, they had already come to the conclusion that he was a god. Although they hated men and strove to kill them at every opportunity, they greeted Bellerophon hospitably and worshipped him as a divinity. They swore their devotion and gave him tokens which would prove their subservience. The youthful hero had successfully accomplished yet another task.

Reconciliation

In desperation Iobates now sent a group of his own soldiers to ambush and kill Bellerophon. But Poseidon (who, you remember, may well have been the hero's father) drowned them all in a flood. After this occurred, the King finally decided to abandon his attempts to carry out the death sentence his father-in-law had demanded. He had long ago come to recognize the great merits of Bellerophon and to admire his accomplishments which he knew could not take place without the blessing of the gods. He welcomed the young man into his family, gave him his daughter in marriage, and made him heir to half his kingdom. If our story ended here, it would be a happy one indeed, and our hero would have lived out his life in contentment like Perseus. But it does not.

Disaster

After living happily for many years, Bellerophon decided that, because of his great deeds, he was surely an equal to the gods and belonged on Mt. Olympus. He mounted Pegasus and flew toward the sacred mountain. Zeus, greatly angered by the presumption of this mortal hero, unleashed a lightning bolt which caused the horse to bolt and threw the brash intruder back down to earth.

Injured by his long fall, defeated for the first time in his life, and now seemingly as much cursed by the gods as he was once blessed, Bellerophon isolated himself completely from human society and ended his life in sorrow as a lonely wanderer.

Pegasus continued on to Mt. Olympus where he served Zeus as bearer of his lightning bolts and was eventually transformed into a constellation still visible to us today.

Sources

The best ancient versions of the story are: Homer's **Iliad**, Book 6, and Pindar, **Olympiad** 13.

Questions

1. What parts of the heroic myth pattern does this story reveal?

2. In what ways does divine intervention influence human action? What does it contribute to the story?

3. How is the motif of family conflict important in this story?

4. Discuss the different ways in which this is a civilizing myth, i.e., advocates the values of civilization over barbarism.

5. In what ways are the tasks of Bellerophon similar? In what ways different?

6. What elements of magic are present in this story?

7. What is the offense of Bellerophon which alienates the gods? How is his punishment pertinent to us all?

8. What are the limits of human endeavor, and how are we to know them?

26. HERACLES

A. Characteristics

B. Conception

C. Family background

D. Birth

E. Early exploits

F. The Twelve Labors

G. Other deeds

H. Marriage

I. Iole

J. Death

K. Deification

L. The Heraclidae

Characteristics

The greatest and most popular of the Greek heroes was Heracles, better known by his Latin name, Hercules, and sometimes called Alcides after his supposed grandfather, Alcaeus. Early in his life he was given a choice symbolized by two women: one represented Vice with a life of ease, the other Virtue with a life of hardship. His choice was virtue, and his life exemplifies its difficulty.

Heracles was a large and muscular man of great strength who constantly performed superhuman tasks. He dressed in a lion skin and carried a club, a bow, and a quiver full of arrows. Supremely talented in all athletic skills, he used his ability to clear the world of evil (monsters and villains of various types), although, because of his quick temper and great strength, he was sometimes like a "bull in a China shop" and did unintentional harm to inoffensive bystanders. The innocent might also suffer when Heracles experienced his periodic fits of madness which were inflicted by the goddess Hera.

His character is most often taken seriously by writers in antiquity, although he is sometimes shown as a mere muscle man with little intelligence, and sometimes, because of his large appetite for food and drink, he is portrayed as a comic figure.

His tales are associated with many bronze age sites since, because of his greatness, popularity, and eventual divinity, many towns wanted to claim Heracles as their own (comparable today to the assertions of various places that "Washington slept here" or "Lincoln stopped here") and families wished to show that they were descended from the hero.

Conception

Heracles' father was the great god, Zeus, and his mother was Alcmene, the beautiful and virtuous wife of the illustrious hero, Amphitryon. She was, supposedly, the last mortal woman with whom Zeus had a love affair. The couple were living at the time in Thebes. Amphitryon was away fighting in a war when Zeus assumed his form and told Alcmene that he was just returning from battle. Zeus had chosen Alcmene carefully because he wanted someone special to be the mother of the great hero he was envisioning. He made the night with her three times its ordinary length, and no sooner had Zeus departed when the real Amphitryon actually returned from the war. He was somewhat disappointed and puzzled that his wife was not more pleased to see him after what he considered his long absence. The result of that extraordinary night was that Alcmene conceived twins: Heracles by Zeus and Iphicles by Amphitryon.

Family background

Althought Zeus was his father, Heracles was born into a human family which could trace itself back to Perseus and another divine conception.

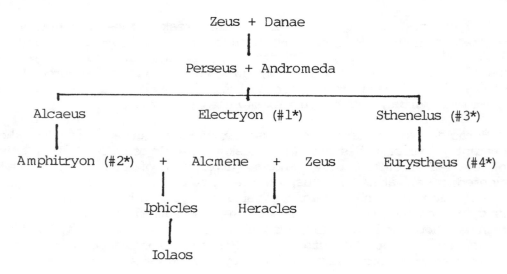

* = a king of Mycenae

Electryon, a son of Perseus and the first king of the town of Mycenae, was waging war against the Teleboans, a people of western Greece. In this struggle, all of Electryon's sons were killed. When the Teleboans withdrew before Electryon had an opportunity to react, he decided to pursue them into their own land. So that he would not leave Mycenae rulerless in his absence, he appointed his nephew, Amphitryon, as king. He also gave the young hero his daughter, Alcmene, to marry. Unfortunately, soon after these happy events, Amphitryon accidentally killed Electryon; he was forced to give up the kingship and, as was the custom with the nobility in those days, go into exile. Sthenelus, another son of Perseus, became the third king of Mycenae.

Amphitryon and Alcmene went to Thebes where they found the land of King Creon to be devastated by a savage fox to whom the Thebans had to offer a human sacrifice each month. This horror was compounded by the knowledge that the fox was destined never to be caught. From his friend Cephalus of Athens, Amphitryon borrowed a hunting dog who was able to catch any animal after which it had been sent. Thus was set up the dilemma: an uncatchable fox pursued by an inescapable hound. Zeus solved the problem by turning both animals into stone.

With the aid of the Theban army, Amphitryon now left to take the revenge on the Teleboans which his uncle, Electryon, had been prevented from doing by his death. The Teleboan king, Pterelaus, and his people were invincible provided that a golden hair was never removed from the king's head. His daughter, Comaetho, standing day by day on the walls of her father's beseiged city fell in love with the noble Amphitryon -from a distance- and decided to betray her family and her country in order to win favor with her beloved. As her father slept, she removed the golden hair. The king died, and his people were defeated by the forces of Amphitryon who, rather than returning the love of Comaetho, had her killed for her treachery. It was from this campaign that Amphitryon was returning on the night when Heracles and his brother Iphicles were conceived.

Birth

Hera, the wife of Zeus, was naturally jealous of Alcmene and of Zeus' feelings toward this mortal woman. She could do nothing against her omnipotent husband, so she sought vengeance against the much less powerful mortals. While the name "Heracles" means the "glory of Hera", it was the antipathy of this goddess which caused many problems for our hero, as we shall see.

When the time came for the birth of the twin sons of Alcmene, Zeus proclaimed: "The descendant of Perseus born on this day shall become king of mighty Mycenae and ruler of all Greece!" To frustrate her husband, Hera delayed the birth of Heracles until another descendant of Perseus was born: Eurystheus, son of King Sthenelus. Because of the goddess' vindictiveness, it was Eurystheus who became the next king of Mycenae (succeeding his father), and Heracles eventually served him.

While our hero was still a seemingly helpless infant, Hera again revealed her hostility: she sent a pair of enormous snakes to kill him while he slept in his cradle. But Heracles sensed the danger. He awoke, confronted the two serpents courageously, seized them, and strangled them to death. Surely a sign of coming greatness!

Early exploits

As he grew to manhood, Heracles was taught all of the skills and arts by the best teachers available; however, he was rash even in his youth, and, in a fit of temper, he killed his music teacher, Linus, a son of Apollo, by hitting him over the head with his lyre. A bad note indeed!

Heracles spent all of his adult life in heroic endeavors. His first exploit was to kill a lion which was preying on the cattle of Amphitryon and on that of Thespius, the king of a small town near Thebes. While on this adventure, Heracles was entertained by Thespius for fifty days. The king sent a different one of his fifty daughters to Heracles' bedroom each night so that they might conceive noble sons. Some say, indeed, that all fifty were sent to our hero on the same night and that nine months later fifty sons were born. But perhaps the myth exaggerates.

Heracles next helped Creon, the king of Thebes, win a battle against a long time oppressor. As a reward for his assistance, King Creon gave his daughter, Megara, to Heracles as his wife. The two lived together contentedly for some time and had three children. But Hera, always hostile to our hero, could not tolerate his happiness. She caused him to experience a fit of madness during which he killed Megara and his children, imagining them to be monsters. When he regained his senses and realized to his horror what he had done, he went to the oracle of Apollo at Delphi to discover if there were any way in which he could expiate his crime. Note that he accepted full responsibility for the murders even though he was not in control of his actions at the time. The priestess of Apollo spoke: "You must present yourself as a slave to your cousin, King Eurystheus of Mycenae, and perform twelve tasks during twelve years of service. If you are able to complete these labors successfully, you will not only expiate your crime, you will eventually become a god." Heracles at once accepted the sentence and set out for Mycenae.

The Twelve Labors

The Twelve Labors vary both in content and order; the description below is, however, fairly standard. The Greek word for labors is athloi which means contests undertaken for a reward. The prize in this case was immortality, as the priestess of Apollo had promised. The Labors are accompanied by many secondary adventures, and are followed by countless Deeds.

Labors which take place in the Peloponnesus

1. The Nemean lion

The first task ordered by Eurystheus was to kill a huge lion which was destroying the territory around the town of Nemea. Not only was the animal especially strong and savage, but its hide was impervious to weapons. Heracles tracked the beast down, and, after trapping it in a cave, and trying unsuccessfully to kill it with his club, he eventually had to resort to his bare hands with which he strangled it to death. He used the animal's claws to flay it, and the hide became our hero's impenetrable cloak.

2. The Lernean Hydra

The second labor of Heracles was to destroy the Hydra, a poisonous snake with nine heads (of which one was immortal) which lived in the swamps near the town of Lerna. Heracles was aided in this mission by his nephew Iolaus, the son of Iphicles. As soon as our hero attacked the fearsome monster, he saw -much to his dismay- that when he cut off one head, two more grew in its place! He happened to be using Iolaus to keep the other heads at bay with a huge torch while he attacked one at a time, and, he somehow discovered -perhaps with the aid of the gods- that if he had Iolaus burn the severed neck right after decapitation, he could prevent new "sprouts" from appearing. Thus was the monster dispatched. Heracles buried the one immortal head under an enormous rock which only someone with his strength could lift. He then dipped his arrows in the venom of the beast so that they became lethal from that time on.

Some say that the Hydra was not a monster at all but rather a multitude of springs near Lerna which would yearly flood the area and that Heracles' real task was to devise a system to control the unruly waters.

During this struggle with the Hydra, the ever-spiteful Hera sent a giant crab to bite at the feet of Heracles and increase the difficulty of his task. Heracles killed this monster as well, but Hera changed it into a constellation which we know today as Cancer.

3. The Cerynean Stag

For his third labor Heracles had to catch and bring back alive to Mycenae a stag exceedingly fast with golden horns and bronze hooves which lived in the forests on Mt. Cerynea. The animal was sacred to Artemis and could not be harmed without incurring her wrath. Our hero pursued the beautiful beast for days that lengthened into weeks, and weeks that lengthened into months, until finally, after a year, he caught his exhausted quarry and without doing it any harm brought it to Mycenae.

4. The Erymanthian Boar

Eurystheus determined now to send Heracles on another chase, this one more difficult than the last. He ordered the hero to bring back alive the wild boar which lived on the slopes of Mt. Erymanthus. This animal was one of the world's most dangerous beasts. With its razor-like teeth and its long, sharp tusks, it could tear, rip and slash an opponent with amazing speed. It could outrun a horse for short distances, and could easily kill both horse and rider. Eurystheus was convinced that while Heracles might be able to kill the animal, he could never manage to bring it back alive. But Heracles did indeed accomplish the task by forcing the animal to wear itself out by running through the deep snow on the mountainside. He then captured the boar in his net and brought the tired animal back to Mycenae. When Eurystheus saw the tusks and teeth of the monster, he ran in terror to hide.

A side adventure with this task has Heracles being entertained by the centaur, Pholus. A misunderstanding developed and a group of centaurs attacked Heracles who responded by driving them off. In this struggle Chiron, the one sensitive creature among this crude and savage race, was accidentally struck by one of Heracles' poisoned arrows. His agony was terrible, and, since he was immortal, he could not stop his pain through death. Prometheus, no stranger to suffering, intervened and persuaded Zeus to transfer Chiron's immortality to himself and allow the centaur to end his torment.

5. The Augean Stables

King Augeas had vast herds of cattle, and the stalls in which the animals were kept had never been cleaned. The fifth labor which Eurystheus devised for Heracles was to clean these stables. Heracles accomplished this tremendous feat in a single day by diverting two nearby rivers, the Alpheus and the Peneus, through the barns. Augeas had agreed to pay Heracles for this task, but he broke his promise, and, as a result, years later after all of the Labors had been completed, Heracles returned at the head of an army and killed the deceitful ruler.

It was after this battle that Heracles instituted the athletic festival called the Olympic Games in the territory of King Augeas. He determined that various contests (running, jumping, discus throw, javelin toss, and wrestling) should be held every four years in honor of Zeus. He supposedly marked out the length of the stadium and planted the olive tree which provided the wreathes given to winners. Although the first recorded Olympic Games were held in 776 B.C., this story moves their origin back to heroic times.

6. The Stymphalian Birds

For his sixth labor Heracles was told to kill or drive away the giant, man-eating birds which were living near the town of Stymphalus. Athena aided our hero by forcing the birds out of their cover, and Heracles quickly shot them with his poisoned arrows. It was a difficult and perilous task both because they were so numerous and because they kept attacking him with their pointed beaks and sharp claws.

The labors outside of Greece

7. The bull of Crete

King Minos ruled the island of Crete, some 90 miles south of Greece. The king had once promised to sacrifice a certain bull to the god Poseidon and had then broken his promise and offered another. Poseidon punished Minos by having the bull cause destruction throughout the island and terrorize all of the inhabitants. This same animal was also the father of the dreaded monster, the Minotaur. For his seventh labor Heracles was ordered to tame the bull and bring him to Greece. He sailed to Crete and from sunrise to sunset hunted the bull and was hunted by him. They had many contests of strength, and, finally, after nearly a year, the animal, tamed, sailed home with our hero. The beast was then turned loose and eventually came to Marathon, a town close to Athens where, sometime later, Theseus, an Athenian hero, caught and sacrificed it.

8. The horses of Diomedes

Diomedes, a son of the war-god Ares, was a king in Thrace, a country to the north of Greece. To keep his racing horses swift, he fed them on the human flesh of unsuspecting guests whom he had murdered. As his eighth labor, Heracles was ordered to subdue these man-eating animals. Heracles killed Diomedes and fed him to his own horses which immediately tamed them.

9. The belt of Hippolyta

Heracles was commanded to sail eastward into the Black Sea until he found the land of the Amazons, a race of fierce and greatly feared women warriors who hated and killed most men whom they encountered. He then had somehow to obtain the belt of Hippolyta, their queen, and bring it back to Mycenae.

Heracles' renown as a courageous warrior, as a wise, prudent and courteous man, and as a lover of justice preceded him. The Amazons received him kindly, asked him to tell them of his adventures, and in turn told him of their society and laws. Hippolyta freely gave the belt which Heracles had come for, and all would have ended happily except for Hera's intervention. The goddess spread a false rumor that Heracles was planning to seize Hippolyta and take her with him. Such a suspicion soon became fact in the minds of the male-hating Amazons and caused them to mount an attack secretly against our hero as he was leaving. Heracles mistakenly thought that the queen had intended all along to trick him in this way and thus catch him unawares, so he reacted with great violence and killed Hippolyta along with many of her warriors. It was only later that -to his sorrow- he learned the truth.

In a side adventure connected with this labor, Heracles stopped at the city of Troy where he found that King Laomedon had cheated the gods Apollo and Poseidon out of the pay he had promised them for building the enormous walls of the city. Apollo, as a result, had sent a terrible plague on the Trojans, and Poseidon had forced King Laomedon to sacrifice his daughter, Hesione, to a horrendous sea-monster. The girl was chained to a rock and was awaiting her savage death. Heracles offered to save her, and Laomedon promised a fine reward. In a fierce struggle, Heracles killed the monster and saved both the girl and the city, since Apollo lifted the plague in honor of Heracles' victory. But, once again, Laomedon refused to pay what he had promised. Heracles left, but as with King Augeas, he returned with an army after the Labors were completed, captured the city, and killed King Laomedon.

10. The Cattle of Geryon

As his tenth labor, Heracles had to go far to the west to an island located in the Atlantic Ocean and bring back the cattle of the three-bodied monster called Geryon. On his very long journey our hero set up mountains on both sides of the Strait of Gibraltar which even today are called the Pillars of Hercules. Helios, a god of the sun, provided him with a golden cup in which to sail from the mainland to the dreaded island of Geryon. He killed the monster in a fierce struggle, obtained the cattle, sailed back with them in his special boat, and, after many difficulties, drove them to Mycenae.

One of the most famous of the adventures in the long journey home was the encounter with Cacus, a son of the fire god, Vulcan, who lived in a cave on the site which would eventually be Rome. Cacus tried unsuccessfully to steal some of Heracles' cattle and to hide them in his cave. Our hero discovered the theft and killed Cacus for his boldness. This small story was connected with the religious worship of Hercules at Rome many centuries later.

11. The golden apples of the Hesperides

The eleventh labor consisted in obtaining the golden apples of the Hesperides who were three daughters of the Titan, Atlas. The fruit grew on a tree which was tended by the women and guarded by the serpent, Ladon.

Ignorant of the location of the Garden of the Hesperides, Heracles went north into the Caucasus mountains where he found Prometheus still suffering because of his disobedience towards Zeus. Heracles first killed the eagle which daily attacked the god and then broke the chains which bound him. Prometheus, in turn, since he had prophetic powers, told Heracles that the enchanted garden he sought was located in North Africa and that his brother, Atlas, would provide necessary assistance. It is at this time that Prometheus agreed to take on the immortality of Chiron (the fourth labor) so that the centaur could die and end his excruciating pain.

On his journey to the Garden of the Hesperides, Heracles encountered King Antaeus of Libya. Antaeus was a son of Poseidon and an invincible wrestler as long as he was in contact with the ground. He challenged all travellers to a match and would quickly defeat and kill them. He then used their skulls to build a temple to his father. Heracles accepted the challenge of this notorious bully, soon discovered his weakness, and broke his back with one of his famous holds.

Heracles finally reached his destination where he sought the aid of Atlas, since only he could remove the apples from their enchanted garden. The Titan agreed to help him in his quest, and Heracles, in turn, took on the enormous weight of the sky in his absence. When the Titan returned, he was so pleased with his newly acquired freedom that he decided to make the substitution a permanent one. Heracles, finding that his burden was growing increasingly heavy, and not wishing to replace the Titan for a longer time, asked to be relieved briefly so that he might get a pillow to place on his shoulders. Atlas agreed —giants are always simpleminded— and reassumed the sky, only to have Heracles take the apples and leave forever.

12. Cerberus

As his final labor Heracles was ordered to bring Cerberus, the three-headed dog who guards the Land of the Dead, to the gates of Mycenae. Because of his great reputation, the hero was allowed to enter the Underworld where he asked permission of Hades to bring the fearsome beast to the earth's surface. The request was granted, provided that no weapons were used to capture the animal. Heracles fought the monster, defeated him, and led him up to Eurystheus who, after a quick and fearful glance, sent him speedily back to the Underworld.

While he was in the Land of the Dead, Heracles saw the heroes Theseus and Pirithous imprisoned there because they had foolishly attempted to carry off Persephone, the queen of the Underworld. Heracles was able to free Theseus, but Pirithous had to remain a captive until his actual death.

Heracles also met the ghost of the noble Meleager who described his tragic end. Out of sympathy for the youth, Heracles agreed to marry his sister, Deianira. It was this action which would begin a series of events leading eventually to his own death.

Other deeds

Heracles accomplished innumerable feats in addition to the twelve labors and the adventures attached to them. We have seen that he raised armies to take revenge on King Augeas and King Laomedon because they broke their word to him. Other expeditions are likewise associated with him in which he killed many other criminals and monsters. He also fought for Zeus and the other Olympians in their long struggle against the Giants.

Heracles accompanied Jason and the other Argonauts in their quest for the Golden Fleece, but he abandoned the journey when his comrade, Hylas, disappeared during a brief stop. Some say that when Hylas had attempted to take water from a pond, the nymph who lived there fell in love with him and drew him to the bottom to be with her. In any case, Heracles would not leave without a thorough and lengthy search, so the Argonauts left him behind. He eventually accepted the death of Hylas and returned to Greece alone.

Marriage

Heracles kept the promise he had made to the spirit of Meleager which he had encountered in the Underworld (twelfth labor): he sought marriage with Deianira, Meleager's sister. There was, unfortunately, another suitor for the woman, a river god by the name of Achelous, so the two met in a wrestling match to see who would become the husband. Achelous had two advantages: he had sharp horns and he could change himself into any shape he wished. Despite these assets, the strength of Heracles prevailed, and he defeated his rival. In the struggle he had broken off one of the god's horns which he then returned to him as a gesture of reconciliation. In gratitude Achelous gave Heracles the famous horn of Amalthea which supplied its owner with as much food and drink as he desired. From this object has come our cornucopia, or "horn of plenty."

After the wedding Heracles began the journey to Tiryns -where he was currently living- with his new bride. When they came to the river Evenus, he entrusted Deianira to the centaur Nessus who carried her on his back across the stream. Nessus, in the lustful and impetuous manner of centaurs, was so impressed by Deianira's beauty that he began to show his sudden affection in a violent and physical manner. Heracles in growing anger witnessed the centaur's moves from the opposite shore. He quickly took his bow and shot him with one of his poisoned arrows. As he was dying, Nessus persuaded Deianira to take some of the blood now flowing from his wound; he told her that it could be used as a love potion if she ever needed it in order to win back her husband's affection. In actuality the blood contained the deadly venom of the Hydra (second labor) which Heracles had placed on his arrows.

Heracles and Deianira lived happily at Tiryns for several years where they had two children: Hyllus, a son, and Macaria, a daughter.

Iole

At some time after the above events, Heracles in his travels met and fell in love with a beautiful young woman called Iole, a daughter of King Eurytus. Since there were many suitors for the young woman, her father decided to hold an archery contest with the winner receiving Iole as his prize. Heracles participated and, of course, won. But the king hedged and refused to give him his daughter. Heracles left the country in a rage, vowing vengeance.

Soon afterwards the son of King Eurytus, Iphitus by name, paid a visit to Tiryns. Heracles, his bitterness at the recent insult of Eurytus intensified by a fit of madness, threw the innocent young man to his death from the walls of the city.

When Heracles came to his senses, he left Tiryns in sorrow at what he had done and went to the shrine of the god Apollo at Delphi to find how he could rid himself of this curse of madness. When the priestess refused to respond, Heracles seized the sacred tripod and walked away with it, determined to found his own oracular site. Apollo immediately intervened to prevent the theft, and the two of them began to fight. Zeus appeared and mediated the dispute by ordering Heracles to return the tripod and Apollo to answer the hero's inquiry.

The Pythia told Heracles that to end his periodic madness he must be sold as a slave and serve for one year. The highest bidder was Omphale, queen of the Lydians in Asia Minor, and Heracles performed various heroic feats under her direction.

After his year of servitude, Heracles returned to Greece and took vengeance on King Eurytus by killing him, sacking his city, and seizing his daughter, Iole.

Death

Word of Heracles' feeling for Iole came to Deianira who felt that she now had need to recapture her husband's love. She sprinkled the blood of Nessus on a tunic and sent it as a gift. As soon as the unfortunate man put on the poisoned clothing, a terrible searing sensation began in every part of his body. The garment seemed alive: it ate steadily inward with the lethal and acidic poison of the Hydra. It could not be removed. Suffering beyond all measure! He ordered his son Hyllus to build a funeral pyre for him on Mt. Oeta where he – raging in torment– had himself carried. Only Poeas, a shepherd, would light the funeral pyre of the great, suffering hero; all others hung back in terror and grief. As a reward, Heracles gave him –his last action– the bow and arrows which had served him so well during his life.

Deification

Heracles' mortal life ended on Mt. Oeta, but when the flames of the pyre reached his body, in a flash of lightning he was taken to Mt. Olympus where, finally reconciled with Hera, he became a god and married Hebe, Hera's daughter.

The Heraclidae

There are many stories about the Heraclidae, the descendants of Heracles. Essentially, they are forced to live in exile from the Peloponnesus for several generations until they eventually return and seize power in several cities. This "return of the Heraclidae," as it is called, is generally associated with the historical event of the invasion by the Dorians about 1200 - 1100 B.C.

Sources

Some of the best ancient versions of parts of the story are found in Sophocles' **Trachinian Women,** Euripides **Heracles,** Apollonius' **Argonautica,** and Seneca's **Hercules Furens** and **Hercules Oetaeus.** Bits and pieces of the story are scattered throughout much of Greek and Roman literature.

Heracles' foster father, Amphitryon, has received considerable literary attention as well. Jean Giraudoux, a modern French playwright, wrote **Amphitryon 38** because he believed the play to be at least the thirty-eighth version of the events surrounding Heracles' conception. Others who have written on the topic include Plautus (Roman), Dryden (English), and Moliere (French).

Questions

1. What elements of the heroic myth pattern does this story reveal? What does each element add to the story?

2. Show how the myth represents the triumph of civilization over barbarism.

3. What does the animosity of Hera add to the story?

4. If one considers just the twelve labors and their related adventures, what adjectives could be used to describe Heracles?

5. In what ways is the myth related to Thebes, Mycenae, Delphi, and Tiryns?

6. Show how Heracles' marriages ended in tragedy. What does this feature add to the myth?

7. Show the importance of centaurs in the myth.

8. Which of Heracles' feats can be considered symbolic conquests of death?

9. Is Heracles deserving of immortality more than any of the other heroes? If so, why? If not, why not?

10. Over eighty films have been made with Heracles as the main character. Why do you think he has become such a popular figure for a modern audience?

27. THESEUS

A. Mythic history of Athens

B. Birth

C. The journey to Athens

D. The Minotaur

E. Theseus the king

Mythic history of Athens

The mythological history of the early kings of Athens offers many variants, since ancient writers changed it to meet their purposes. It was generally agreed that Cecrops was the first king. He was pictured as being snake-like in the lower part of his body which demonstrated in a visual way the idea that he had been born from the earth, and thus was native to the area and not an immigrant. A point of pride for the Athenians.

Cecrops founded the city of Athens and set the boundaries of Attica. He allowed the Athenians (then called Cecropians, since he had named the city after himself) to vote on which of two gods they wanted as their proctector: Athena or Poseidon. Each of them performed a miracle to win votes: Athena, as a symbol of her love and bounty, caused an olive tree to grow on the Acropolis, the high hill which dominates the area; Poseidon, to demonstrate his power, struck a rock with his trident and caused salt-water to gush forth. In the election most of the women voted for Athena, most of the men for Poseidon. Since there were more women in the city, Athena won. Poseidon was so greatly angered by this apparent slight, that he caused a flood which threatened the very existence of the new town. When Cecrops asked the god what might be done to conciliate him, Poseidon replied that he would only be appeased if the vote were taken away from the women, since they had grievously insulted him by favoring Athena. To save his people, Cecrops did as the god requested: the vote was denied to the women of Athens from that time on.

As Athena performed various tasks for her new people, she attracted the notice of Hephaestus, the craftsman of the gods. At first he felt admiration and affection for the goddess, but this quickly developed into a lustful passion. Athena was aware of the god's feelings, but she was a virgin and did not wish to have a lover. Gea, goddess of the earth, agreed to be a substitute for her, and soon became pregnant by Hephaestus.

Gea gave birth; the child was similar to Cecrops in that he combined human and serpent features. Athena named the infant Erechtheus and placed him in a chest which she gave to the daughters of Cecrops warning them not to open the container. The girls' curiosity intensified each day, and they finally looked inside. When they saw the human-snake creature within, they went mad and leaped from the edge of the Acropolis to their death on the rocks below. One would think that having a father with the same snake-like features would have accustomed them to the sight, but apparently it did not. Or perhaps the gods drive mad those whom they wish.

Erechtheus became the next king, placed on the throne by Athena. Even today we can see the ruins of the Erechtheum, a temple built in his honor, on the Acropolis. A sacred snake was kept there to recall the serpentine features of this primitive ruler. The contest between Athena and Poseidon for control of Athens was believed to have taken place nearby.

Erechtheus had two beautiful daughters: Procne and Philomela. Procne married King Tereus of Thrace, a wild and rugged country to the north of Greece. She soon became homesick and longed to see her family. Tereus agreed to go to Athens and bring Philomela to Thrace for a visit with her sister. On their journey back, Tereus developed a violent passion for Philomela. He expressed his feelings to the young woman, but she strongly rejected him. Unable to achieve his wishes through persuasion, he attacked and raped the maiden. When the savage act was completed, Philomela asked that he kill her to end her sorrow and her shame. "If you do not," she said, "I will tell what you have done." The threat had its effect. To insure her silence, the brutal Tereus did not murder the woman, but instead cut out her tongue and imprisoned her in a remote part of his kingdom. When he returned home, he told Procne that her sister had died during the journey.

Despite her confinement, Philomela devised a way in which she could communicate. She wove the story of Tereus' crime into a tapestry and secretly sent it to her sister. When Procne learned the truth -and she was stunned at its savagery- she found her sister's prison, released her, and the two plotted a horrible revenge on Tereus. They killed Itys, the son of Tereus and indeed of Procne herself, tore apart his body, then cooked and served it to Tereus. When the king discovered what had been done, he drew his sword and rushed after the two women. The gods intervened: Procne was changed into a nightingale which mourns eternally, while Philomela was transformed into a swallow which tries to tell its story with incoherent chirping.

Pandion, the son of Erechtheus, followed his father as king of Athens. He in turn had several sons, one of whom, Nisus, became king of Megara, a city near Athens. At one point his city was beseiged by King Minos of Crete, a very powerful ruler. Nisus was unafraid, since he was invincible as long as no one cut his lock of purple hair. He was, however, unaware that his daughter, Scylla, had developed a passion for King Minos and thought that he would love her in return if she helped him to overthrow her father. As Nisus slept, she crept into his chamber and cut the magic lock of hair from her father's head. When she told Minos what she had done, he was horrified at her treachery. After he sacked the city and killed Nisus, he drowned Scylla by attaching her to the back of his ship as he sailed away.

Another of Pandion's sons was Aegeus who became king of Athens when his father died. It is Aegeus (probably an eponym for the Aegean Sea and a humanization of the god Poseidon) who became the mortal father of our hero, Theseus.

Birth

Disturbed, because after two marriages he still had no children, Aegeus decided to consult the oracle at Delphi. His inquiry was given a puzzling response: "Do not open the wineskin until you return home!" How did such a statement have anything to do with his question about childlessness? Aegeas had no idea what action to take, so rather than return home in confusion, he decided instead to discuss his problem and the enigmatic reply of Apollo with his old friend, Pittheus, king of Troezen, a city on eastern shore of the Peloponnesus.

Pittheus, sympathizing with his friend's problems, entertained him with a lavish banquet at which much wine was served. After Aegeus had retired, Pittheus sent his daughter, Aethra, to him. She had silently loved Aegeus since she had first seen him, years ago. After the two had made love, they fell asleep, but some say that Aethra had a vision in which she was told to swim to a nearby island. She rose from the bed and did as the dream had instructed. When she reached the island, she entered the small temple of Poseidon which had been built there, and -miraculous to say- the god himself visited her on this extraordinary night. It is because of these events that Theseus was thought to have both a human and a divine father.

On the next day Aegeus brought Aethra to a huge rock under which he placed his sword and sandals. He said to her: "If you bear a son, raise him without revealing who his father is. When he comes of age, bring him to this rock. If he can lift it, send him with the sword and sandals to me at Athens where he will claim his birthright."

Aethra did indeed give birth to a son whom she named Theseus. She supervised his education at Troezen (never revealing his father's identity) and watched with pride as he developed into a strong,

-130-

courageous, and intelligent young man. When Aethra thought that he was old enough, she brought him to Aegeus' rock. The future hero lifted it without difficulty and found the sword and sandals beneath. She told her son to bring these things to Athens and show them to the king who would explain their meaning.

The Journey to Athens

Theseus decided to go to Athens immediately, and, since he wished to perform heroic actions based on the model of the famous Heracles and to rid the country of those who made the roads unsafe, he planned to take the dangerous overland route which was filled with murderers and thieves, rather than travel more safely by ship. Theseus also resolved that on his journey he would never be the first to attack, but that he would always deliver a punishment to fit the crime.

There are six famous deeds —often called the Labors of Theseus— associated with our hero on the way to Athens. The murderers whom he met were inventive in the manner in which they dispatched their victims, and Theseus, true to his resolve, killed each of them in the same fashion in which they had disposed of others.

First met was Periphetes, a son of Hephaestus. He beat his victims to death with a bronze club. In a fierce struggle, Theseus seized the weapon and killed the villain with it. Because of this adventure, our hero is often pictured with a club (much like Heracles).

Next encountered was Sinis who disposed of people by bending two pine trees toward each other and tying the arms of his victim to one and the legs to the other and then releasing the trees to spring apart with terrific force. Our hero defeated Sinis in a fight and then split his personality.

In his third adventure, Theseus speared a huge, man-eating pig which was terrorizing the people who lived near the isthmus of Corinth.

The next murderer was Sciron who forced all who came by to wash his feet while kneeling at the edge of a road along a cliff. After the victim had been forced to perform his disagreeable task, Sciron would kick the unfortunate person over the cliff where a huge turtle would be waiting to devour the body broken on the rocks below. Sciron was now forced to wash the feet of another, and his fractured corpse formed a feast for the monster which he had been nourishing for so long.

The fifth episode involved Cercyon, a wrestler who forced all travellers to fight to the death with him and who had always been victorious until Theseus accepted his challenge. This accomplishment recalls Hercules' match with the invincible wrestler, Antaeus (eleventh labor).

Finally came Procrustes who, after lavishly entertaining passers-by, forced them to lie upon his bed, and if they were too long for it, cut off their limbs, and if too short, stretched them until they achieved a perfect fit. Procrustes was killed in his own bed.

Theseus eventually arrived in Athens where, because the news of his great deeds had preceded him, the populace greeted him warmly as a great hero, and King Aegeus invited him to the palace.

Now Aegeus had some years earlier provided sanctuary for the beautiful sorceress, Medea, and she in turn had promised to end the king's childlessness. They soon had a son called Medus. Because of her special powers, Medea at once recognized Theseus as the legitimate heir of the king and determined to kill him so that Medus might inherit the throne of Athens.

Medea arranged to have the young stranger sent to tame the Cretan bull which Heracles had brought into Greece (seventh labor) and which had again become wild and was devastating the countryside around Marathon. Theseus, like Heracles, tamed the bull through repeated struggles with him. He then killed the animal and sacrificed it to Poseidon.

Failing in this attempt to kill the young hero, Medea next attempted to persuade Aegeus that Theseus had been sent by the king's enemies to do him harm. In this deception she was successful. A lavish banquet was scheduled for Theseus in honor of his killing of the bull, and at the feast she planned to serve him a goblet of poisoned wine. The plan would have worked except that Theseus for the first time brought out the sword which had been left under the rock, and Aegeus, recognizing his old weapon, was just able to prevent his son from drinking the poison. Medea, with her plot exposed, was forced to flee, while Aegeus rejoiced in his son from Troezen whom he made heir to the throne.

The Minotaur

It was now time for Theseus to undertake his greatest labor and the one for which he is the most famous: the struggle with the dreaded Minotaur. So that we can better understand the significance of this task, we shall look briefly at the island of Crete in those early times.

Crete is the largest of the Aegean islands and is about ninety miles south of the mainland. It is 160 miles long by 36 miles wide at its broadest point. The early civilization which existed there was thought until this century to be derived from that on mainland Greece, called Mycenaean, because one of its major towns was Mycenae. Sir Arthur Evans, a British archaeologist, began in 1900 a thirty year excavation of Knossos, the largest site on the island, and soon determined that the culture of Crete was not taken from that on the mainland but was instead the dominant one which greatly influenced the less well developed Mycenaeans. Evans gave the name Minoan to the civilization on Crete.

Minoan civilization was apparently palace-centered with towns built around many such structures scattered over the island. The floor plans of the palaces are all similar to that at Knossos which is the largest and which many believe to be the main site and perhaps the residence of the island's ruler. The art work which survives at the palaces reveals a highly sophisticated culture. The ruins at Knossos also show considerable knowledge of engineering techniques.

Minoan culture seems to have reached its height from about 2000 to 1400 B.C. and then to have declined. Judging from the relatively unfortified nature of their palaces and towns, the Cretans appear to have depended heavily upon their navy for defense. There is no literature remaining, but many inscribed clay tablets have been found. These often contain short messages followed by numbers, apparently some sort of palace bookkeeping system. There are two kinds of script used in these accounts: Linear A (about 1750-1400 B.C.) which is still undeciphered and must be a Cretan language different from any that we know, and Linear B, a later script which was recently deciphered and appears to be a primitive form of Greek.

The bull seems to have been a favorite animal among the Minoans and was perhaps a national as well as a religious symbol. There are many wall paintings of bulls, and it is clear that some sort of acrobatic feats were performed with the animal by Cretan (or foreign?) athletes in the large courtyard found in all of the major palaces on the island.

It now appears that the Mycenaeans probably conquered Crete -or at least Knossos- around 1450 to 1400 B.C., after some terrible natural disaster had weakened the Minoans. A current theory connects the tremendous volcanic eruption which destroyed most of the island of Thera, some sixty miles north of Crete, with this fatal weakening of Minoan civilization. The eruption, apparently one of the most powerful the earth has ever witnessed, and the accompanying earthquakes, tidal-waves, and fall-out of ash would have been more than enough to devastate the Minoan palaces and cities which were mostly located near the coast while leaving the Greek cities, located farther inland and on elevated sites, relatively unharmed.

Some have connected the destruction of Thera with the end of Atlantis as described by Plato in his dialogues, the **Timaeus** and the **Critias,** and have attempted to find the topography of the "lost continent" in that of Thera which was an outpost of the Minoans. This theory holds that the advanced civilization of Atlantis was really that of Crete.

The historical events of this time are endlessly fascinating and all the more mysterious since we can be certain of so little. It does appear, however, that the myth of Theseus is directly connected with this time of change and upheaval in the relationship between Mycenaean Greece and Crete.

There are myths about the Minoans as well. Let us look briefly at some of these.

One day, while the beautiful maiden Europa, the daughter of Agenor, king of Phoenicia, was strolling along the seashore, Zeus, much taken with love of this mortal woman, appeared before her in the form of a bull. Europa, attracted by the beauty and gentleness of the creature, approached it and eventually sat upon its back. Suddenly, the animal jumped into the sea and swam with the young woman to the island of Crete where Zeus assumed human form and changed the bull into the constellation Taurus which can still be seen today. With Europa the god produced three heroes, the most famous of whom was Minos, king at Knossos and thereby ruler of the entire island. Some think that Minos rather than being a name is actually a title for the ruler, much like "pharaoh" in Egypt.

Minos governed Crete with honesty and fairness (so much so that after his death he was made a judge in the Underworld). He married Pasiphae, a daughter of the sun god, Helios. They had many children, the most famous of whom –for our purposes– were two daughters, Ariadne and Phaedra, and a son, Androgeus.

Minos was especially devoted to Poseidon, and he once prayed that the god would send him a special animal worthy of sacrifice to the divinity who had provided Crete and its ruler with such good fortune for so many years. As if in answer to his request, the waves parted and a huge bull emerged from the sea. Minos was so struck by the beauty of this animal that, despite his entreaty to Poseidon, he could not bring himself to kill it. He hid the bull among his cattle and offered another in solemn sacrifice. But we know that mortals cannot deceive the gods. Poseidon did not punish Minos directly for his deception, rather he caused his wife, Pasiphae, to develop a growing and uncontrollable passion –horrible to relate– for this bull which had come from the sea. How could she satisfy such unspeakable lust? Even her sense of shame and her concern for her good reputation were overcome; she revealed her feelings to Daedalus in hopes that he could help her.

Daedalus was a famous Athenian craftsman and inventor. He had come to Crete in exile after committing a murder in his native city. Minos had kept the engineer busy with projects at Knossos, and he is credited with designing much of the palace. Pasiphae's request for aid was surely his strangest commission. He constructed a hollow wooden cow, covered it with hides, and wheeled it into a pasture. Pasiphae hid inside it. The cow was so lifelike that the bull was deceived, and eventually the queen gave birth to the Minotaur, a monster with the head of a bull and the body of a man. The creature was so horrible that just to see it struck terror in the hearts of the Minoans; it devastated the countryside and fed on human flesh.

Since no one dared to kill the monster which was believed to be sacred to Poseidon, Daedalus designed a labyrinth in which the animal was to be kept and from which it could never escape. We should note that while "labyrinth" today is a synonym for "maze," it has the etymological meaning of "double-headed ax," another of the religious and national symbols of Crete. We should also note that the complicated floor plan at Knossos would surely appear to be a maze to a Greek accustomed to much simpler living quarters.

Daedalus carefully supervised the construction of the labyrinth. The Minotaur was tricked inside and could not find his way out of the intertwined passageways. He was fed with prisoners who were forced to enter the labyrinth and would eventually be located and consumed by the beast.

Shortly after these events, Androgeus, the son of King Minos, was killed while participating in the Panathenaic athletic contests. Minos suspected that there was treachery involved, and he declared war on Athens. It was during this war that he sacked the city of Megara after the magic lock of hair had been cut from the head of King Nisus by his daughter. He then moved on to Athens where the city had been advised by the oracle at Delphi to give Minos whatever he wished as restitution for the death of his son. Minos demanded that the Athenians send seven males and seven females annually (the period varies) to Crete to be fed to the Minotaur. The Athenians resented this appalling demand; however, they had no choice but to comply. Each year the Athenians put the names of all the young men and women living in the city into an urn and drew by lot the fourteen who must go.

Theseus arrived in Athens after Aegeus had been complying with the harsh order of Minos for several years. He volunteered to be one of those to go to Crete, despite the pleas of his father who believed that his newly found son would face certain death. The Athenians, on the other hand, cheered and admired the courage of the young hero. The ship carrying the Minotaur's victims was fitted with a black sail symbolic of the death which they faced; however, Aegeas also gave his son a white one which he told him to hoist on the return voyage, if he was successful in his task. In that way the king, who would watch for the ship on the high cliffs of Sunium in the southernmost part of Attica, could know long before the vessel docked whether his son was alive or dead.

As soon as the ship arrived at Crete, Ariadne, the daughter of Minos, saw Theseus and fell madly in love with him. When she learned through informers that he was the son of the king and had come to kill the Minotaur, her passion increased along with her admiration for his courage. So overwhelming were her feelings that she determined to help the handsome young man accomplish his mission even though it would mean betraying her father. She arranged to have Theseus meet secretly with Daedalus to study the design of the labyrinth. She also provided him with a ball of cord which he could unravel as he entered the maze so that, if successful, he might find his way out again.

Theseus entered the labyrinth, located the Minotaur, and killed the beast in a fierce struggle. Some say he used a sword which Ariadne had given him, others that he killed the monster with his bare hands. He followed the cord out of the maze, and, with the other Athenians and Ariadne, he rushed to the ship and sailed away before Minos realized what had happened.

Theseus was not as loyal to Ariadne as she had been to him. During a stop on the island of Naxos, the hero -for no apparent reason- abandoned the woman who had given up everything for him. Some say that she was later found by the god, Dionysus, and that he made her his immortal wife. Others say that it was Dionysus who forced Theseus to leave the woman behind. But the myth provides no clear explanation for such apparently heartless behavior.

Meanwhile, back on Crete, since he suspected them of assisting their fellow Athenian, Minos had imprisoned Daedalus and his son, Icarus. Daedalus had not anticipated Theseus' success or he would have sailed away with him, and now an escape by sea was blocked by Minos' strong navy. However, the noted inventor had prepared for such an emergency. He had secretly built sets of wings for Icarus and himself. They would fly from Crete, since they could not sail. Daedalus bribed a guard to let them out of the prison, attached the wings to both Icarus and himself, and -to the astonishment of all who saw them- flew from Minos' island. He had warned his son to be careful to follow a middle course, not too high up into the heat of the sun, or too far down into the waves of the sea, but Icarus, delighted by the new experience, forgot his father's instructions and soared upward. The heat melted the wax holding the feathers, the wings disintegrated, and, with his father watching helplessly, the boy plunged into the waters below and drowned. This part of the eastern Aegean near the Asian coast has ever since been called the Icarian Sea. The body, washed ashore, was found by Heracles who was returning to Greece after his year of slavery with Queen Omphale. He performed the funeral rites and named the place Icaria. Daedalus continued on alone with Minos and his fleet in close pursuit. The king eventually caught up with the winged craftsman in Sicily, but was himself killed there by a ruler who had agreed to protect the inventive genius. Daedalus remained in Sicily for some time and designed many projects for the man who had saved his life. He also travelled to Italy and Sardinia. Many believe that the record of his accomplishments actually reflects the spread of Cretan culture westward and northward through the Mediterranean.

Theseus, in his eagerness to return home, forgot to change his sail from black to white, and Aegeus, seeing the ship on the horizon with its dark sail and thinking that his son was dead, threw himself in despair from the high cliffs at Sunium into the water below. The eastern Mediterranean has ever since been called the Aegean Sea. The wisdom of the prophecy at Delphi was now revealed for, after having been warned not to consume wine until he returned to Athens, Aegeus had ignored the oracle at the palace of King Pittheus and had conceived Theseus who now indirectly caused his death.

Theseus the king

After the death of Aegeus, Theseus became king of Athens. He was a wise and judicious ruler who developed a democracy of a sort and permitted considerable political freedom. He aided the weak and unfortunate and helped the worthy. He is essentially portrayed as a civilizing leader, much like King Arthur in British myth; however, the mythological material continues to show a heroic spirit, restless for new adventures and reluctant to assume a more sedentary role.

Theseus traveled to the land of the Amazons, the women warriors who lived in the wilds of Asia. Some say that he accompanied Heracles, others that he made a separate journey. He brought back their queen, Antiope, as his wife, and their marriage produced a son, Hippolytus. Such happiness was short lived. The Amazons left their far distant land to invade Greece and attack Athens, because they believed (rightly!) that Theseus had carried off their queen by force. The Athenians were nearly conquered before they finally defeated the Amazons and drove them out of Greece. Many were killed in the fierce struggle, including, unfortunately, Queen Antiope herself.

Theseus now developed a strong friendship with Pirithous, a ruler of the Lapiths in Thessaly, and a restless man who -like himself- had a longing for new and varied challenges. They fought in the struggle which developed between the Lapiths and the Centaurs at the tragic wedding of Pirithous where his bride was killed. To help alleviate the memory of this great sorrow, each man vowed to help the other obtain whichever wife he desired. The two kidnapped the still unwed Helen of Sparta in hopes that she would become Theseus' wife, but she was rescued by her brothers. They entered the Land of the Dead to accomplish the foolhardy task of kidnapping Persephone to become the bride of Pirithous. Hades imprisoned them both, Pirithous permanently, and Theseus until he was rescued by Heracles when the hero came to obtain Cerberus as his twelfth labor.

At some time before he entered the Underworld, Theseus had married Phaedra, the last daughter of King Minos and sister of Ariadne. She was much younger than Theseus, more the age of her stepson, Hippolytus, with whom she fell in love while Theseus was imprisoned in the Underworld. Hippolytus, the son of Theseus and Antiope, knew nothing of the force of passion. He was devoted to hunting and the worship of the maiden goddess, Artemis. He rejected the illicit suggestions of his stepmother, and Phaedra in humiliation hanged herself, leaving a note which accused Hippolytus of rape. Theseus returned about this time, and, when Hippolytus despite his innocence was not able to make any kind of defense, he believed the accusations contained in the letter of his dead wife. He called upon Poseidon to punish his son. Soon afterwards, when Hippolytus was driving his chariot along the beach, a huge bull suddenly rose out of the sea causing the horses to bolt in terror. They overturned the chariot and trampled their master to death. Only after this tragic event, did the grief-stricken father learn the truth of the matter.

Theseus fell out of favor with the Athenians. He had brought on a disastrous war when he had kidnapped Helen earlier, and, during his long absence in the Underworld, another king supplanted him. He went in voluntary exile to the bleak island of Scyros where some say that the treacherous king, Lycomedes, pushed him off a cliff, others, that he merely slipped and fell to an accidental death.

Centuries later the Greeks believed that Theseus' spirit assumed human form again and was seen during the Battle of Marathon in 490 B.C. He supposedly fought at the front of the line and led the Athenians to victory against the Persians. The oracle at Delphi was consulted, and, based on that advice, the Athenians brought back what were thought to be Theseus' bones from Scyros and gave them an honored place in the city.

Sources

Some of the best ancient versions of the myth are: Plutarch's **Life of Theseus**; Ovid's **Metamorphoses**, Book 2 for the Europa story and Book 8 for the story of Daedalus and Icarus; Catullus 64 and Ovid's **Heroides** for the tragic love of Ariadne; and, Euripides' **Hippolytus** for the Theseus-Phaedra-Hippolytus triangle.

Questions

1. What elements of the heroic myth pattern does the story contain?

2. Show how the myth of Theseus reflects the forces of civilization triumphing over barbarism.

3. Discuss the impact of Poseidon on the myth.

4. List the ways in which the myth of Theseus may well reflect the actual historical circumstances of the time.

5. Examine the impact which women have upon the life of Theseus.

6. How does the entire myth reflect Athenian patriotism?

7. List the parallels between the myth of Theseus and that of Heracles.

8. How is the Hippolytus-Phaedra story similar to the one about Bellerophon and Queen Antia?

9. In what ways is the ending of Theseus' story similar to the that of Bellerophon's? What purpose does such an ending serve?

10. In what ways is the Minos-Scylla story similar to that of Amphitryon and Comaetho in the Heracles myth? Are both stories making the same point?

11. In what ways is Scylla similar to Ariadne?

28. THE THEBAN SAGA

A. The founding of Thebes

B. The children of Cadmus

C. Oedipus

D. The Seven Against Thebes

E. Creon and Antigone

F. The Epigoni

G. Tiresias

Some of the most famous of all of the Greek myths come from Thebes, and its saga was very popular in antiquity. Unfortunately, much of the literature (epic poems and tragedies) which presented the stories has been lost to us, unlike, for example, the Trojan legend where a good bit remains. The stories are generally tragic and often depict innocent men and women who are given seemingly undeserved punishments by the gods, yet who themselves remain courageous and enduring throughout their trials.

The founding of Thebes

Agenor, the king of Phoenicia, was much disturbed over the disappearance of his daughter, Europa, so he sent his four sons to find her. One of the young men, Cadmus, traveled as far as Greece in his quest. He had heard of the great reputation of the oracle of Apollo at Delphi, so he went to the shrine to ask for assistance in his task. The reply was unexpected: "Stop your futile search for your sister, and instead find a cow with markings of full moons on its side. Follow this animal until it becomes tired and rests, and at that place build a city!" Cadmus obeyed without hesitation. His wanderings took him into the area of Greece called Boeotia (cow-land) where he founded the city of Thebes.

After some of his men had been attacked by a dragon, an offspring of Ares which guarded a nearby spring, Cadmus killed the monster. Athena appeared and told him to pull the dragon's teeth, give half of them to her, and plant the others. As soon as Cadmus had plowed the teeth under, an armed man grew from each one. As they advanced against him, he threw a stone in their midst, and all but five were killed as they fought among themselves. These five made peace with each other and with Cadmus. They promised to help build his city, and they became founders of the five leading families of Thebes.

Because he had killed the dragon, Cadmus was compelled to serve Ares for eight years. At the conclusion of the sentence, the god gave him his daughter, Harmonia, as his wife, and Athena proclaimed him king of the new city which he had founded. The marriage of Cadmus and Harmonia was blessed by the attendance of the gods, a compliment they paid only to one other mortal couple, Peleus and Thetis, the parents of Achilles.

Cadmus, like Theseus of Athens, is portrayed as a king who brought civilization to the Greeks. He introduced among other things, the alphabet, the worship of Dionysus (and thus the cultivation of the grape vine), and various kinds of mining.

Cadmus and Harmonia had four daughters and a son. Late in their lives the two left Thebes and went to western Greece to inspire the people there to many victories in battle. They were eventually transformed into snakes by Ares (a reward!) and sent to Elysium.

The children of Cadmus

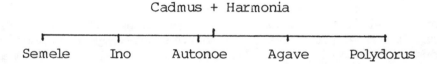

Cadmus + Harmonia

Semele   Ino   Autonoe   Agave   Polydorus

The four daughters of Cadmus led tragic lives. The beautiful Semele had attracted the eye of Zeus who visited her in human form, and although the union would produce the god, Dionysus, Semele was killed in the process. Hera had visited her in disguise and created doubts in the young woman's mind about her lover's divinity. Semele, having already exacted a promise from the god that he would grant any request, asked Zeus to reveal himself in all of his brilliance and glory. Zeus was compelled to keep his word, and the woman was consumed by the fire of the divine aura.

Zeus saved the infant Dionysus who was given to Ino, Semele's sister, for a short time. For her part in caring for the god (a seemingly generous action), Ino was driven to madness and suicide by Hera, after unsuccessfully attempting to kill her step-children, Phrixus and Helle. The youngsters escaped from her clutches on the back of a golden ram. This marvellous beast could also fly, and it carried the children eastward until Helle fell off and drowned in the waters which still bear her name: the Hellespont (= Sea of Helle). Phrixus managed to ride the animal to the eastern shore of the Black Sea, to a land called Colchis, where he sacrificed the ram and hung its golden fleece on a tree. It became the object of a quest by Jason and the Argonauts in the next generation.

Autonoe, another daughter of Cadmus, had a son by the name of Actaeon. While out hunting one day, he accidentally looked upon Artemis and her nymphs as they were bathing. For this unintentional offense Actaeon was transformed into a stag by Artemis and torn to pieces by his own hunting dogs.

Agave and her son, Pentheus, both refused to accept the divinity of Dionysus. They were driven mad by the god for their impiety. Agave led a group of women worshippers of the god in an attack on her own child. The ecstatic bacchants killed Pentheus and ripped his body into shreds. Later, Agave returned to her senses and realized -in unbelieving horror- what she had done.

Polydorus, the only son of Cadmus, became king of Thebes and ruled the city well, but he died while his son, Labdacus, was still an infant, so a man by the name of Lycus became regent until the youngster came of age.

Although Lycus was a good king, he and his wife, Dirce, treated his niece, Antiope, harshly. He refused to believe that she had become pregnant by Zeus, and when she gave birth to twins, he abandoned them in the wilderness. As is usual in such stories, they were found and secretly raised, in this instance, by a shepherd. When the boys -Amphion, a noted musician, and Zethus, a fierce warrior- came of age, they killed Lycus and Dirce in revenge for the treatment they and their mother had received. The twins then became regents, since Labdacus had died after a short reign and left a son, Laius, who was still too young to rule.

Amphion built the wall around the city -with its famous seven gates- by causing the stones to move into place through the magical beauty of his lyre playing. Zethus married Thebe who gave her name to the city (which had been called Cadmea up to that time), while Amphion married Niobe, a daughter of Tantalus.

Niobe, as we have seen earlier, had seven sons and seven daughters of whom she was so proud that she claimed -unwisely- to be superior to Leto, the mother of Artemis and Apollo, who had only the two children. Such pride would not go unpunished. Leto sent Artemis and Apollo to kill all of Niobe's children. No pleading would save them; they were all slaughtered. So great was the mother's grief that even when she was transformed into a rock so that she would no longer feel the pain of what she had done, water still came forth, the tears of Niobe.

Oedipus

When Amphion and Zethus died, Laius was old enough to become king of Thebes. He married the gracious Jocasta who soon conceived a child. But their happiness was marred by a terrible prophecy: their child would kill his father and marry his mother. When Jocasta gave birth, they quickly abandoned the infant on the desolate slope of a mountain. Despite their precautions, a shepherd found the baby and took him to the childless King Polybus and Queen Merope of Corinth where the royal couple raised him as their own. They named the child Oedipus (= Swollen-foot) because of the condition of the infant's feet which had been tied together by his parents.

Oedipus grew to manhood thinking that Polybus and Merope were his parents. When the legitimacy of his birth was questioned by someone who suspected he might actually be the son of one of the king's mistresses, Oedipus decided to settle the matter by appealing to the oracle at Delphi. But, when he inquired who his parents were, the terrible response was that he would kill his father and marry his mother.

Stunned by this hateful utterance, Oedipus determined never to return to Corinth until his parents had died. He started instead on the road to Thebes without realizing that this was indeed his true home. Along the way an argument developed between Oedipus and a nobleman accompanied by his slaves who demanded more than their share of the narrow road. Words led to blows, and, in the bloody fight which ensued, Oedipus killed them all. Without realizing it, the unfortunate hero had already fulfilled the first part of the prophecy, for the wealthy man had been his father, King Laius, who had been on his way to Delphi to seek advice from the oracle.

Oedipus continued on to Thebes where he found that the city was being threatened by the Sphinx, a creature part lion, part woman, with the wings of an eagle. (It was this menace which had sent Laius to Delphi). The Sphinx posed a riddle to any Theban whom it encountered outside the city walls: what walks on four legs in the morning, two legs at noon, and three legs at night? Failure to give the correct answer resulted in immediate and painful death. Oedipus sought out the monster and gave the correct reply. The riddle refers to man in three stages of his life: infancy, when he crawls on all fours; maturity, when he walks upright; and old age, when he walks with a cane. The curse of the Sphinx was removed, and Oedipus was welcomed into the city as a great hero. He was offered the kingship as a reward, and presented with the recently widowed Jocasta for his wife.

Oedipus and Jocasta lived happily for many years and had four children: two sons, Eteocles and Polyneices, and two daughters: Antigone and Ismene.

Suddenly a plague descended upon the city. Oedipus took action at once and did all in his power to discover what had caused the anger of the gods and what must be done to remove the disease. Through his efforts he came to see that his real parents were Laius and

Jocasta and that, although unknowingly, he had killed the one and was living incestuously with the other. Jocasta hanged herself with the knowledge of what she had done. Oedipus gouged out his eyes and went into exile, a wandering outcast, avoided by everyone.

Years later, as an old man, he was accepted by Theseus into Athenian territory where he died in a mysterious fashion and was worshipped as a kind of demigod.

The Seven Against Thebes

When Oedipus' sons, Eteocles and Polyneices came of age, they decided to alternate the rule of Thebes annually. Eteocles, who ruled first, refused to give up the throne, so Polyneices persuaded King Adrastus of Argos, his father-in-law, to help him organize an army to attack his native city. This expedition was led by seven great heroes and is one of the most celebrated actions in Greek myth; however, as we have mentioned, most of the ancient literature describing the event has been lost so that the Theban war does not seem as significant to us as do some of the other sagas.

The army organized by Polyneices marched on Thebes, having many adventures along the way. The seige of the city continued for some time until, after a single combat in which Polyneices and Eteocles killed each other, the invading forces lost heart and returned home. Of the seven generals who led the expedition, only King Adrastus survived.

Creon and Antigone

Creon, the brother of Jocasta, now became king of Thebes. One of his first actions was to issue an edict forbidding the burial of Polyneices because he had acted as a traitor by leading enemy forces against his native city. In the religious beliefs of the times an improper burial not only prevented the spirit of the person from obtaining its proper resting place in the Underworld, but was also a disgrace for the family. Antigone, Polyneices' sister, determined to disobey Creon's law and perform funeral rites for her brother. She was apprehended by the king's guards and sentenced to the death penalty of being enclosed in a cave. When Creon finally heeded the warning of the prophet Tiresias that he had acted improperly both in denying a burial for Polyneices and in sentencing Antigone to death, he attempted to recover the daughter of Oedipus from her entombment, but she had already died. Creon's son, Haemon, then killed himself over the loss of the woman he loved, and Creon's wife, Eurydice, likewise committed suicide when she was informed of her son's death. By issuing a law which he thought perfectly justifiable, Creon saw the lives of his loved ones and his own fortunes totally destroyed.

The Epigoni

Ten years after the initial attack upon Thebes, the sons of the original seven generals who are called the Epigoni (After-born) organized another expedition against the city. This time the invaders were successful. The city was sacked and burned.

Tiresias

Tiresias, perhaps the most famous prophet in myth, is associated with the city of Thebes from its founding until its destruction with the attack of the Epigoni. Although born a male, he experienced life as a female for several years, and was then restored to manhood by the gods. In an argument which Zeus and Hera were having as to whether the male or female derives the greater pleasure from the sexual act, it was decided to call upon Tiresias for an answer, since he had experienced life in both sexes. Tiresias claimed that the female experiences much more pleasure than the male. His reply greatly irritated Hera who had been arguing the opposite point of view. In her anger she blinded Tiresias, but Zeus rewarded the young man by giving him prophetic powers and a life nine times longer than the ordinary. The blind prophet is present in almost all of the stories connected with Thebes. His advice like that of most prophets, while often sought, is often ignored.

Sources

The best ancient versions of the Theban myths can be found in three plays by Sophocles, **Oedipus the King**, **Oedipus at Colonus**, and **Antigone**; in the play **The Seven Against Thebes** by Aeschylus; and in the epic poem **Thebais** by Statius.

Some of interesting modern adaptations can be found in plays by Jean Cocteau: **The Infernal Machine**; Andre Gide: **Oedipus**; and, Jean Anouilh: **Antigone**. T.S. Eliot's drama, **The Elder Statesman**, is based on Sophocles' **Oedipus at Colonus**.

Questions

1. Describe the major tragedy in the life of each of Cadmus' daughters.

2. How is the punishment of Niobe typical of the gods?

3. Is it the gods who punish Oedipus? If so, why?

4. Why is Creon punished?

5. Show how prophecy is important in this myth. What does prophecy tell us about the nature of the world and the gods?

29. JASON AND THE ARGONAUTS

A. Phrixus and Helle

B. Aeson and Pelias

C. Preparations for the quest

D. The voyage to Colchis

    1. The Lemnian women
    2. King Cyzicus and the Doliones
    3. Heracles and Hylas
    4. Amycus
    5. Phineus
    6. The Symplegades
    7. The Stymphalian birds

E. The Argonauts at Colchis

F. The voyage back to Thessaly

    1. Circe
    2. The Sirens
    3. Scylla and Charybdis
    4. The marriage of Jason and Medea
    5. The Libyan desert
    6. Crete and Talos
    7. Iolcus and Pelias

G. Corinth

Phrixus and Helle

As we have already seen when we looked at the stories from Thebes, Ino was a daughter of Cadmus who married King Athamas. In a fit of madness and jealousy she tried to kill Phrixus and Helle, her husband's children by a previous marriage. Her stepchildren were saved by a golden-fleeced ram which took them on its back and flew away. When they reached the strait between Europe and Asia near the site of Troy, Helle fell from the ram and was drowned. That place today is still called the Hellespont (= Sea of Helle). The long flight ended in the land of Colchis at the far eastern end of the Black Sea, a destination apparently determined by the gods. The kingdom was ruled by Aeetes, son of Helios (god of the sun), and a brother to Pasiphae (wife of Minos of Crete) and to Circe (a sorceress most noted in her connection with Odysseus). Despite the Colchian reputation for hostility toward strangers, the king graciously welcomed Phrixus and even gave him one of his daughters as a wife.

The young man settled down happily. He sacrificed the ram to Zeus and gave its golden coat to Aeetes who hung it on a tree in a grove sacred to Ares. With his special powers, Aeetes arranged to have it guarded by an ever-watchful dragon, since there had been a prediction that he would rule only as long as the fleece remained in his domain.

Aeson and Pelias

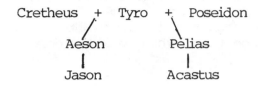

Cretheus + Tyro + Poseidon

Aeson   Pelias

Jason   Acastus

    Cretheus was the king of Iolcus, the largest city in Thessaly, an area located in the northeastern part of the Greek peninsula. When Cretheus died, his older son, Aeson, should have become king; however, Aeson's half-brother, Pelias, usurped the throne. Pelias was a son of Poseidon and Cretheus' wife, Tyro. Being the son of a god gave him a greater right, he thought, to rule the city. Although his life had been temporarily spared, Aeson feared that Pelias would try at the first opportunity to kill both him and his young son, Jason, so he spread the false story that Jason had died, while he secretly sent him to be educated by the centaur, Chiron.

    Since Pelias had received a prophecy that he would one day be deposed -and indeed even killed- by a person wearing one sandal, he was most uneasy as king. After several years Jason appeared at one of Pelias' festivals with a sandal missing, having lost it in helping an old woman cross a stream. The woman was actually Hera in disguise, a goddess who continued to favor Jason throughout his quest and who was hostile to Pelias because he had neglected her rites. Indeed, some say that the basic motivation behind this entire legend is Hera's desire to bring Medea to Iolcus so that the sorceress could kill the neglectful king.

    When he arrived at the festival, Jason forthrightly announced to Pelias who he was, told him that he might keep whatever wealth he had acquired, but that he, Jason, wished to claim his rightful kingdom. Although Pelias recognized the danger which Jason represented, he was hesitant for political reasons to kill the youth outright. He decided, finally, to send the hero upon a dangerous and -what he hoped would be- fatal mission: he challenged Jason to bring back the Golden Fleece from distant Colchis, alleging that the ghost of Phrixus had appeared to him in a dream and ordered that it be done.

Preparations for the quest

Jason accepted the task, although he realized that the voyage would be the farthest ever attempted by the Greeks -filled with innumerable perils- and that the Colchians themselves would offer much resistance to his quest.

While the saga of Jason probably originated in Mycenaean times (some say it is merely a romanticized version of a Greek pirate raid to steal Colchian gold), it was surely enlarged by Greek expansion into the Black Sea beginning in the eighth century B.C., and the journey to Colchis and back, which offers stories from almost every geographical area in the Greek world, may well be reflective of actual trade routes.

Because of the length and rigors of the voyage, a large and sturdy ship had to be constructed. Jason obtained the services of Argus, a famous shipwright, as designer and builder. Athena assisted in the construction, and the goddess even placed a wooden figurehead which could actually speak in the ship's prow. The vessel was named **Argo** (= swift) in honor of its designer.

A call for volunteers was sent to all of the cities of Greece and fifty great heroes were selected (the number of rowers in a Greek warship). There is wide variation in just who the fifty were, since later Greeks considered it an honor to be descended from one of these men, and new names would be added to fit the wish. Among those generally included were Heracles, Meleager, Castor, Polydeuces, Orpheus, Admetus, Peleus (the father of Achilles), and Telamon (the father of Ajax). From the names it can be seen that this adventure took place in the generation before the Trojan War. The fifty heroes were called the Argonauts (= Sailors on the **Argo**).

The quest for the fleece has three parts: the expedition to Colchis, the adventures there, and the return trip. The saga, because of its journey format and because of its popularity in antiquity has had innumerable incidents accumulate around the outward and return voyages. Many local myths are in this way attached to the main narrative. We shall describe the major adventures.

The voyage to Colchis

1. The Lemnian women

Lemnos is an island in the northern Aegean about halfway between Thrace and Troy. Some years earlier, because they had not properly worshipped her, Aphrodite had punished the women of this kingdom by causing them to give off an unpleasant smell. They were avoided by their husbands who brought other women home from their raids on the mainland and began to have children by them. Anger and jealousy caused the wives to rise up as a group and kill both the women who had been brought in and their own husbands. Their anger still not sated, they killed all remaining males, including their sons. The women and their queen, Hipsipyle, now regretted their actions —Aphrodite had removed her curse— and were quite susceptible to the charm and talents of Jason (who was always irresistible to females) and his handsome crew. The Argonauts remained on the island for some time and helped to repopulate it.

2. King Cyzicus and the Doliones

The Argonauts sailed eastward through the Hellespont into the Sea of Marmara which is adjacent to the Black Sea. Here they were greeted hospitably by the Doliones and their young king, Cyzicus. The Argonauts disposed of a group of six-armed giants who were threatening the Doliones. Unfortunately, after the task was completed and the **Argo** had departed, the ship was blown back by adverse winds. The Doliones had been troubled by sea raiders in the past, and, because of the darkness and the storm, they did not recognize the Argonauts and thought them to be marauders. The Greeks, on the other hand, did not know where the wind had taken them; they defended themselves against the savage onslaught of the Doliones and finally drove them off. When —with the dawn— both sides discovered what had happened, they were filled with sorrow at the mistake which they had made. The Argonauts remained for the funeral rites of King Cyzicus who had been killed by Jason in the struggle.

3. Heracles and Hylas

The Argonauts continued their eastward voyage along the Asiatic shore. They stopped at the port of Cios after Heracles had broken his oar. While the great hero went into the woods for new lumber, Hylas, his friend, went to a spring to draw water. The nymph who dwelled there saw the handsome youth and was so taken by his beauty that she pulled him to the bottom to be with her forever. Heracles was wild with grief at the loss of his companion. He searched everywhere in the vicinity and was unwilling to depart without him. The Argonauts reluctantly had to leave the great hero behind.

4. Amycus

The Argonauts next encountered Amycus, a mighty son of Poseidon, who challenged all visitors in his land to a boxing match which inevitably ended with the death of his opponent. Polydeuces, a son of Zeus and Leda, willingly accepted the challenge for the Argonauts. The bout continued for some time, but Polydeuces finally struck Amycus a fatal blow which ended the threats of the previously invincible bully.

5. Phineus

The Argonauts next came upon Phineus, the blind king and prophet, who, because he had offended Zeus by revealing too much of the god's plan for the human race, was being plagued by bird-women creatures called Harpies (= Snatchers). These hybrids would swoop down at every mealtime to seize and defile the king's food so that he was rapidly starving to death. The Argonauts drove the monsters away with the aid of Zetes and Calais, who, because they were sons of Boreas, the god of the north wind, were able to fly. In gratitude, Phineus told Jason how he could successfully make his way through the Symplegades (= the Clashing Rocks), two great boulders located near the entrance to the Black Sea which rushed together and crushed any ship which tried to pass between them.

6. The Symplegades

When the Argonauts came to the Symplegades, they released the dove which Phineus had given them. It flew between the rocks which immediately reacted and came together with great force. As the boulders began slowly to move back, the Argonauts rowed through the passage with all the strength they possessed. Phineus had told them that the rocks would have to withdraw completely before they could close again in response to the **Argo.** They were successful -only a decoration on the ship's stern was damaged-, and, because of their success, the Symplegades were fixed in position from that time on and were never again a threat to mariners.

7. The Stymphalian birds

Jason and his men continued to sail along the shore of the Black Sea. They rowed past the country of the Amazons without incident, and came to the Island of Ares where they found the Stymphalian birds: fierce, man-eating creatures which Heracles had driven out of Greece (sixth labor). The Argonauts kept the birds at a distance by clashing their shields together while they rescued the four sons of Phrixus who had been shipwrecked on the island.

The Argonauts at Colchis

The **Argo** finally arrived at Colchis on the far eastern shore of the Black Sea. Through spies and informers, Aeetes knew who the Argonauts were and why they had come. He was determined to frustrate their plans. The king at first concealed his true feelings and welcomed Jason and his men with a banquet. Jason told the king the reason for their journey, that they meant him no harm, and that, if he would give them the fleece, they would leave at once, since that was the only purpose for their voyage. Aeetes was impervious to the request of the Argonauts, and, indeed, was so angered by their presence that he would have killed them all right there at the banquet were he not concerned about the punishment Zeus might inflict upon him for violating the law of hospitality. He craftily told Jason that he would give up the fleece if the young man could pass certain tests of valor which he had devised. The bold adventurer readily agreed -what else could he do?- and Aeetes presented the tasks: first, he must yoke a pair of fire-breathing bulls, then plow a field with them, and, finally, plant the teeth of a dragon. Although Jason did not know it, the teeth were those that remained from the dragon which Cadmus had killed when he founded the city of Thebes; they produced the same crop, as you will see. The Argonauts were dismayed when they heard Aeetes describe the challenges; not even Jason, they thought, would be able to complete such labors successfully.

The goddess Hera realized what Aeetes intended, and so, to help her favored youth compete against a much more powerful opponent, she caused Medea, the beautiful young daughter of Aeetes and a sorceress with many magical powers, to fall in love with the hero. Medea arranged to meet secretly with the handsome leader, and, since Jason was at his best with women, their encounter only made her passion increase. She provided him with an ointment to spread over his body which would protect him from the fire of the bulls. She warned him that armed men would grow from the dragon's teeth, but she indicated that they could be defeated by throwing a stone in their midst which would cause them to fight and kill each other (a technique also used by Cadmus, as we have seen).

Despite the aid provided by Medea, the tasks were extremely difficult and required enormous courage and strength. Jason possessed both qualities, and, to the consternation of Aeetes, he successfully completed what had been required. The king, however, still refused to surrender the prize, since he suspected that his daughter had aided the hero.

Medea realized that her father and the Colchians were plotting treachery against the Argonauts, so she secretly led Jason to the sacred grove where the object of his quest was located. After Medea had drugged the guardian dragon and Jason had seized the fleece from a low hanging branch, the two of them rushed to the **Argo.**

Aeetes was soon informed that the fleece had been stolen and that his daughter had betrayed him. His fleet was prepared; he pursued the Argonauts in force. But Medea had anticipated this eventuality and had placed her young brother, Apsyrtus, on board the **Argo.** Without hesitation she killed the child, dismembered his body, and threw the pieces into the sea. Aeetes was forced to stop so that he could collect the parts of the corpse and provide his son with a proper burial. In the meantime, the Argonauts escaped to the open sea.

The voyage back to Thessaly

The homeward voyage has an itinerary which is very confusing and contains many variations. The Argonauts sailed in almost all waters known at the time. Many of their adventures are repetitious either of the outward journey or of episodes found in Homer's **Odyssey.**

Although the Colchians stopped to perform the funeral rites for Apsyrtus, they did not abandon the pursuit of the Argonauts, and the Greeks, for their part, attempted to choose routes which would keep them from the clutches of the far more numerous enemy. Moreover, the wondrous figurehead of the **Argo** -which could speak- told Jason that he and Medea would have to visit Circe who lived on the distant Italian coast (near the future site of Rome) in order to have their guilt for the murder of Apsyrtus removed.

1. Circe

The Argonauts left the Black Sea by sailing up the Danube River which they followed to another of its mouths at the top of the Adriatic Sea. The route is unclear, but it seems that they entered the Po River and somehow followed it to the Rhone which carried them back into the Mediterranean. They then sailed south along the Italian coast until they arrived at Circe's island where the sorceress (Medea's aunt) purified them of the blood of Apsyrtus.

2. The Sirens

As Jason and his men sailed farther south along the coast of Italy, they came to the island of the Sirens, bird-women who lured seafarers to destruction by singing beautiful and irresistible songs. Once the enchanting melody was heard, sailors were compelled to turn their ships toward the source where they would meet a watery death on the treacherous rocks. The Argonauts passed by safely because Orpheus was able to counter the Siren-song with a more captivating one of his own.

3. Scylla and Charybdis

Continuing their southward journey, the Argonauts came to the narrow passage between Italy and Sicily (the strait of Messina) where the monsters Scylla and Charybdis were located. Scylla was a woman to the waist, but the rest of her body was formed by six snakes with the head of a ravenous dog at the end of each. Sailors who came too close to her lair were seized from the deck and consumed. But to sail on the other side of the narrows resulted in being captured by Charybdis, a female monster who took the form of an enormous and powerful whirlpool. At the request of Hera, Thetis and the other Nereids (= sea-nymphs, daughters of Nereus), guided the **Argo** safely through the treacherous area.

-152-

4. The marriage of Jason and Medea

The Argonauts sailed around the southernmost part of Italy, across the Ionian Sea, to the island of Corfu where King Alcinous and the Phaeacians received them hospitably. It was here that a large contingent of Colchians caught up with the Greeks and demanded the return of Medea. When it became known to Jason that Alcinous was prepared to grant the demand of the Colchians unless he and Medea were married, he quickly arranged the necessary ceremony. The two spent their wedding night in a cave sacred to Dionysus. When Alcinous was informed that Jason and Medea were indeed man and wife, he so informed the Colchians who reluctantly accepted his decision and gave up their pursuit.

5. The Libyan desert

As the Argonauts began their voyage around the Peloponnesus, a great storm lashed their ship and pushed it southward toward Africa where a gigantic wave carried it far inland and left the vessel stranded deep in the Libyan desert. The men were exhausted and downhearted; nevertheless, at Jason's urging, they carried the **Argo** on their backs for nine days to Lake Triton. But, once there, they did not know how to get from the lake to the sea, since the whole area was a marsh, and it was impossible to tell which stream led to open water. Suddenly, the god Triton, the son of Poseidon, came to their aid. He pushed the ship through the maze of small tributaries out into the Mediterranean. The Argonauts rejoiced and offered a sacrifice in thanksgiving to the god.

6. Crete and Talos

As they sailed north, Jason and his men planned to stop at the island of Crete, but they were kept away by Talos, a bronze giant who hurled huge rocks at them. Zeus had given Talos to Europa as a guard for her island. As he circled the perimeter, the giant kept unwanted visitors away because of his vigilance, size and strength. The Argonauts were able to land under cover of darkness, and, after Medea had drugged the monster into a deep sleep, she directed Jason and his men to remove a bronze nail from Talos' heel. As soon as this was done, the vital fluid which coursed through the giant's veins poured out onto the ground, and the bronze body cracked and fell to pieces.

7. Iolcus and Pelias

Much to Pelias' consternation, the **Argo** and its crew finally returned to Iolcus only to discover that the stubborn king was unwilling to give up the throne despite the successful accomplishment of the quest. There were even rumors that he was plotting to kill Jason.

Medea took matters into her own hands. She showed Pelias' daughters how she was able to restore an aged ram to youthful vitality by dismembering it and placing it in a cauldron boiling with magic herbs. She said: "I will do the same thing for your aged father!" The naive girls readily agreed to the plan. Pelias was killed, his body dismembered and placed into the bubbling container. This time, however, Medea did not add the magic ingredients, and Pelias —much to his daughters' dismay— was not restored to life. Yet the murder did not accomplish what Medea had hoped. The savagery of the crime so alienated the citizens that they turned against Jason and Medea and forced them to flee from the country. Acastus, Pelias' son, became king.

Corinth

After leaving the Golden Fleece in a temple of Zeus, Jason and Medea went as exiles to the city of Corinth where Medea gave birth to two children. Jason, restless and always ambitious, arranged with Creon, the king of the city, to marry his daughter, Creusa. When Medea was informed of this ungrateful and heartless action, she determined to take revenge. She pretended to be reconciled to the forthcoming marriage and even sent a gift of a beautiful robe and a crown to the princess. But they were poisoned, and, when Creusa put them on, they burned deeply into her flesh and killed her. Moreover, when Creon tried to remove the poisoned gifts, he too was consumed in their searing flame.

Jason rushed from the palace to confront the treacherous Medea only to discover another terrible punishment: she had killed their two children. The sorceress escaped the wrath of Jason —some say in a flying chariot drawn by fiery dragons— and went to Athens where King Aegeus had agreed to provide her with asylum. There she remained until Theseus arrived, when she was forced to flee once again, this time back to her homeland where she ruled successfully for many years, giving her name to the people called the Medes.

Jason like Bellerophon seemed to lose the favor of the gods. His glory had come when he was young. Some time after the tragedy at Corinth, as he sat brooding on the shore next to the beached **Argo**, a piece of rotting wood fell from the ship and killed him. Whom the gods wish to raise up, they raise up, and whom they wish to destroy, they destroy. Ours is not to question, but to endure.

Sources

The best ancient version of the story can be found in the **Argonautica** by Apollonius of Rhodes and in a poem by the same name by Valerius Flaccus. Pindar refers to the story in the **Fourth Pythian Ode,** and Euripides describes the episode at Corinth in his play, **Medea.**

There have been many modern adaptations of the story. Two of the best are a novel by Robert Graves entitled **Hercules, My Shipmate,** and an epic poem by John Gardner, **Jason and Medeia.**

Questions

1. What elements of the heroic myth pattern can be found in the story of Jason?

2. Compare and contrast: Medea and Ariadne (Theseus myth).

3. Show how Jason's effectiveness with women both helps and hinders him.

4. Compare and contrast: Jason and Bellerophon.

5. Show how this myth is connected in its narrative with other heroic stories and characters.

6. Show what impact the gods have on the myth.

7. Medea can be viewed either as an evil sorceress or a wronged woman. Develop both points of view.

8. List the geographical areas used as background for the story.

9. How does the myth develop the contrast between civilization and barbarism?

10. How does this myth examine ambition and its effect on men's lives? Consider Pelias and Aeetes as well as Jason.

30. A FEW LOVE STORIES

A. Meleager and Atalanta

    1. Meleager and the log
    2. The call for heroes
    3. Atalanta
    4. The Calydonian boar hunt
    5. The death of Meleager

B. Atalanta and Hippomenes

    1. The contest for the bride
    2. The golden apples

C. Pygmalion and Galatea

D. Baucis and Philemon

E. Alcestis and Admetus

    1. Apollo's favor
    2. The day of death
    3. Heracles' struggle

F. Caeneus and Poseidon

G. Cephalus and Procris

H. Narcissus and Echo

I. Hero and Leander

J. Pyramus and Thisbe

Meleager and Atalanta

1. Meleager and the log

The famous King Oeneus of Calydon married his niece, Althea; however, the beautiful princess attracted the attention of Ares, and it was with the god as father that she gave birth to Meleager. Soon afterwards she was visited by the three Fates who told her that her infant son would die when a log which was then on the fire was completely burned. Althea quickly pulled the piece of wood from the hearth, smothered its flames, and stored it safely away.

2. The call for heroes

Some years later King Oeneus offended Artemis by neglecting her rituals. The angry goddess sent an enormous boar which tore up the crops, killed both humans and animals, and so frightened the Calydonians that they would not go out into the fields. Meleager was by this time a young man and had indeed just returned from the long journey to Colchis with the Argonauts. He organized a hunt for the vicious animal by sending out a request for assistance to the great heroes, many of whom, like himself, had been on the **Argo**. Jason, Theseus, Castor, Polydeuces, Telamon, Peleus, and many others came to Calydon. There was -to everyone's astonishment- one woman, Atalanta, who heard and answered the call. Meleager fell madly in love with the maiden and insisted that she be allowed to stay despite the grumblings of some of the heroes who resented a female's presence in such an endeavor.

3. Atalanta

Atalanta was the daughter of King Iasus of Arcadia, a mountainous area in the central Peloponnesus. Since the king wanted a son, he gave orders to have his infant daughter abandoned in the woods. She was found and nursed by a she-bear and eventually raised by a family of hunters from whom she learned the skills necessary to survive in the wilds. She became especially talented in archery and foot-racing. Because of her strength and athletic skills, Atalanta was allowed to participate along with men in some of the great adventures of the time. Her fame and identity eventually came to the attention of her father who now graciously welcomed home the child he had earlier tried to kill.

When Meleager's herald announced the hunt for the Calydonian boar, Atalanta set out at once to join the expedition.

4. The Calydonian boar hunt

There was a long chase after the boar with many adventures, injuries, and deaths along the way. Atalanta drew first blood with one of her arrows, several other heroes wounded the animal with their spears, and Meleager finally killed the beast. The hide was voted to Meleager as a symbol of his accomplishment, but he gave it instead to Atalanta, because it was she who had first injured and slowed the boar. The re-awarding of the trophy greatly irritated several of Meleager's relatives who had been on the hunt. "It is not right," they said, "that the award should be given to someone outside the family. We have all done at least as much as the woman!" An argument developed. Words changed to blows, fists to weapons, with the result that two of Meleager's kinsmen were killed.

5. The death of Meleager

When Althea -back at the palace- heard the news that two of her brothers had been killed by her son, in a fit of anger and grief she took the fatal log out of the place where it had remained since the visit of the Fates and threw it on the fire. As the wood burned, Meleager, miles away in the mountains, suddenly felt a sharp pain for which there seemed to be no cause. His companions were terrified as the hero fell to the ground writhing and screaming in agony until he died a most horrible death. When Althea recovered her sanity and realized what she had done, she hanged herself in despair. Thus, both the love affair and the great adventure of the Calydonian Boar Hunt ended in tragedy.

Source

A version of the Calydonian Boar Hunt can be found in Ovid's **Metamorphoses**, Book 8.

Questions

1. Meleager's life span is determined by a piece of wood. What other stories have we seen in which the length of a person's life is determined by some external object?

2. The boar is sent to punish King Oeneus. What other stories have we seen where monsters are sent as punishment from the gods?

3. How is the abandonment of Atalanta typical of such motifs, and how is it different?

4. Is Meleager an example of an innocent man killed, or does he deserve his fate?

5. What does the myth imply about the role of women?

Atalanta and Hippomenes

1. The contest for the bride

When Atalanta returned home from the hunt for the Calydonian boar, her father insisted that it was time for her to marry. The maiden, who preferred the single life but was unwilling to oppose paternal wishes, devised a scheme whereby she could achieve both ends. She said that she would marry any man who could defeat her in a foot race, but, to keep out the undeserving, the penalty for losing the contest should be death. Her father agreed, and the announcement was sent out.

Because of Atalanta's great beauty, many hopeful suitors came to compete, but none of them was a match for the maiden's speed. At the conclusion of each race, the audience watched in horror as the loser was decapitated and his head placed on a post to serve as a gruesome warning to future competitors.

2. The golden apples

It happened that a young man by the name of Hippomenes had come to watch the races rather than to participate himself, but once he saw Atalanta, he was so overwhelmed by her beauty that he immediately entered his name in the competition. The night before the race he prayed fervently to Aphrodite for assistance, and in a dream he saw what he must do. When he awakened, he found, as the vision had forewarned, three golden apples under his cot.

When the race began, Hippomenes threw a golden apple to the side of the course where Atalanta, curious as to what the glittering object was, ran to get it, confident that she could still win the contest. Three times Hippomenes threw the apples, and three times Atalanta ran to get them. In the end she miscalculated (deliberately?), was not able to return in time, and lost the race. The victorious Hippomenes jubilantly claimed his bride.

Sources

Atalanta's race is described in Ovid's **Metamorphoses**, Book 10. A modern interpretation is found in Swinburne's poem, **Atalanta in Calydon.**

Questions

1. What other stories have we seen which involve a struggle or contest to obtain a woman?

2. Why would Aphrodite be interested in helping Hippomenes?

Pygmalion and Galatea

Pygmalion of Cyprus was both king and sculptor. He was unable to find a bride out of all the women on his island and so decided to sculpt his ideal wife in statue form. He carved a marble woman so wondrous that he fell in love with his own creation and prayed to Aphrodite to find him someone as beautiful. The goddess more than granted his request, for she brought the statue to life, and Pygmalion married her.

Sources

The best ancient telling of the story can be found in Ovid's **Metamorphoses,** Book 1Ø. Two modern adaptations are those by George Bernard Shaw in his play, **Pygmalion,** and by Lerner and Lowe in the musical, **My Fair Lady.**

Question

How does this brief story touch on the relationship between art and life?

Baucis and Philemon

Zeus and Hermes in disguise were wandering through Bithynia, a country on the Asian coast of the Black Sea. They had been refused hospitality in countless homes. Finally, they came to the poor hut of Baucis and Philemon located on a hillside above a town that they had found to be particularly unfriendly. The elderly couple welcomed the strangers and gave them whatever they wished to eat from their meager supplies. When the hosts noticed that their wine bowl kept refilling itself, they realized that the guests were more than they seemed to be. The gods led the couple to the top of the hill. When they looked down, they saw that the inhospitable town had been destroyed by a flood and that their own home had been changed into a temple. Zeus asked what wish the couple might have. They requested simply that they might be keepers of the shrine which had just been miraculously created, and that when death came, neither would outlive the other. Zeus granted the request. Baucis and Philemon became caretakers of the temple, and, at the moment of death, they were transformed into trees which grew side by side.

Source

The story is told in Ovid's **Metamorphoses,** Book 8.

Questions

1. In what ways would this myth teach religious piety?

2. In what ways does this myth teach the values of civilization?

3. How is this myth similar to that of Deucalion and Pyrrha? Or to that of Noah?

Alcestis and Admetus

1. Apollo's favor

As we have seen, Hippolytus, the son of Theseus, had been killed through the curse of his father. When Theseus discovered that his son was innocent, he asked Asclepius, the great physician, to restore Hippolytus to life. Asclepius performed the miracle, but Zeus, angered at having someone brought back from the dead, killed both Asclepius and Hippolytus with a thunderbolt. Apollo, who was outraged at the death of his noted son, killed the Cyclops responsible for the thunderbolt. Zeus could not allow such a challenge to his authority to go unpunished. He ordered Apollo to spend a year in servitude under a mortal's command. Since an unscrupulous person could easily take advantage of the situation, the god had to consider carefully where he would stay. He chose to serve his sentence with the kindly King Admetus, and his choice proved a wise one for he was most graciously treated. At the end of the year to show his appreciation to the good-hearted ruler, Apollo granted him a special favor: Admetus might live beyond the day appointed for his death, if he found someone to die in his place.

2. The day of death

The fatal day came sooner than expected for Admetus. He angered Artemis by neglecting to invite her to his wedding feast, and the goddess punished the king by inflicting a deadly illness upon him. Admetus searched throughout his city for a substitute, but everyone refused, even his own father and mother, everyone, that is, except his beautiful young wife, Alcestis, who offered to die for her husband. Immediately Admetus grew stronger, Alcestis weaker, until she succumbed.

3. Heracles' struggle

On the very day of Alcestis' death it happened that Heracles was passing through the country on his way to tame the horses of Diomedes in Thrace (eighth labor). Admetus concealed his great sorrow, received his friend hospitably, and acted in every way as a host should toward a guest. Only by chance from a servant did Heracles learn of the actual situation. Without hesitation he went out to meet Death who was coming to claim the spirit of Alcestis. He offered a bargain: a wrestling match between himself and Death. If he should win, he would keep Alcestis in the land of the living; if Death should win, he would claim Heracles as well as Alcestis for his prize. Death could not refuse the contest. He was invincible; no mortal had ever defeated him. The match began. It was long, it was difficult, but in the end Heracles prevailed, and Death was conquered. The hero restored the beautiful Alcestis to her astonished and grateful husband.

Sources

Euripides' play, **Alcestis,** is the best ancient telling of the myth. There have been over twenty operas based on the story of Alcestis and Admetus of which Gluck's **Alceste** (1767) is the most famous. Thornton Wilder retells the story in the trilogy, **Alcestiad** (1955). T.S. Eliot's drama, **The Cocktail Party,** is an excellent adaptation of the myth.

Questions

1. Why does Admetus think his life is worth more than that of another? Or does he think so?

2. Can one die for another? Is anything worth dying for?

3. What does Heracles' victory in the wrestling match symbolize?

4. How does this myth affirm the values of both love and friendship?

Caeneus and Poseidon

Caenis was the beautiful daughter of a king in Thessaly. She attracted the attention of Poseidon who, when she refused to be seduced, raped her. Later, ashamed of what he had done, the god offered to grant the young woman whatever she might wish. She asked to be transformed into a man so that such an offense could never again be committed against her. Not only did Poseidon comply with her request, but he made Caenis -who was now called Caeneus- invulnerable to weapons. Caeneus fought against the centaurs in the famous battle with the Lapiths at Perithous' wedding. When the centaurs saw that the young man was unable to be harmed by arrows, spears, or swords, they began to hit him over the head with heavy logs until they had driven him into the ground. Some say that he died there, others that he was transformed into a bird.

Source

The story is told in Ovid's **Metamorphoses,** Book 12.

Questions

1. Name another mythic character who undergoes a sex change and describe his story.

2. Name other characters associated with Poseidon who are apparently invincible but who are defeated.

Cephalus and Procris

Procris was the daughter of Erechtheus, an early king of Athens. After several love affairs, including one with King Minos of Crete from whom she received a spear that could not miss the object at which it was aimed, she settled down with Cephalus, a great hunter. It seemed fitting that she gave him the spear as a wedding gift.

Cephalus had also had several love affairs before his marriage, the most famous of which was with Eos (called Aurora by the Romans), the goddess of the dawn. Since he was often absent from early morning until dusk on his hunts, Procris began to doubt her husband's fidelity. She decided to follow him secretly on one of his expeditions. After a vigorous but unsuccessful chase of a boar, Cephalus, out of breath, rested in a clearing and shouted for air. Procris thought that he was surely calling the name of a woman, so she jumped up from behind the bush where she was hiding. Cephalus heard the rustling and believed it was the animal which he had been pursuing. He spun about and threw the spear which never missed. Procris was killed instantly.

Source

Ovid tells the story of Cephalus and Procris in the **Metamorphoses,** Book 7.

Questions

1. How does Procris' own life and character contribute to her death?

2. What comment is the myth making about trust?

Narcissus and Echo

Narcissus was a handsome youth with whom the nymph, Echo, fell in love. Because she had aided Zeus in one of his love affairs by talking with Hera and thus distracting her, Echo had been given a special punishment by the queen of the gods: she could only repeat what the last person had spoken to her. With such an impairment, the nymph was unable to attract Narcissus. She wasted away with unrequited love until all that was left was a voice.

No one was found appealing by Narcissus, until one day he stopped to drink at a clear pool in the forest. He saw his own reflection in the water and fell immediately in love with it. He sat each day looking at the face which would vanish with the night and reappear with the dawn. Now he in turn languished with a love that could not be satisfied. Finally, the gods pitied him and changed him into a flower, the narcissus, which often grows at the side of ponds.

Source

The story is told by Ovid in the **Metamorphoses,** Book 3.

Question

Look up a definition of narcissism and show how it is related to the myth.

Hero and Leander

The beautiful Hero, a priestess of Aphrodite, lived in a tower by the sea near the town of Sestos on the European side of the Hellespont. On the Asian side in the town of Abydus lived the handsome young man, Leander. They met at a festival and fell hopelessly in love. Leander promised to swim the Hellespont each night to be with his beloved, while Hero in turn would place a lamp high up in her tower to guide him across the water.

Throughout the summer the lovers were able to be together, but with the winter months came stormy weather and rough seas. One fatal night Leander felt his strength fail as he fought against the huge waves, and, because the howling wind would not allow Hero to keep the lamp lighted, he had no sense of which direction to swim in order to save himself. With the dawn, as Hero anxiously looked everywhere across the sea, in horror she saw Leander's body lifeless on the shore below. Griefstricken, she leaped from her tower into the sea so that she and her lover might be united forever in death.

Sources

Ovid tells this story in the **Heroides,** a collection of imaginary letters of mythical heroines. Vergil refers to the tragedy in the **Georgics,** and the Greek poet, Musaeus, of the fifth century A.D. wrote a small epic based on the myth. In more recent times, many poets of the nineteenth century found the story appealing, among them, Byron, Keats, Tennyson, Rossetti and Schiller.

Questions

1. The plot line of this story is often considered romantic. What does this mean?

2. List as many stories as you can from modern literature which present one lover dying for love of another.

Pyramus and Thisbe

Pyramus and Thisbe lived in ancient Babylon in houses next to each other. Pyramus loved Thisbe, and she loved him, but their parents were opposed not only to their marriage but even to their seeing one another. The romance was kept alive, however, by whispered conversations held through a chink in the garden wall which separated the two houses. Not wanting their love to continue in this stealthy manner, the two determined to elope and planned to meet each other at a tomb outside the city on a certain night.

Thisbe arrived first at the appointed place but was frightened away by a lion whose jaws were all bloody from a recent meal. The lion found the cloak which Thisbe had dropped in her hasty flight and ripped it apart. When Pyramus arrived, he found the torn and bloody garment and thought that Thisbe had been slaughtered by a savage beast. Overcome with grief, he drew his sword and plunged it into his heart. Thisbe soon returned only to find his body. Not fully understanding the tragedy, but not wishing to outlive her beloved, she took the same sword and ended her own life with it. The two lovers were united finally in death.

Sources

The story can be found in Ovid's **Metamorphoses,** Book 4. Chaucer tells the story in **The Legend of Good Women,** and Shakespeare uses it in **A Midsummer's Night Dream.**

Questions

1. How is this story similar to and how is it different from that of Hero and Leander?

2. In what ways could this myth be considered a partial source for Shakespeare's play, **Romeo and Juliet?**

31. TROY

A. The legend

B. The discovery

C. The nine cities

The legend

The legend of Troy was considered by the Greeks to be one of the most glorious of their myths. It presents through noble actions the Hellenic endeavor to avenge one of their rulers whose wife had been taken from him by a Trojan prince. It was the culmination of the Mycenaean Age, the final burst of energy before the entire civilization receded into the darkness of barbarism.

The discovery

Until the last century, there was serious question as to whether Troy actually existed or was an imaginary creation of ancient writers. It had the same questionable status as Atlantis does today. Then, in 1870, a German by the name of Heinrich Schliemann, using the topographical references in Homer's Iliad as a guide, began excavations at the mound of Hissarlik and found what almost everyone now considers to be the ancient city of Troy.

The nine cities

Schliemann found nine cities on the site.

```
Troy I      3000 - 2500
Troy II     2500 - 2300
Troy III    2300 - 2200
Troy IV     2200 - 2050
Troy V      2050 - 1900
Troy VI     1900 - 1300
Troy VIIA   1300 - 1250
Troy VIIB   1250 - 1100
Troy VIII   sixth century B.C.
Troy IX     first century A.D.
```

The appearance of Troy was very sudden, and we know very little about the people who settled there. The site expanded outward from a strong citadel, and it was always characterized by heavy fortifications. Those of Troy VI were the most elaborate of all, far superior to anything in Greece. It is clear that a siege would be necessary to take the city. Attacks on the walls would be futile.

Troy I presents a gradual development from primitive beginnings. There is no sharp break between it and Troy II which was destroyed militarily, perhaps in a civil war. Troy III, IV, and V were settled by the same people as earlier, but they offer a more primitive level of culture than had evolved with Troy II. Schliemann called them "wretched hamlets", but they do show a gradual increase in civilized attainment.

Troy V met a quick and violent death at the hands of outside invaders, perhaps the same people who were invading Greece at the time. If this is so, then the Greeks during the Trojan War may well have been fighting the descendants of the very tribes which helped to form themselves as a people. Such an hypothesis is strengthened by the similarities in names for both Trojans and Greeks as found in Homer.

Troy VI was settled by the conquerors. While it was the most culturally sophisticated as well as the longest-lived city on the site, its culture was not original but was imported chiefly from Greece and Crete. The great wealth of the town seems to have been acquired through a tax which was imposed on ships entering and leaving the Black Sea. Unromantic as it sounds, the cause of the Trojan War was probably economic: the Greeks wanted to seize the fabled riches of their eastern neighbor.

Troy VI was heavily damaged by a violent earthquake about 1300. It was clearly a natural disaster which brought the city down; there are no signs of battle. However, the site was hastily rebuilt (Troy VIIA). The walls were repaired in a make-shift way. Squatters huts were placed in the middle of former streets, as those who farmed or worked outside of the city walls sought the protection of the fortifications. Large containers were placed in holes dug under the floors of houses both to conserve space and to store food, water, and other necessities. The Trojans were clearly expecting an imminent siege, and Troy VIIA was indeed destroyed by an invading army. There are many traces of harsh fights, violent deaths, and a long siege. Most scholars believe that it is the destruction of Troy VIIA which is reflected in the saga of the Trojan War. The archaeologcal date for the fall is approximately 1250 B.C., the traditional date in legend is 1184.

Barbarians took over the site after the destruction (Troy VIIB). They enslaved the few inhabitants who were left and built their hovels in the burned-out ruins. By 1100 the fomerly glorious city was abandoned to the wind and dust of the centuries.

The Greeks attempted to colonize the area in the sixth century B.C. (Troy VIII). They were not successful. After a brief habitation, the city was again abandoned.

The Roman emperor Augustus tried to revitalize the city in the first century A.D. (Troy IX) in order to remind his people of their legendary origin. This effort also ended in failure, and the site was forgotten through the centuries until Schliemann brought it once again to prominence.

Sources

There are many sources for the Trojan Saga. Almost every writer has something to say about it somewhere in his works. The major names are: Homer, Hesiod, Aeschylus, Sophocles, Euripides, Pindar, Apollodorus, Apollonius, Vergil, Ovid, Seneca, Hyginus, Dares, and Pausanias.

There was also a group of many long poems called the Epic Cycle. These poems were written in imitation of Homer and have all been lost except for fragments and brief summaries. Even in this mutilated form, they provide us with many details of the Trojan saga not given by Homer, Vergil, or the dramatists.

The **Cypria** presented events prior to the Trojan War and from its opening years.

The **Aethiopis** presented episodes in Achilles' life from the funeral of Patroclus to his own death and burial.

The Little Iliad and **The Sack of Troy** described actions in the final year of the conflict.

The Nostoi described the homecomings of various Greek leaders, and **The Telegony** continued the adventures of Odysseus after his resumption of power in Ithaca.

Questions

1. Who rediscovered Troy in modern times? What did he use as a guide to the location?

2. How many different cities have been found on the site of Troy?

3. What is the date for the first settlement at Troy?

4. What architectural feature distinguishes Troy from the very beginning?

5. What is the archaeological designation, and what are the dates for the longest-lived city at Troy?

6. What is the archaeological designation, and what are the dates for the city at Troy which fell to the Greeks?

32. THE LEADING FAMILIES IN THE TROJAN WAR

A. The family of Peleus

B. The family of Atreus

C. The family of Tyndareus

D. The family of King Priam of Troy

The Family of Peleus

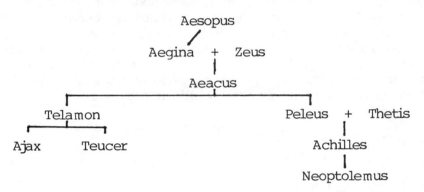

```
                    Aesopus
                      /
            Aegina  +  Zeus
                      |
                   Aeacus
        ┌─────────────────────────────┐
     Telamon                    Peleus  +  Thetis
     ┌──────┐                           |
   Ajax    Teucer                    Achilles
                                         |
                                    Neoptolemus
```

Aesopus was a river god whose daughter, Aegina, was carried off by Zeus to an island which later bore her name. Aeacus, their child, became king of the island, and had to contend with a terrible plague which had been sent by Hera, who, unable to punish her husband directly for his infidelity, chose to work out her anger on the mortal offspring. The populace was devastated. Aeacus prayed to Zeus for assistance, and the great god took pity on the suffering of his son. He ended the disease and repopulated the island by turning ants into humans. The Greek word for ant is "myrmex", and the newly created inhabitants were called Myrmidons.

Aeacus had two sons: Telamon and Peleus. Both were noted warriors themselves as well as being fathers of great heroes in the Trojan War. As we have seen, the two men were members of the crew on the **Argo** and took part in the Calydonian Boar Hunt. Telamon was a good friend of Heracles and accompanied the great hero on the expedition to punish King Laomedon of Troy who had refused to pay the promised fee for the rescue of his daughter, Hesione, from a sea-monster. Telamon received the woman as his reward.

Telamon became king of the island of Salamis (off the coast from Eleusis) and his son, Ajax, led the Salaminians to Troy. Next to Achilles, Ajax was considered the greatest warrior among the Greeks;

however, in the final year of the war, after Achilles met his doom, Ajax expected to be awarded his armor, and when the Greek chieftains gave it instead to Odysseus, Ajax went mad and killed himself.

Telamon's other son, Teucer, was the most famous archer at Troy (after Achilles, of course). He survived the war but when he returned home, his father repudiated him, because he believed that he could have prevented the suicide of his brother. Teucer went into exile and eventually founded the city of Salamis on the island of Cyprus where he became the first king.

Peleus, the other son of Aeacus, led those Myrmidons who wished to accept his leadership into Thessaly where he became king of the city of Phthia. He was awarded the Nereid, Thetis, as his wife and the two became the parents of Achilles, the greatest of the Greek heroes at Troy. After Achilles met his death in the last year of the war, he was replaced by his son, Neoptolemus, who distinguished himself in battle even at his very youthful age.

Questions

1. Who were the Myrmidons, and how did they get their name?

2. Why did Ajax kill himself?

3. Why did Telamon reject Teucer?

4. Of which island did Teucer become king?

5. Who were the parents of Achilles? Explain what a Nereid is.

The Family of Atreus

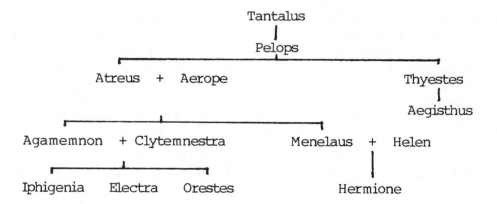

-170-

Tantalus

Tantalus was a mortal son of Zeus and a king of Lydia (in modern day Turkey) who unfortunately proved unworthy of his birth. To test the omnipotence of the gods he invited them to a banquet at which -horrible to relate- he cooked and served the flesh of his son, Pelops, whom he had killed for this insane purpose. The gods at once realized the substance of the gruesome feast, except for Demeter who was griefstricken over the loss of Persephone and distractedly ate a small portion of Pelops' shoulder. The enraged deities threw Tantalus into the Underworld where he was condemned forever to stand in water which receded whenever he attempted to slake his unending thirst, and to have branches ripe with fruit hang over his head which also withdrew from his grasp whenever he sought to end his eternal hunger.

Pelops

The gods immediately restored Pelops to life, and Demeter replaced the portion of his body which she had eaten with a piece of ivory. The young man left Lydia to go to Greece where he had heard about the great beauty of Hippodamia, the daughter of Oenomaus, King of Pisa (located near Olympia). Oenomaus had been warned in a prophecy that he would be killed by the man who married his daughter, so he set up a most difficult test for prospective husbands. Each suitor had to take Hippodamia in his chariot and ride toward a distant goal. Oenomaus pursued them in his own chariot. If he caught the unlucky man before he reached the end of the course, the king killed him, decapitated him, and put his head over the entrance to his palace as a warning to others. Many such had been disposed of; no one had successfully competed.

Although Pelops was confident he could win, he considered prudence to be an important part of valor, and so, when he discovered that Myrtilus, the king's charioteer, was also in love with Hippodamia, he promised him half of the kingdom and a night in Hippodamia's bed, if he would betray his master. Myrtilus quickly accepted the offer and placed weak supports on Oenomaus' chariot. Before the king had gone far in his pursuit of Pelops, a wheel suddenly fell off; he was thrown to the ground and dragged to death by his horses.

Pelops had won the contest for the bride and the kingdom, and he had no intention of sharing either. Before Myrtilus could collect on their bargain, Pelops threw the unsuspecting charioteer into the sea, where, as he was drowning, he cursed Pelops and all his descendants. No small matter, since Myrtilus was a son of Hermes. Indeed, throughout the rest of his life Pelops was in fear of this curse, and he made great efforts to be purified of the murder. To no avail. Many of the terrible difficulties which his children and grandchildren experienced were traced back to the deadly words of Myrtilus.

Atreus and Thyestes

Pelops had two sons, Atreus and Thyestes, who were sent into permanent exile from their homeland because of a charge of murder set against them. It so happened at this time that the people of Mycenae were without a king and had been advised by an oracle to choose one of these men. They selected Atreus, because of two signs of divine favor which he presented. First of all, he showed the Mycenaeans that he possessed the golden fleece of a lamb which had been given to him by the gods, and then, with Zeus' assistance, he forced the sun briefly to reverse its movement in the sky.

Thyestes was jealous of his older brother and was soon able to find an outlet for his feelings. Atreus had married Aerope, and although she bore him two sons, Agamemnon and Menelaus, she loved not him but Thyestes, and had met secretly many times with her brother-in-law.

Atreus eventually discovered the adultery of his wife. He had her put to death and then carried out a savage punishment on his brother. He murdered the children of Thyestes, dismembered them, and served them to their unknowing father during a banquet. At the conclusion of the meal, Atreus revealed what he had done, and drove the horrified father from Mycenae.

Aegisthus was the only son of Thyestes to avoid the murderous banquet. He was raised in secret by his father, and the two of them plotted their vengeance. After several years they were able, through treachery, to kill Atreus. Although Thyestes then became king of Mycenae, he was soon driven from the throne by Agamemnon and Menelaus, Atreus' sons. An old man, he died shortly after, but Aegisthus lived to take his father's vengeance on another day.

Agamemnon and Menelaus

Agamemnon became king of Mycenae. He married Clytemnestra, sister of the beautiful Helen, and they had several children.

Menelaus was chosen to be the husband of Helen and later replaced her father as king of Sparta. It was Menelaus' wife who was taken by Paris of Troy, and it was Agamemnon, as Menelaus' elder brother and as king of the most powerful city in Greece, who was chosen to lead the expedition against the Trojans. But, as we shall see, the curse of Myrtilus had not yet played itself out on the unhappy family of Tantalus.

Questions

1. What was Tantalus' crime, and what was his punishment?

2. Describe the contest for Hippodamia which Oenomaus had devised. Describe other such contests.

3. Who was Myrtilus and why was he important for the rest of the descendants of Pelops?

4. With what miracles did Atreus take the throne of Mycenae?

5. Of what action against his brother was Thyestes guilty? How was he punished? Who was the lone survivor in Thyestes' family?

6. Who is Clytemnestra? How is she related to Helen?

7. Who became the king of Mycenae during the Trojan War? Of Sparta?

The Family of Tyndareus

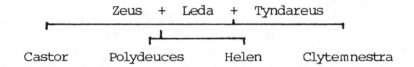

Zeus + Leda + Tyndareus

Castor   Polydeuces   Helen   Clytemnestra

Leda and Zeus

Our story begins when the beautiful Leda became the wife of King Tyndareus of Sparta. One night, several years after their marriage, Zeus visited Leda in the form of a swan and mated with her. Later that same night, her husband also made love to her.

Leda gave birth to twin sons, Castor and Polydeuces, and two daughters, Helen and Clytemnestra. Some say that the children were hatched from eggs. In fact, one of the eggs became a sacred relic which Pausanias, a traveller in the second century A.D., reported seeing in a Spartan temple. Usually, Polydeuces and Helen are considered children of Zeus, while Castor and Clytemenestra are offspring of Tyndareus.

Helen and Clytemnestra

The two daughters of Tyndareus married the two sons of King Atreus of Mycenae. Helen, famous for her great beauty, married Menelaus who replaced Tyndareus as king of Sparta. It was her later abduction by Paris which led to the Trojan War. Clytemnestra became the wife of King Agamemnon of Mycenae, the commander-in-chief of the Greek forces during the same war.

Castor and Polydeuces

Castor became famous as a tamer of horses and a soldier, while Polydeuces became a noted boxer. Usually, Polydeuces, the son of Zeus, was thought to be immortal, while Castor, the son of Tyndareus, was mortal. The two invented the war dance and war-like music. They were good friends and undertook many heroic missions. They accompanied Jason on his quest for the Golden Fleece, and they participated in the hunt for the Cayldonian boar. They also rescued their sister, Helen, after she had been abducted by Theseus (before her marriage to Menelaus).

In their last adventure Castor and Polydeuces seized the two daughters of Leucippus —whom they wanted for their own brides— on the day of their marriage to two other men, Idas and Lyncaeus. Lyncaeus, who had exceptionally good vision, spotted the Spartan twins escaping with the women, even though they were many miles away. The deprived bridegrooms chased the two heroes and caught them. A tremendous fight developed during which Castor was killed. Polydeuces, after taking vengeance, begged Zeus that he be allowed to share his immortality with his dead brother, a wish which the god granted. The result was that the two brothers were permitted to spend one day on Olympus and the next in the Underworld. Some say, however, that Zeus showed his approval of the brotherly love by placing the two in the sky as twin stars where they are known as the Gemini, the twins. In this aspect, they are worshipped as protectors of sailors. The two are often called the Dioscuri, the sons of Zeus.

At the Battle of Lake Regillus in 496 B.C., when things were going badly for the Romans, the two gods suddenly and mysteriously appeared at the head of the army and led it to victory. The Romans in gratitude adopted the twin deities as their own and called them Castor and Pollux. They built a temple in their honor near the spot in the Forum where the two supposedly stopped to water their horses. Columns from the structure can be seen today. Statues of Castor and Pollux can be found on the Capitoline Hill as well.

Questions

1. In what way is Zeus directly connected with the family of Tyndareus?

2. How are Helen and Clytemnestra related to each other and to Agamemnon and Menelaus?

3. What are the special skills associated with Castor? With Polydeuces?

4. How was Castor killed?

5. What are the two variants of Zeus' reply to Polydeuces' offer?

6. Explain the titles "Gemini" and "Dioscuri".

7. In what ways are Castor and Pollux closely associated with the Romans?

The Family of Priam

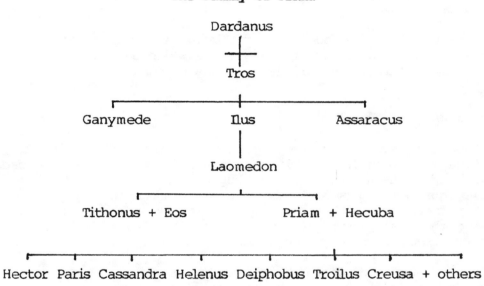

Dardanus

Dardanus, who was a son of Zeus and Electra (a mortal daughter of Atlas), survived the great flood and floated on a raft to the region that was later identified with Troy. He married the daughter of King Teucer who ruled there and eventually became king himself. He changed the name of the people from Teucrians to Dardanians, both of which are used as synonyms for the later Trojans who regarded him as their earliest ancestor.

Tros

Tros was a grandson of Dardanus who gave the most familiar name to the city and the people. He had three sons: Ilus, Ganymede, and Assaracus.

Ilus, Ganymede, Assaracus

Ilus, the actual founder of Troy, gave it another of its names: Ilium or Ilion. As Cadmus did, so Ilus followed a cow until it rested, and there he built his city. When he prayed to Zeus for a sign that he had found the proper place, the god permitted a small statue of Athena -called the Palladium- to fall from the sky. Ilus built a temple to house the symbol of divine favor, and later discovered through an oracle that as long as the statue remained within the walls, the city could not be captured by a foreign enemy.

Zeus sent his eagle to carry off the handsome Ganymede, another of Tros' sons, to become cupbearer of the gods on Mt. Olympus. The young prince was later transformed into the constellation, Aquarius, the waterboy.

Assaracus was the founder of the family which ruled at Dardania, a neighbor to Troy. It was this royal line which eventually led, as we shall see, to Aeneas, who carried the Trojan gods to Italy.

Laomedon

Laomedon became king of Troy after the death of his father. We have already seen how he is characterized as a liar and a cheat. Poseidon helped him to build the huge fortifications of Troy, while Apollo guarded his sheep. When it came time to pay the gods, Laomedon refused. As a punishment they sent a sea-monster to attack the town, and only the sacrifice of Laomedon's daughter, Hesione, could appease the beast and save the city.

It so happened that Heracles was present at the time in connection with his visit to the country of the Amazons (ninth labor), and he indicated his willingness to intervene and fight the monster for the price of a pair of the king's horses. Laomedon agreed without hesitation. Heracles disposed of the beast in a savage fight and saved Hesione. When he demanded his pay, Laomedon again refused to honor his bargain. Heracles was unable to remedy the situation at the time, but he later mounted an expedition, captured the city, and killed Laomedon. He awarded Hesione as a prize to his companion Telamon (she bore him a son, Teucer, who fought in the Trojan War), and he installed Priam, one of Laomedon's sons, as king of Troy.

Tithonus

Eos (or Aurora for the Romans) fell in love with Priam's brother, Tithonus. She took him to her abode far in the east where the two lived so happily that Eos asked Zeus to grant immortality to her lover. The gift was given, but Eos had neglectfully forgotten to request that Tithonus would not age, and so, while he would never die, he continued to grow old and feeble until all that was left was a babbling voice which Zeus assigned to the insect called the cicada.

Priam

Priam became the last king of Troy after his father, Laomedon, was killed by Heracles. He and his wife, Hecuba, had many children, and he had many more from his harem. It was he who ruled the city during the Trojan War. He saw most of his children killed in that conflict, and he himself was slain on the final night of the struggle.

Hector

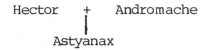

Hector was Priam's eldest son, as well as being the best of the Trojan warriors. He married Andromache, and the two had a young son, Astyanax, who, like his father, did not survive the conflict. Although Hector strongly objected to the action of his brother Paris which led to the lengthy war, he remained at the front of those who fought for the city.

Paris

When Hecuba was pregnant with Paris, she had a nightmare in which she dreamed that she gave birth to a burning torch. A prophet interpreted the vision to mean that her child would cause the destruction of his city. Priam and Hecuba gave the child to a shepherd to abandon on the slopes of Mt. Ida. The servant could not bring himself to leave the child to die, so he raised him as a member of his own family. The child grew to become strong and handsome, and because of his courageous actions he was given the additional name of Alexander (Defender of men).

One day, when he was in the city, he encountered Cassandra, his sister, who, although she had never met him previously, recognized him as her brother through her divinely inspired intuition. Priam and Hecuba joyously welcomed their son as if he had been restored from the dead and brought him to the palace to live as a prince of the royal house. The prophecy of so long ago was forgotten or ignored.

Cassandra

Cassandra was a daughter of Priam and Hecuba with whom Apollo fell in love. He taught her the art of prophecy in hopes of winning her favor, but to no avail. The frustrated god then condemned her to the punishment of never being believed even though she would always see future events accurately. She predicted, for example, that Paris' journey to Sparta to visit Helen and Menelaus would bring destruction on the city, yet she was ignored by Priam; and, at the end of the conflict, she warned the Trojans that the wooden horse was filled with Greeks, but they continued to pull it within the city walls.

Helenus

Helenus was a son of Priam and Hecuba, and, like Cassandra, he had prophetic powers. Late in the war he was captured by the Greeks and made predictions for them as well. He indicated, for example, that Troy would fall only if Pelops' bones were brought to the city, if the Palladium were removed from within the walls, if Neoptolemus (Achilles' son) would replace his dead father, and if Philoctetes would use the bow and arrows of Heracles on the side of the Greek forces. All of these conditions were met. After the war Helenus founded Buthrotum in northern Greece and married Andromache, Hector's widow.

Deiphobus

Deiphobus was a son of Priam and Hecuba. He assumed Hector's position of leadership in the fighting at Troy after his brother's death. When Paris was killed, Helen was awarded to him. In the final battle, Deiphobus was killed by Menelaus.

Troilus

Troilus was a son of Priam and Hecuba. Little more is known of him other than he was ambushed and killed by Achilles. His story was much expanded by medieval writers on Troy and by Chaucer and Shakespeare.

Creusa

Creusa was a daughter of Priam and Hecuba who was married to Aeneas, a leader of the Dardanian allies of the Trojans. She bore a son, Iulus, and was killed as she and her husband were attempting to escape from Troy on the final night of the city.

Questions

1. Explain the origins of the titles "Teucrians" or "Dardanians" as applied to the Trojans.

2. How is the founding of Troy similar to the founding of Thebes?

3. To what does Ilium or Ilion refer? How did the names originate?

4. What was the Palladium, and what was its significance?

5. With what constellation is Ganymede associated? Why?

6. Who founded the family associated with Aeneas? At which town?

7. Why was Hesione threatened by a sea-monster?

8. How did Heracles punish Laomedon?

9. What is the meaning of the story of Tithonus?

10. Who was Priam? Hecuba?

11. Who was the major Trojan warrior? To whom on the Greek side would he be equivalent?

12. Who were the parents of Paris? Why was he abandoned? Who saved him? What is another name for Paris?

13. How was Paris restored to his parents?

14. What was Cassandra's special gift? What was her punishment? Why was she punished?

15. Which daughter of Priam became the wife of Aeneas?

16. Who was the son of Priam who prophecied for both Trojans and Greeks?

17. Who led the Trojan army after Hector's death?

33. PRE–WAR EVENTS

A. The marriage of Peleus and Thetis

B. The judgment of Paris

C. The seduction of Helen

D. The oath of Tyndareus

E. Odysseus and Palamedes

F. The search for Achilles

G. The departure from Aulis

H. Philoctetes

When the ancients sought a divine cause for the long and bloody war at Troy, they concluded that Zeus had brought about the conflict to reduce the overpopulation of the earth and to "empty the world." The series of events leading to the conflict is usually thought to begin with the marriage of Peleus and Thetis.

The marriage of Peleus and Thetis

Thetis was a sea nymph, one of the Nereids, and had been a favorite of Zeus, until he received an ominous warning about her from Prometheus: she would bear a child greater than his father. Zeus quickly arranged to end his romance with the nymph and to have her marry Peleus whom he judged to be the worthiest mortal of that time.

The hero first had to capture his prospective bride. No easy task, since Thetis could change into any form she wished at any moment. Peleus found the Nereid sleeping in her cave and held on to her while she went through many transformations. She finally agreed to wed him.

As with the marriage of Cadmus and Harmonia, all of the gods were invited to celebrate that of Peleus and Thetis, all, that is, with the exception of Eris, a minor divinity who was the goddess of discord. She came nonetheless and brought a golden apple on which was inscribed: For the Fairest. Hera, Athena, and Aphrodite each made immediate claims on it, and they went to Zeus for a decision. The god realized that whatever choice he made would appear biased and would greatly anger the other two goddesses, so he assigned the decision to Paris, a son of King Priam of Troy, and the most handsome man then living.

The Judgment of Paris

Hermes brought the three contenders to Paris whom he found guarding sheep on the slopes of Mt. Ida near Troy. Each goddess offered a reward if the young man would choose her. Hera promised him unlimited political power, Athena assured him that he would always be victorious in battle, and Aphrodite offered him Helen, the most beautiful woman in the world, as his wife. Paris was young and romantic, so with only slight hesitation he gave the apple to Aphrodite. Serious decisions have serious consequences. The goddess of love became his constant ally, while Hera and Athena became his (and Troy's) permanent enemies.

As we have seen, Paris had been abandoned at birth by his parents, King Priam and Queen Hecuba of Troy, because of a prophecy that he would cause the destruction of his city. He was raised by a shepherd who could not bring himself to allow the child to die in the wilderness. Sometime after the visit by the goddesses, Paris happened to be in the city of Troy and was recognized by his sister, Cassandra, through the special powers given to her by Apollo. Priam and Hecuba were overjoyed to find their son -whom they had presumed dead- not only to be among the living, but to be valorous and handsome as well.

In this happy glow of reunion Paris requested that he be given a ship to sail to Sparta so that he might claim the prize he had been awarded by Aphrodite. King Priam was astonished by the request. He pointed out that Helen was already married to Menelaus who would surely attempt to retake her. Paris replied that Troy was much stronger than Sparta and had nothing to fear from such a small and rustic town. Cassandra and her brother Helenus, both of whom had prophetic powers, warned their parents that the young man's action would cause the destruction of the city, but Paris laughingly reminded his father that prophets were wrong as often as they were right. In the end, Priam reluctantly complied with his son's request and -with a sense of impending doom- watched from the high ramparts of the city as the ship disappeared over the horizon.

The seduction of Helen

Paris was greeted hospitably by King Menelaus and his queen at Sparta. They assumed that he was on a diplomatic mission to establish better relations between their two cities. After several days, Menelaus had to leave to attend a funeral of a relative in Crete, and he asked his wife to replace him as host. Aphrodite now began her irresistible work. Some say that Helen fell madly in love with Paris and agreed to leave her husband and go with him to Troy. Others believe that she was able to withstand the young hero's considerable charm and had to be taken forcibly. The myth is ambiguous on this point. They did, at any rate, take a large amount of Menelaus' wealth with them.

The standard version of the voyage to Troy is that the two lovers leisurely sailed along while enjoying each other's company. A variant has their ship blown south by a storm to Egypt where the gods substituted a double of Helen whom Paris took to Troy. The real woman was kept in Egypt during the long years of the war, until she was eventually found by her husband. It is this latter story that is usually attached to the version that an innocent Helen was taken from Sparta against her will.

When Paris and Helen reached Troy, they were greeted with profound sadness by King Priam and his people. When the young man had sailed, there was hope that what he wished to accomplish would somehow not happen or would be done properly in some way. But Paris had behaved in the worst possible manner. Everyone knew that this action by the young prince would bring both divine (Paris had violated Zeus' sacred law of hopitality) and human retribution. The Trojans began to prepare for the war which they knew would come. Hector, Paris' eldest brother and a noted warrior, was placed in charge.

The oath of Tyndareus

When Menelaus returned from Crete to find his wife and much of his wealth missing, he went immediately to his brother, Agamemnon, in Mycenae and asked him to organize an expedition to recover what had been stolen and to punish the Trojans. Agamemnon decided to invoke the oath of Tyndareus. He sent heralds to the chief cities to remind the kings of what they had sworn.

Tyndareus was the former king of Sparta and the father —although some say it was actually Zeus— of Helen. Because of her great beauty, Helen had attracted many suitors from among the leading families of the time. Although it was the custom in those days for a father to choose his daughter's husband, Tyndareus was reluctant to name any one of the candidates as his choice because of what the others might do to him. He asked the wise leader, Odysseus, for advice. The wily Greek recommended that the suitors should make a solemn promise that they would come to the aid of Helen and her husband if anyone did them injury. The princes all agreed with the plan and swore to abide by the oath of Tyndareus. The king then chose Menelaus to become Helen's husband. Although no one had suspected that it would be a foreigner who would cause harm to Menelaus, each of the chieftains was now reminded of what he had pledged.

The Greek kings met and chose Agamemnon —because of the power and prestige of Mycenae— to be their leader. They each agreed to raise an army, to build ships, and eventually to assemble at the town of Aulis which provided a sheltered harbor for the vast armada.

They would then all sail together for distant Troy. Although Odysseus and Achilles were notably missing from the assembly, the Greeks were determined to have them join the expedition.

Odysseus and Palamedes

Odysseus (the Romans called him Ulysses) was king of the island of Ithaca, off the coast of western Greece in the Ionian Sea. He was known not only for his courage and strength, but also for his cleverness, imagination, and wisdom. He had recently married Penelope, and she had just given birth to their son, Telemachus. Odysseus was most reluctant to leave his young bride and his infant son to fight in a foreign war over a matter that was of no concern to him. He decided to feign madness.

Palamedes led a group of Greeks who were sent to Ithaca to remind Odysseus of his obligations under Tyndareus' oath, since he had been one of Helen's suitors before he married Penelope. When Palamedes arrived, he found Odysseus plowing his fields with salt. But the envoy was convinced that it was a trick. He seized Telemachus out of his mother's arms and placed him in the path of the plow. If Odysseus continued, he would trample and crush his son; if he stopped, he would prove that he was sane and would be forced to leave and fight in the war. What would he do? Would the father kill his own son? The plow came closer and yet closer to the infant, and then...it stopped. Palamedes was exultant. He had won the battle of wits! He had been able to trick the cleverest of the Greeks.

The Search for Achilles

Achilles was the child of Peleus and Thetis, and he proved the truth of the prophecy that Thetis would bear a son more famous than his father. Shortly after his birth, Thetis dipped the infant into the River Styx which made him invulnerable to weapons except for that portion of his heel by which she held him. Peleus gave the child to Chiron the centaur to train in all of the heroic skills, and the youngster's great ability exceeded the fondest hopes of both his father and Chiron.

There were two prophecies concerning Achilles which troubled Thetis. She knew her son had been given a choice of fates: he could live a long but mediocre life or a short but glorious one, and she was also aware of the prophecy which told the Greeks that they would need Achilles to be victorious at Troy.

Thetis realized that her son would choose to go to Troy and thereby have a short life of glory. She wanted both to keep the news of the impending struggle from her child and to prevent the Greek chieftains from knowing his whereabouts. She hid the young Achilles on the island of Scyros in the Aegean Sea with King Lycomedes who had only daughters in his family. She asked the king to dress Achilles as though he were one of his own girls. Achilles (and the girls) must have been aware of the difference, because sometime later one of Lycomedes' daughters gave birth to a son, Neoptolemus, the only child of Achilles.

Since Odysseus was now part of the force preparing to go to Troy, he determined to find Achilles in order to insure their predicted success. Odysseus had heard a rumor that the young man was hidden on Scyros, so he disguised himself as a merchant and visited the palace of King Lycomedes. He had two large chests placed in front of him. He opened one to display fine cloth and jewelry; Lycomedes daughters swarmed around it. He opened the other to display military gear; only one "girl" was interested in the weapons. Odysseus knew he had found Achilles. He told the youthful hero about the coming war and indicated how badly the Greeks needed his services. Although he had been too young to be one of Helen's suitors and was, therefore, under no obligation to fight, Achilles immediately accepted the invitation to glory (as his mother had feared he would). He returned home to gather his soldiers, the Myrmidons, and then went to Aulis accompanied by his good friend, Patroclus.

The departure from Aulis

The Greek armada began slowly to assemble as each king arrived with his ships. There were predictions by the prophets that the war would be a long one, which, indeed, the elaborate fortifications at Troy also forebode.

Finally the armada set sail from Aulis, but with much confusion as to just where Troy was located. The Greeks landed on the coast of Asia Minor near Mysia which they thought to be Troy. The Greeks destroyed the city before they realized their error. They then returned to Aulis, dejected and confused.

Now it happened that the king of Mysia was Telephus, a son of Heracles. He had been grievously wounded in the fight and was informed by an oracle of Apollo that he could be healed only by Achilles who had inflicted the wound. Telephus went to Aulis and offered to show the Greeks the way to Troy, if Achilles would treat his wound. Achilles agreed and healed Telephus by touching his father's spear to the festering sore. The king was now prepared to chart the course to the city of the Trojans. But still another obstacle lay ahead.

As the armada began preparations for its second departure, the wind suddenly died. Day followed day with not even a breeze. Surely an ominous sign! Agamemnon's prophet, Calchas, was consulted, and his response was terrifying: Artemis had been grievously offended when Agamemnon and Menelaus had killed one of her sacred deer while they were hunting. That they could not have distinguished the special nature of this particular animal from any other was of no matter. They had killed it; they were guilty. The penalty demanded by the goddess was blood for blood. As the sons of Atreus had killed one of her family, she demanded the sacrifice of the eldest child of Agamemnon: his daughter, Iphigenia. Unbelievable horror! Could a goddess be so cruel? The priest was consulted again and again; the response was the same.

Agamemnon was in anguish over the fate that had befallen him. What should he do? Give up the command? Offend Zeus by not punishing those who had violated the sacred law of hospitality? Or kill his innocent daughter to appease a heartless and bloodthirsty goddess for an offense that had not been intentional? He seemed doomed no matter which choice he made. Was it, indeed, the old curse which had run through his family for generations? He vacillated; the ramifications of his decision filled him with dread. But, in the end, he could not surrender power.

Agamemnon sent a message to his wife, Clytemnestra, in which he told her that Achilles wished to have Iphigenia sent to him so that he might marry her before he sailed to Troy. Both wife and daughter were overjoyed. What could be more of an honor for their family than to be chosen by the greatest of warriors? Iphigenia came to Aulis looking forward to the happiest moments of her young life. She found instead sorrow, pain, and death through the sacrificial knife. Pleas were useless before an unheeding father. Her innocent blood was shed, and the wind at once rose and blew seaward.

The Greeks were subdued as the armada embarked, for they realized what a price had been paid to the harsh goddess. Such acts do not go unpunished. Indeed, when the news reached Clytemnestra of her daughter's death and her husband's deception, whatever love she may have had for Agamemnon turned to bitter hatred. She vowed in her rage to kill him if he survived the war, and she took a lover, Aegisthus -a bitter enemy to Agamemnon- to help and encourage her in the plot.

Philoctetes

Philoctetes, who had inherited the bow and arrows of Heracles, was king of the Malians (from central Greece) and led seven ships to Troy. When the armada stopped at a small island sacred to an obscure divinity by the name of Chryse, Philoctetes unintentionally violated holy ground and was bitten by a poisonous snake. The wound was very painful and soon began to fester and give off a foul smell.

The Greek chieftains found the constant cries of pain and the offensive odor coming from the wound were having a very negative effect upon the morale of the soldiers soon to be landing at Troy. They decided that it was necessary to leave Philoctetes behind. They stopped at the deserted island of Lemnos, and, while Philoctetes was sleeping after one of his spasms of intense pain, they sailed away, abandoning him with his bow and arrows.

For the ten long years of the war the deserted hero remained alone on the island, enduring the pain of the festering wound, and feeding himself on whatever he could find or kill with his bow. In the tenth year of the war a prophecy declared that, in order for the Greeks to be victorious, Philoctetes must bring the bow and arrows of Heracles to Troy. Odysseus and Neoptolemus (the son of Achilles) were sent to bring him. When Philoctetes finally arrived, the doctors were able to heal his wound, and he became a noted fighter. It was he who killed Paris with one of his poisoned arrows.

Shortly after abandoning Philoctetes the Greeks sent Menelaus and Odysseus as ambassadors to Troy to attempt to persuade the Trojans to return Helen and the stolen wealth. Priam and some of his wiser counsellors wanted to comply and so avoid what they knew would be a long war, but the majority were not only opposed, but were so violent in their feelings that they nearly killed the envoys.

Questions

1. Describe the various ways in which Thetis is connected with the Trojan saga.

2. What do the actions which the goddesses take to influence Paris' decision tell us about the culture of the time?

3. How is Paris characterized by the myth? How is the prophecy concerning him fulfilled?

4. What is the story of Cassandra? What are her special powers? What is her curse? Why is she being punished?

5. What are the two versions of Helen's departure from Troy? How is Egypt connected with them?

6. What was the oath of Tyndareus? How does it influence the myth?

7. What is the relationship between Agamemnon and Menelaus? Why was Agamemnon chosen to head the expedition rather than Menelaus?

8. Describe how Odysseus and Achilles were brought into the war. Why is cleverness rather than strength more important in each case?

9. Why does Thetis hide Achilles? How is her action connected with his fate?

10. What does the false start to Mysia contribute to the myth? What does it tell us about the times?

11. How is Artemis characterized at Aulis?

12. How is Agamemnon doomed no matter which choice he makes? Does he make the right one?

13. Why do you think human sacrifice is part of the myth?

14. How is the treatment Philoctetes receives from the gods similar to that which Agamemnon receives?

15. Of what might the wound of Philoctetes be a symbol?

34. THE WAR AT TROY

A. The landing

B. The first nine years

C. The wrath of Achilles

D. Patroclus

E. Achilles and Hector

F. The death of Achilles

G. The prophecies

H. The wooden horse

The landing

Hector led the vast forces of the Trojans out of the city to oppose the landing of the Greek armada. Even though there had been a prediction that the first Greek to step on Trojan soil would die, the courageous Protesilaus ignored the warning, jumped over the side, and led the Trojans onto the beach. In the savage hand-to-hand fighting which occurred, he was indeed killed by Hector.

With a great loss of life on both sides, the Greeks were slowly able to force the Trojans back and to establish a beachhead. Eventually, they set up fortifications and pulled their ships onto land.

The first nine years

As they had already been warned, the Greeks saw that the walls of Troy were massive and unbreakable. A seige was necessary, and the sooner they could cut off Trojan supplies from the neighboring towns, the quicker the city would be forced to capitulate. Led by Achilles, the Greeks conquered nearly two dozen of the villages allied with Troy. Not only did they isolate the fortress, but they provided food and plunder for themselves. There were occasional forays by the Trojans, as they marched out to attack the invaders, and there were many single combats among the leaders. Except for the mounting and terrible toll of deaths on both sides, the struggle was inconclusive and the Trojans were somehow able to endure the seige. It was in the tenth year of the war that Troy was fated to fall, and it is in this year that most of the major events occur.

The wrath of Achilles

In one of the raids which the Greeks had made on nearby settlements, Achilles had taken a woman, Briseis, to share his tent with him. It was a custom in those days for this sort of thing to be done. Over the years of the war, Achilles and Briseis had developed a feeling of affection -perhaps even of love- for one another. Now the gods ordained that another woman, Chryseis, similarly obtained by Agamemnon, had to be restored to her father. When the king stubbornly refused to do so, a plague -some say it was sent by Apollo- began to spread among the soldiers. Agamemnon was warned by his prophet, Calchas, that he must comply and return Chryseis. It was with a bitter feeling of humiliation that he gave up the woman, since it seemed to him that the commander-in-chief now had less than the other kings. He decided to use his authority to select someone of comparable beauty from one of the chieftains under his command. For some reason -perhaps it was envy- he chose Briseis. As he might have expected, Achilles objected violently, and, indeed, some say that if Athena had not intervened, he would have killed Agamemnon. To take his woman was to impugn his honor, and nothing was more sacred to Achilles than his honorable reputation. In the harsh words that were exchanged, Achilles swore that he would never fight again.

News of Achilles' withdrawal spread throughout the Greek army. Various other leaders attempted to inspire the soldiers: Menelaus, Ajax, Diomedes, Odysseus, and even Agamemnon himself, all fought valiantly, but the Trojans, encouraged by Achilles' absence, forced the Greek troops slowly to retreat toward the beached ships. Destruction of the armada seemed only a short time away. With advice from his council, Agamemnon relented and sent representatives to Achilles to attempt to win him back to the cause. He would restore Briseis and provide an enormous treasure besides. Achilles rejected the offer. His mind was set. Nothing would compensate for the arrogant abuse of power by the commander-in-chief.

Patroclus

After the disheartened envoys had left, Patroclus, Achilles' companion since youth, proposed a compromise. "Allow me," he suggested, "to wear your equipment into battle. The Trojans will think that Achilles is back in the field, and will surely withdraw in terror!" (It was the armor of a chieftain which identified him, since the helmet covered most of his face).

The great warrior was hesitant, but, when he saw one of the Greek ships set on fire by the Trojans, he relented. "Remember, Patroclus, who you are," he said. "Remember, you are not Achilles. Only drive the Trojans from the ships, and then return."

The sight of Achilles armor had a sudden and pervasive impact on both sides. The Trojans were demoralized not only because the great hero was back, but because they thought his absence had been a trick to draw them far from the city; the Greeks, on the other hand, were infused with a new energy to see their best fighter at the front again.

The Trojans were forced into a hasty and bloody retreat toward the walls of their fortress. Patroclus, lusting for battle and encouraged by his success, completely forgot the warning of Achilles and soon put himself far in front of his troops. It was then that he met his fate, for he found himself opposed by the mighty Hector. The two fought; Patroclus was a courageous and skilled warrior, but no match for the great champion. Hector suddenly found an opening and drove his spear into Patroclus' body. The hero groaned and dropped to the dust with a mortal wound. It was only when Hector stripped the armor from his dying opponent (another custom of the time) that he realized he had not killed his archrival. The Greek soldiers finally came up, and, after a fierce struggle, they recovered Patroclus' body. Ajax brought the corpse to Achilles.

Achilles and Hector

Achilles was griefstricken at the death of his friend. He contemplated suicide, but then, after being consoled and advised by his mother, Thetis, he decided to renew the battle and make the Trojans pay a heavy price for what they had done. Gone now was any thought of Agamemnon or of his oath not to fight. All that he felt was a desire for blood and vengeance and for Hector's death.

Achilles appeared on the field in new armor designed by Hephaestus. He briefly made public amends with Agamemnon who restored Briseis to him. Then, with a terrible cry of battle, he rushed toward the enemy lines in his chariot.

Despite their rapid retreat, the Trojans were not able to avoid the raging warrior. The plain in front of the fortress and the River Xanthus were soon filled with corpses. Finally, the survivors of this onslaught found shelter behind the walls of the city; Hector, alone, remained outside, waiting for the climactic duel.

The Greek forces drew back to watch the fight between the champions, and the Trojans stood on their ramparts looking down on the scene. Priam and Hecuba begged their son to withdraw and fight another day, but Hector knew that the time had come. He trembled as he saw Achilles approach in his blazing armor. He threw his spear; it was harmlessly deflected by his opponent's shield. He drew his sword and attacked. He fought with all the strength and courage he possessed, but Achilles was not to be denied. He parried every thrust, avoided every blow, and when the smallest of openings was given, he plunged his sword into Hector's body and saw the great hero go down into the dust of Troy. It was over. Or was it? To the astonishment of both sides, Achilles tied the ankles of Hector's corpse to the back of his chariot and began to drag it back and forth in front of the walls, taunting the Trojans to come down and fight him, if they did not like what they saw. There was no response. No one dared. Only loud groans of sorrow filled the air. With a final show of contempt, Achilles dragged the body back to his compound.

On the next day Patroclus' body was cremated and various funeral rites were performed, while Hector's corpse lay untended. King Priam, unable any longer to endure his overwhelming grief, left the protection of his city, walked alone through the Greek camp —some say the gods made him invisible— and came to the tent of Achilles where, as a father, on his knees, he begged the great warrior to restore his son's corpse to him so it could have proper burial. Achilles could have killed Priam —the king was unguarded, but he did not; he could have imprisoned him for great ransom, but he did not; he could have rejected his plea, but he did not. The hero was instead moved to compassion by the old man and his fatherly love. He sent the body back to Troy with the king and declared a twelve day truce for funeral rites.

The death of Achilles

New allies joined the Trojans during this tenth year of the war. Penthesilea, queen of the Amazons, brought her women warriors to Troy. She was killed in combat with Achilles who did not know that he was fighting a woman until he had removed her armor after the fatal blow. Memnon, the son of Tithonus (Priam's brother), brought the Ethiopians to the war. He, too, fell before Achilles. Shortly after these two victories, when Achilles was fighting near the Scaean gate of the city, he was struck in the heel by a poisoned arrow which Paris fired at him from a place of concealment. Some even say that the incident was a deliberate ambush and that the arrow was guided by Apollo. Much to the dismay of the Greeks, there was nothing which could be done to save their wounded champion. The missile did its lethal work quickly. With his death, the great hero had fulfilled the prophecy: his was a short and most glorious life. Indeed, his fame lives to this very day, as we see by this telling.

The Greek leaders wished to give the armor of Achilles to their best and most courageous leader, and they decided that this man was Odysseus. Their choice caused Ajax, who felt that he was second in all things only to Achilles, to go mad with his sense of lost honor and esteem. There seemed to him to be no other recourse but death. He fell upon his sword in dismay.

The prophecies

It was prophesied that Neoptolemus, Achilles' son by one of the daughters of King Lycomedes of Scyros, would have to be present at Troy in order for the Greeks to be victorious. When the very young man arrived at the city, Odysseus gave him the arms of his illustrious father, and the novice warrior -following the heroic tradition of his family- put them to effective use.

Helenus, the prophetic son of Priam, had been captured by the Greeks, and he seemed just as willing to use his powers for them as for the Trojans. He indicated that three actions would have to be taken before Troy would fall. First, the bones of Pelops, a famous ancestor of Agamemnon and Menelaus, would have to be brought to Troy. This was done. Secondly, Philoctetes would have to bring the bow and arrows of Heracles to Troy. This was done, and Philoctetes, among other feats, killed Paris with one of his arrows. Thirdly, the Palladium, a small statue of Athena, would have to be removed from the city. This was accomplished with great personal danger by Odysseus and Diomedes.

The wooden horse

Odysseus now put his creativity to work in order to end the war that would not end. He ordered the Greeks to build an enormous wooden horse. The horse was to be hollow so that chosen soldiers under Odysseus' command could hide within it. The Greeks then pretended to give up the seige. They put their ships back into the sea, abandoned their battle lines, and sailed away, leaving only the gigantic wooden horse on the field in front of the city.

The Trojans rushed out onto the deserted plain. For many of them it was their first time outside the walls in ten years. They stared in wonder at the huge horse, and a noisy argument developed as to whether they should take it within the fortifications as a trophy of what they now believed to be their victory.

Suddenly, Laocoon, a Trojan priest, burst out from the crowd; he grabbed a spear from one of the soldiers and hurled it into the side of the horse. There seemed to be a faint rumble of armor from within. "Beware of the Greeks," he shouted, "especially when they bring gifts!" Many Trojans now wanted to tear open the horse and to examine its contents when yet another disturbance caught the crowd's attention.

A Greek soldier had been captured. He identified himself as Sinon and told them that he was a deserter. He had escaped from an intended human sacrifice and now hated the Greeks for what they had planned to do to him. (He had, in reality, been carefully chosen as someone who, because of his great rhetorical skills, might best be

-192-

able to convince the Trojans to take the horse into the city). He was willing to answer any questions which the Trojans might wish to ask him. He said that the Greek chieftains had sailed back to their kingdoms, since they had been ordered by the gods to sacrifice on their home altars if they wished to conquer Troy. (The fleet had actually sailed to the far side of a nearby island called Tenedos). The horse, Sinon claimed, was an offering demanded by Athena to make up for the theft of the Palladium from Troy, and it had been made so large because of a prophecy by the priest Calchas that if it were taken within the city, then, regardless of what the Greeks did, the Trojans would be victorious.

More noisy debate among the Trojans. Was Sinon speaking the truth? What about Laocoon's warning? Should they bring the horse into the city? Suddenly, a scream of terror rose above the loud argument! A woman pointed in frozen horror to the sea. Two huge serpents were skimming across the surface of the water. They slithered up onto the beach -the crowd watched in stunned silence- and went directly toward Laocoon and his two sons who stood beside him. They caught them in their monstrous coils and slowly and painfully strangled all three. Then they left their broken victims and disappeared within the temple of Athena in the city. The crowd came alive again. This action had clearly been a divine response; Laocoon had been punished for his blasphemy, for violating the sacred horse with his spear. The Trojans quickly built a mobile platform and pulled the massive horse within the city walls.

On that very night, with the Trojans rejoicing in their victory and much relaxed from their usual vigilance, Odysseus and his men stealthily climbed from the belly of the horse, killed the few guards on the fortifications and opened the main gates of the city. As the Greeks sailed back from Tenedos, they saw the torch waving from the high walls of Troy and they knew that Odysseus' plan had been successful. They poured in through the open gates, past the now undefended walls which had for so long been an unconquerable obstacle. The Trojans, many of whom were sleeping, were taken completely by surprise and were slaughtered. King Priam like the captain of a sinking ship went down with his city. He was killed by Neoptolemus. There were few male survivors, and most of the women and children became slaves to their Greek masters. The great city which had existed for nearly two thousand years fell to its utter destruction on that one fatal night.

Questions

1. Of what is Protesilaus a symbol?

2. Explain the cause of Achilles wrath.

3. How did Patroclus help the situation? What mistake did he make?

4. What caused Achilles to re-enter the battle?

5. Why did Achilles act as he did against Hector?

6. Who killed Achilles and how?

7. What conditions had to be met before Troy would fall?

8. Whose idea was the wooden horse?

9. How did Sinon accomplish his task?

10. How did the gods apparently assist Sinon and the Greeks?

35. THE RETURNS

A. The division of the spoils

B. The return of Nestor

C. The return of Neoptolemus

D. The return of Philoctetes

E. The return of Diomedes

F. The return of Idomeneus

G. The return of Teucer

H. The return of Ajax the Lesser

I. The return of Menelaus

J. The return of Agamemnon

The division of the spoils

The war at Troy is often portrayed as a double tragedy. Not only were there countless deaths on both sides during the long years of the struggle, but, when the city was sacked on the final night, the Greeks also committed many offenses against the gods which led to divine retribution. Shrines and temples were heedlessly desecrated. Neoptolemus, for example, killed King Priam while he sought sanctuary next to an altar of Zeus in his palace, and Ajax the Lesser (a different warrior from the man who killed himself) raped Cassandra in the temple of Athena. It was this latter action which was especially harmful to the Greeks, for it turned Athena, their benefactor, against them, and she destroyed many of their homeward-bound ships.

It took some time after the fall of the city to divide the huge mass of riches. Most of the women and children were assigned as slaves to various masters. Some were killed. Astyanax, Hector's young son, was hurled from the walls so that there would be no one left of royal blood who might rebuild the city or seek vengeance on individual Greek leaders. Polyxena, one of Priam's daughters, was killed so that her corpse could be placed on the tomb of Achilles. It was thought that the noble hero had fallen in love with her shortly before he died and now wished to have her spirit with him in the Land of the Dead. Some say, in fact, that Achilles was slain not in fighting at the Scaean Gate but in an ambush by Paris and Deiphobus when he had gone to the house of Polyxena to ask parental permission to marry the young woman.

The return of Nestor

Nestor, the king of Pylos, had led ninety ships to Troy. He was already an old man at the start of the war. Known for his wisdom (and also his wordiness), the Greek leaders often sought his advice. He was one of the few chieftains to have a safe voyage home and to regain his kingdom without any difficulty.

The return of Neoptolemus

Through the assistance of his grandmother, Thetis the Nereid, Neoptolemus was able to avoid the storms which did so much damage to many of the other Greeks. He arrived home safely and took over his father's kingdom of Phthia. Later he conquered Epirus in western Greece. He had three children by his slave, Andromache (Hector's former wife), but eventually, according to some versions, he gave her to Helenus, another of his slaves and a son of Priam. Some say that he married Hermione, the daughter of Helen and Menelaus, others that he was killed in a fight with Orestes, Agamemnon's son, over the woman.

The return of Philoctetes

Because of his horrible wound, Philoctetes, as we have seen, was left on the island of Lemnos until the final year of the war. Perhaps because he had already suffered so greatly, the gods allowed him to sail home safely to Malis. But he soon grew restless and took whoever wished to accompany him to the eastern coast of Italy where he established two new towns.

The return of Diomedes

Diomedes was the king of Argos. As one of the Epigoni, he had sacked Thebes and thus avenged his father's death during the attack on the city which had been led by Polyneices, the son of Oedipus. Diomedes brought eighty ships to Troy. He was one of the bravest of the Greek fighters, always plunging headlong into battle with little regard for his own safety. He fought successfully against great heroes, sons of gods, and even wounded a goddess (Aphrodite) who happened to get in his way.

Diomedes returned safely to Argos but then soon left again to found a new city in southern Italy. Some say that he was forced to leave his home because of the political situation there.

The return of Idomeneus

Idomeneus, the king of Crete, brought eighty ships to Troy. He, like Nestor, was an older man, but he still distinguished himself in the fighting. His ships were seriously threatened by a raging tempest

-196-

on the way home. The king pledged that he would sacrifice to Poseidon the first thing or person he encountered on Crete, if the god would bring them through the storm. The sea at once subsided, and the ships arrived safely at Crete where the first person to greet the king was -horror of horrors- his own son. Idomeneus believed that he must do what he had promised (however rashly); therefore, with great anguish -always hoping that the god would intervene- he sacrificed the young man. The Cretan people were so upset by this savage act that they forced the king to go into exile. He took with him those who were willing to go and sailed to southern Italy where he established a new city.

The return of Teucer

Teucer, the son of Telamon and Hesione (the daughter of King Laomedon of Troy), was a half-brother of Ajax. The two of them brought twelve ships from their father's island kingdom of Salamis, near Athens. Ajax, who was often called the Greater to distinguish him from the other Ajax, known as the Lesser, was one of the best of the Greek warriors. Many thought that he was second only to Achilles. Teucer achieved great fame as an archer. When Ajax committed suicide after his failure to be awarded the arms of Achilles, it was Teucer who defied Agamemnon and several other Greek leaders to insist that his brother be given a hero's funeral.

Teucer's voyage home was safe enough, but his father Telamon would not let him land at Salamis. He claimed that Teucer should have somehow been able to prevent his brother's suicide. The hero was forced to go into exile. He eventually founded a city on Cyprus and became ruler of the island. Kings of Cyprus down to the present century have traced their descent from Teucer.

The return of Ajax the Lesser

Ajax the Lesser was a constant companion to the other Ajax. He had brought forty ships from Locris in central Greece, and was noted especially as a spearman and a runner. His desecration of the temple and statue of Athena on the last night of Troy was a serious one. Odysseus wanted to stone him to death, but Ajax clung to the statue of the goddess he had just violated and begged for mercy.

Ajax's fleet was overwhelmed by a storm on the journey home; his own ship was struck by lightning -a bolt thrown by Athena- and sank. He swam to a nearby rock and boasted -a most unwise action- that he had saved himself despite the gods' enmity. Poseidon then caused a huge wave to impale him on the jagged rock to which he was clinging.

The return of Menelaus

Menelaus, the king of Sparta and the husband of Helen, had been a courageous fighter throughout the war. He would have killed Paris in single combat, if the famous lover had not been saved by Aphrodite. On the last night of Troy, he found Helen in the home of Deiphobus (her husband after Paris' death) whom he killed. He was prepared to do the same to Helen, but once he saw her face -which he had dreamed about for so many long nights at Troy- he could not bring himself to act with any violence against her. Instead, he ordered her to be placed on his ship for the return voyage so that she could be displayed in disgrace to the Spartans.

Menelaus' fleet was constantly ripped by storms during the eight years it wandered about the Mediterranean, unable to reach Sparta. Only five out of the fifty ships survived. Finally, after being driven to Egypt, Menelaus was informed that, if he could defeat Proteus, a minor sea-god who lived near the mouth of the Nile, in a wrestling match, he would be told how to reach home safely. To defeat any god was no easy task, but it was made especially difficult with Proteus since he could change into any form he wished. Nonetheless, Menelaus was victorious, and the sea-god supplied the necessary instructions.

Except for Odysseus, Menelaus was the last of the heroes to arrive home, and, by the time they reached Sparta, he and Helen had become reconciled. Some try to explain their unexpected relationship by saying that Menelaus was simply not able to resist the great beauty and seductive charm of his wife, while others maintain that, while in Egypt, Menelaus discovered to his delight that the real Helen had not gone to Troy at all, but had remained there during the long years of the struggle and had been faithful to him all along.

Menelaus and Helen resumed their power in Sparta with no difficulty and ruled there successfully until they died in old age.

The return of Agamemnon

Agamemnon as commander-in-chief was responsible and had to suffer for any sacrilegious actions committed by those under his authority as well as for any violations of which he himself might be guilty. His fleet was destroyed on the voyage home, except for the one vessel which carried the king, Cassandra (whom he had taken as his slave), and a few soldiers.

Agamemnon's wife, Clytemnestra, had been long preparing for his return to Mycenae. Ever since her husband had deceived her and had sacrificed their daughter, Iphigenia, to appease Artemis, her love for him had been replaced by a deep and bitter hatred. She had taken a lover, Aegisthus, an enemy to Agamemnon and a man who desired to be ruler of Mycenae himself.

Clytemnestra publicly greeted Agamemnon on the day of his return. According to the plan, she led the king to the palace bath. When he was stripped of armor and weapons, she and Aegisthus acted savagely and quickly. They tangled the unsuspecting king in a net and butchered him with an ax. On the very day of his triumphal return, the leader of all the Greeks, the conqueror of Troy lay a naked and mangled corpse in his own palace. Clytemnestra then murdered Cassandra, the prophetic daughter of Priam, who in vain foretold her own death to the unbelieving citizens of Mycenae.

Within a few years Agamemnon's son, Orestes, returned from exile and with the aid of his friend, Pylades, and his sister, Electra, took revenge for his father's murder by killing Aegisthus and Clytemnestra. Such a bloody act was typical of the time and was indeed expected of a murdered man's son. The problem for Orestes was that one of the killers was his own mother. Because of this complication, some say that Orestes was driven mad by the Furies (the spirits who attack any child who slays a parent) and had to be purified of the crime by Apollo at Delphi and then put on trial at Athens where his actions were found to be justified.

Orestes became king of Mycenae. He wished to marry Hermione, the daughter of Menelaus and Helen, as did Neoptolemus, Achilles' son. Orestes claimed a prior and stronger right to the woman which Neoptolemus refused to recognize. The two argued and fought, and, by most accounts, Neoptolemus was killed.

Orestes and Hermione married and had one child who became king of Sparta when Menelaus died. Orestes also arranged a marriage between his sister, Electra, and his friend, Pylades. After so much evil and tragedy, the long account of the family of Atreus finally ended with some order and happiness.

Questions

1. In what ways can the war at Troy be called a tragedy for both sides?

2. What chieftain caused the greatest harm for the Greeks on the last night of Troy?

3. What alternate story for the death of Achilles is presented?

4. Which Greek leaders were able to sail back from Troy without having to endure a storm at sea? Why?

5. Which Greek leader was killed at sea? Why?

6. Which Greek leaders were forced to go into exile when they returned home?

7. Which Greek leaders established new towns? What countries are involved?

8. Which of the returns involves the motif of the "rash promise"? In what way? Can you think of any other stories with this motif?

9. What explanations are given for the reconciliation of Menelaus and Helen?

10. What is Clytemnestra's motivation for killing Agamemnon?

11. From your knowledge of Atreus' family, why is Aegisthus a special enemy to Agamemnon?

12. What is significant about the way in which Agamemnon is killed?

13. Show how vengeance is an important theme in the story of Agamemnon's homecoming.

14. What are the contributions of Orestes to the story of the family of Atreus?

36. THE RETURN OF ODYSSEUS

A. The journey to Ithaca

    1. The Ciconians
    2. The Lotus-eaters
    3. The Cyclops
    4. Aeolus
    5. The Lystrygonians
    6. Circe
    7. The Land of the Dead
    8. The Sirens
    9. Scylla and Charybdis
    10. The cattle of Hyperion
    11. Calypso
    12. The Phaeacians

B. The suitors

C. The later years

The journey to Ithaca

As we have seen, Odysseus (his alternate name of Ulysses comes from the Romans) in addition to having the usual heroic qualities of great courage and strength, was known as well for his cleverness, imagination, and intelligence. Although at first reluctant to go to Troy because of his recent marriage to Penelope and the birth of their son, Telemachus, he was, once committed, one of the leading participants, and it was he who planned the stratagem which led finally to the fall of the city.

Homer's epic poem, The Odyssey, presents the hero's return from Troy to his island kingdom of Ithaca, a journey which took ten years beyond the ten already spent in battle. As we have seen with the story of Jason and the Argonauts, the voyage is a narrative device to which adventures of various kinds can be easily attached. Each episode in The Odyssey, as well as being entertaining, reveals the resourcefulness of its main character.

1. The Ciconians

Odysseus left Troy with a contingent of twelve ships. They made a surprise attack on the city of the barbaric Ciconians in Thrace; however, despite Odysseus' warnings, his crew delayed too long feasting and enjoying their triumph. The Ciconians used the time to regroup and counterattack. In the second battle the Greeks suffered grievous losses before they were able to sail away.

2. The Lotus-eaters

Blown far off course by a storm, the Greeks landed on the coast of North Africa. The people there were friendly and peaceful, but very docile. They ate of a plant called the lotus which deprived them of any energy or initiative. When some of Odysseus' men tried the flower, they lost all desire to return home; they preferred to lie about with no greater ambition than to eat again of the lotus. Odysseus gathered up the few men who had tried the plant and sailed away quickly.

3. The Cyclops

The next episode is perhaps the most famous one of the voyage. Odysseus and a large contingent of his men were trapped in the cave of the giant, one-eyed Cyclops. The monster was a shepherd, and each night he brought his sheep into the cave and blocked the entrance with an enormous rock which only he could move. Unfortunately, the giant had a taste for human flesh, and, once he had trapped the Greek explorers in his abode, he planned to eat them all. The problem for the Greeks was a difficult one: it did not just involve killing the Cyclops in some manner, since they needed him alive to move the huge rock at the entrance so they could make good their escape.

Odysseus developed a plan. The Greeks gave the giant some particularly potent wine which they happened to have with them, and the monster, unaccustomed to strong drink, fell into a drunken sleep. They then drove a sharpened stake through the Cyclops' single eye. The monster roared in pain and fumbled about attempting to seize his attackers, but the Greeks quickly jumped from one place to another to avoid his grasp. When morning came, the blind Cyclops was forced to move the rock so that his sheep could go out to pasture. He stood at the entrace with blood dripping from his ravaged eye-socket and felt with his hands to make certain that only sheep passed through the mouth of the cave. Odysseus had anticipated this action and had tied his men underneath various sheep. They passed the inspection of the monster undetected.

Once the Greeks had reached their ships, Odysseus could not resist taunting the Cyclops by letting him know that they had escaped and by shouting back who it was who had outwitted him. It was a serious mistake. The Cyclops, a son of Poseidon, prayed to his father for vengeance, and the prayer was answered. Many of Odysseus' troubles from this point on were due to the god's enmity.

4. Aeolus

The Greeks next stopped at the island of King Aeolus, the keeper of the winds. He entertained them hospitably and gave Odysseus a bag which contained all of the winds unfavorable to his return home. The ships then sailed to within sight of Ithaca, and all would have gone well except that the crew had seen the bag which Aeolus had given to Odysseus, and they suspected that it contained some treasure which their leader was hiding away. While Odysseus slept, they opened the sack, and, much to their dismay, it contained not treasure, but howling winds which blew them with enormous force away from Ithaca and back to Aeolus' island. This time the king turned them away without additional aid.

5. The Lystrygonians

The Greeks next came to an island city with a calm harbor surrounded by high cliffs to which there was a narrow entrance. Odysseus refused to enter the bay until he knew more about the inhabitants, even though the captains of the other eleven ships had anchored there with no apparent problem. It was a wise precaution, since the Greeks soon discovered that the people were savage cannibals called the Lystrygonians. As the Greeks tried to escape from the port, the barbarians sank their ships by dropping rocks from the high cliffs above. They then speared the swimming survivors –like fish– to eat at a later meal. Only Odysseus and his crew were able to escape from the horror of that island.

6. Circe

With just his own vessel remaining, Odysseus stopped next at the island of the sorceress, Circe, who, as we have seen, was the daughter of Helios. She was at first very hostile, and transformed several of Odysseus' crew into pigs, but, when she tried her magical powers on the hero himself to no avail, Circe immediately understood that Odysseus was more highly favored by the gods than she. The enchantress then changed the crew back into human form and entertained the Greeks hospitably for a year. Some say that Circe and Odysseus became lovers. In any case, through her special powers, the sorceress was able to give the hero warnings and advice about future perils.

7. The Land of the Dead

As advised by Circe, Odysseus sailed to the far western sea which encircles the earth. There he entered the Land of the Dead to obtain the advice of Tiresias, the famous prophet of Thebes, about what he must do to reach home safely. While in the dark land of spirits, Odysseus saw and talked with many of his former comrades from the war at Troy.

8. The Sirens

The Sirens, as we have seen, were bird-like women (often portrayed as possessing human bodies with wings) who lured sailors to death with their beautiful songs. Once the haunting melody was heard, the mariners would either be drowned on the rocks surrounding the Sirens' island or would waste away with all thoughts of home removed from their minds.

Odysseus had been warned by Circe about the threat which the Sirens presented, but he was curious to hear their song. He filled the ears of his crew with wax and had himself tied to the mast with instructions to ignore his commands until they were well past the dangerous island. Thus, the sailors were safe from the sound of the fatal song, and Odysseus, while he heard the irresistible melody, could take no action.

9. Scylla and Charybdis

Circe had warned Odysseus that the next challenge following the Sirens would be to sail between Scylla and Charybdis. As we have already seen with Jason's story, Scylla was a terrible monster: female to the waist, but from there divided into six snakes, each with the head of a ravenous dog which longed for human flesh. Charybdis was a giant whirlpool which sucked anything coming within its grasp to a death at the bottom of the sea. The two monsters existed in the narrows between Italy and Sicily (Strait of Messina), and the difficulty was to sail the tight course of safety between them. Circe had told Odysseus that Scylla would claim one man for each of her six heads, and, although he attempted to prevent these deaths, he was unsuccessful.

10. The cattle of Hyperion

The Greeks next stopped at the island on which Hyperion, the sun god, kept his cattle. Odysseus had been warned not to harm a single head of this herd, and he gave this command in strongest terms to his men. Despite these orders, they killed and feasted on several of the animals. A most unwise action, since, soon afterwards, their ship was ripped apart by a violent storm, and the entire crew was drowned.

11. Calypso

Only Odysseus survived -and just barely- the tempest which killed his men. He swam to a nearby island which was inhabited by the goddess Calypso and her nymphs. Despite the beauty of the goddess, the serenity of her island, and her offer of immortality, Odysseus' thoughts were always of Ithaca, of Penelope, and of Telemachus. After seven years, the gods took pity on him and ordered Calypso to allow him to leave. Odysseus built a small raft and sailed safely toward home until he was seen by Poseidon who immediately caused a storm which again nearly drowned him. He was finally washed ashore on the island of the Phaeacians.

12. The Phaeacians

King Alcinous and the Phaeacians treated Odysseus most hospitably. After feasting and games in his honor, they brought him to Ithaca on one of their ships and left him on the shore. Vindictive Poseidon punished these good-hearted people for helping his enemy by turning their ship into a rock as they returned to port.

The suitors

Unlike Agamemnon who assumed that all was well at home and, unsuspecting, was murdered on the day of his return, the crafty Odysseus disguised himself as a beggar and observed the situation in his kingdom before he took any action.

Odysseus discovered that, except for his wife, son, and a few loyal servants, people believed that he was dead. Princes from Ithaca and neighboring territories had come to his palace seeking to marry Penelope. She had refused all offers, but that did not dissuade them. For three years they had arrogantly remained at the palace: feasting, drinking, abusing the household, and generally wasting the wealth of absent king. Since she was helpless to take action against them, Penelope -with the cleverness of her husband- had devised a plan to put them off. She said that she would choose one of them as soon as she finished weaving a burial robe for Laertes, the father of Odysseus, and each night she would secretly pull out much of what she had woven that day. But she had been caught. The suitors were now insistent: she must make her choice.

Odysseus revealed himself to his son, Telemachus, and the two of them plotted how to take action against such overwhelming odds.

Telemachus announced to the suitors in the great hall of the palace that his mother would choose as her husband whoever was able to string the bow of Odysseus and shoot an arrow through the opening in the heads of twelve axes set in a row. The suitors enthusiastically agreed to such a contest, each one believing that he alone would be able to accomplish the task.

One by one the suitors attempted to string the bow, but each lacked the strength. "It is another trick!" they shouted. "No one can string the bow!" Suddenly, a frail voice from the back of the hall asked to be allowed to try. It was Odysseus in his disguise as a beggar. The suitors protested and mocked the old man, but Penelope permitted him to enter the competition. He came slowly to the front of the hall, and then quickly and with seemingly no effort strung the bow. The noisy and insulting shouts of the suitors suddenly stopped. Their attention became fixed upon the man who held the bow. He drew back the string and fired the arrow through the twelve ax-heads. It struck a metal shield hanging on the wall, and the reverberation sounded loudly through the otherwise silent hall. Then the great hero threw off his disguise and turned to face the arrogant men who for so long had abused the law of hospitality in his palace. Telemachus came quickly to his father's side and brought more weapons. The suitors, unarmed and unprepared, ran for the door, but it had been locked. They were trapped; their doom had come. Odysseus and Telemachus slaughtered them all.

The later years

After the palace had been cleansed following the killing of the suitors, Odysseus and Penelope were reunited for the first time in twenty years. Together they lived happily in Ithaca from that time on. Some say that the hero met his death in old age when he was accidentally killed by Telegonus, his son by Circe. Telegonus, searching for his father, was unaware that he had arrived in Ithaca and led a raiding party onto the island. In the fight that ensued, Odysseus was one of those killed. When the actual identities of all parties had been made clear, Odysseus' family forgave Telegonus. They brought his body to Circe's island where it was buried. Telegonus then married Penelope, and Telemachus married Circe who, apparently, never aged.

Questions

1. To what group(s) in society today might the lotus-eaters be compared?

2. In what ways does the adventure of the Cyclops reveal Odysseus' resourcefulness?

3. How does the adventure of the Lystrygonians distinguish Odysseus from the other captains in his fleet?

4. How does the episode with Circe distinguish Odysseus from the rest of his men?

5. In what ways has Odysseus conquered death?

6. What qualities of Odysseus does the encounter with the Sirens reveal?

7. What qualities of Odysseus does the encounter with Calypso reveal?

8. Compare and contrast: Agamemnon's and Odysseus' homecomings.

9. How does Odysseus' plan help to increase the odds for his success in punishing the suitors?

10. Describe the different ways in which the myth emphasizes the virtues of loyalty and fidelity.

37. THE MYTH OF AENEAS

A. Background

B. The wanderings

    1. Thrace
    2. Delos
    3. Crete
    4. The island of the Harpies
    5. Buthrotum
    6. The land of the Cyclopes
    7. Drepanum
    8. Carthage
    9. Cumae

C. The war in Latium

D. Aftermath

Background

The story of Aeneas is told in the great epic poem, The Aeneid, by Vergil. The Romans looked back on Aeneas as their founder; Rome became the new Troy.

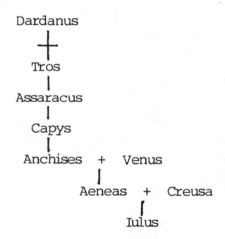

```
        Dardanus
           |
         Tros
        Assaracus
           |
         Capys
           |
   Anchises  +  Venus
              |
       Aeneas  +  Creusa
                  |
                Iulus
```

Aeneas was descended from Assaracus, a brother of Ilus who began the royal line at Troy. Aeneas' family ruled at Dardania, a town close to Troy and allied with it.

Anchises, Aeneas' father, was handsome in his youth, and he attracted the attention of Venus (the Roman name for Aphrodite). The goddess visited him in the form of a mortal woman, and their love produced the great hero. Venus insisted that Anchises should never reveal who the mother of their child was, but he eventually boasted of their romance. Zeus struck him with a thunderbolt which crippled him for life.

During the war at Troy, Aeneas was the leader of the Dardanian troops, and he fought bravely in defense of the city. On the final night, he was warned by the ghost of Hector and by Venus that he must leave to found a new Troy elsewhere. Reluctant to abandon his home and comrades, Aeneas nevertheless obeyed the wishes of the gods. Carrying his father on his shoulders and leading his wife, Creusa, and their young son, Iulus, Aeneas managed to escape with his followers; however, in the confusion of the darkness and the constant threat of enemy troops, Creusa became separated from the group and was killed by the Greeks.

Aeneas gathered the Trojan survivors near Mt. Ida and eventually set sail with twenty ships. Throughout his wanderings, the goddess Juno (the Roman name for Hera) was his implacable foe. She had not forgotten that it was Paris, a Trojan, who awarded the Golden Apple to Venus.

The wanderings

Unlike the other voyages after the fall of Troy, Aeneas was not returning to an original point of departure, but was seeking a new home for the Trojan gods. The location of the reborn city only very slowly became clear.

1. Thrace

Aeneas first planned to establish their new home in nearby Thrace, but Polydorus, a young son of Priam, eerily spoke to them from his grave. He told them that he had been treacherously murdered by the local king and that they themselves were in great danger. The Trojans quickly departed.

2. Delos

Aeneas and his followers next stopped at the island of Delos, the birthplace of Apollo, where they asked the god to reveal where they should settle. The ambiguous response was misinterpreted by the Trojans who thought that it referred to Crete.

3. Crete

After suffering a serious plague, the Trojans realized that Crete was not the site for new Troy, and, in a dream, Aeneas was told to sail to Italy.

4. The island of the Harpies

After several days of stormy weather, the Trojans stopped at an island in the Ionian Sea. They slaughtered cattle they found there, and, just when their feast was all prepared, they were suddenly attacked by the Harpies. These were the same creatures -with the faces of women and the bodies of birds- which had been driven away from King Phineus by the Argonauts. The Harpies seized whatever food they could, and spoiled the rest with their filth. The Trojans were filled with terror at the unexpected attack and with loathing at the horrible nature of the monsters. They fought as best they could against creatures who could fly out of range and who were seemingly impervious to their weapons. Aeneas quickly gave the order to sail away.

5. Buthrotum

The ships were next anchored at the town of Buthrotum in western Greece where they found -to their great surprise- a Trojan ruler. Helenus, a son of Priam, had been given this kingdom by Neoptolemus, the son of Achilles. He had also been given Andromache, Hector's former wife, whom he married. Although Neoptolemus had recently been killed in a fight with Orestes, Agamemnon's son, the Greeks of Buthrotum had been so impressed with Helenus' effectiveness as their king that they wished him to continue. The Trojans were warmly welcomed, and Helenus, who possessed prophetic powers, gave them further information about their journey and destination.

6. The land of the Cyclopes

The Trojans stopped briefly in eastern Sicily near Mt. Etna where they saw -from a distance- several of the Cyclopes, the tribe of one-eyed, giant cannibals. They were able to rescue a Greek sailor who had inadvertently been left behind by Odysseus.

7. Drepanum

The ships next reached the town of Drepanum in western Sicily. The area was ruled by King Acestes who, since he had a Trojan mother, felt a close affinity for Aeneas and his followers. It was here that Anchises, Aeneas' father, unexpectedly died.

8. Carthage

After funeral rites for Anchises, the Trojans set out for Italy, but a tremendous storm (caused by Juno) blew them far off course to the city of Carthage in North Africa. Here Aeneas encountered Dido, the queen of the prosperous settlement. She too, after learning of the murder of her husband, had left her native city (Tyre in Phoenicia) and had led a group of followers to a new home in the western Mediterranean. For nearly a year, the two exiles enjoyed their new-found happiness in each other. Dido urged Aeneas to remain permanently and to share the kingdom with her. Trojans and Carthaginians would become one people; Carthage would be the new Troy. Aeneas was greatly tempted for he had strong feelings of affection for this woman whose life was so similar to his own, but visions and instructions from the gods became clearer and more insistent: Italy, seek Italy. Aeneas was placed in a terrible dilemma between his personal desire to remain with the woman he loved and his sense of duty as a leader of his people. In anguish he obeyed the wishes of the gods and sailed away. When Dido learned what he had done, in a frenzy of rage and hurt and shame, she killed herself.

9. Cumae

After a brief stop again in Drepanum where Aeneas held funeral games for Anchises and left behind those followers who did not wish to continue on the journey, the Trojans sailed to Cumae near Naples. The Cumaean Sibyl led Aeneas into the Underworld where the spirit of Anchises revealed to him the noble race of people for whom he was to be the progenitor.

The war in Latium

Aeneas led his fleet north along the coast until they dropped anchor in the Tiber River, close to the future site of Rome. The area was called Latium and was ruled by King Latinus who hospitably received the ambassadors of Aeneas and was graciously willing to allow the Trojans to settle in his land. He had sometime earlier received a prophecy that his daughter, Lavinia, would marry a foreigner, and he now assumed -correctly- that Aeneas was that man. Unfortunately, before the leaders could meet, Juno caused a needless argument to develop between the two sides which led, in turn, to a long and bloody war. King Latinus abdicated rather than fight, so the noble warrior, Turnus, assumed the leadership of the Latin side. There were many savage battles, many single combats, and, as usual in war, many innocent and unnecessary deaths. The outcome was decided, finally, by a struggle between Aeneas and Turnus in which the Trojan hero killed his Latin counterpart.

Aftermath

Aeneas made peace with the Latins and married Lavinia, King Latinus' daughter. He established and ruled the city of Lavinium. Some say that their son, Brutus, eventually left Italy and sailed to Britain where he founded Londinium (London). Iulus, Aeneas' son by his Trojan wife, Creusa, established the neighboring town of Alba Longa and his descendants ruled there for over four hundred years until the establishment of Rome in 753 B.C. The famous Julian family of Roman emperors claimed that their name could be traced back to that of Iulus.

<h2 style="text-align:center">Questions</h2>

1. What is the name of the Roman epic poem which tells the story of Aeneas, and who is its author?

2. Compare and contrast: the wanderings of Aeneas with those of Odysseus.

3. List similarities and differences between the Aeneas and Odysseus.

4. To which figures in the Trojan War might Aeneas and Turnus be compared? In what ways?

5. List all of the tie-ins with other myths which you observe in this story.

38. ROME

A. The founding of Rome

B. The rape of the Sabine women

C. Tarpea

D. The death of Romulus

E. The kings

F. The overthrow of the kings

G. Roman gods

The founding of Rome

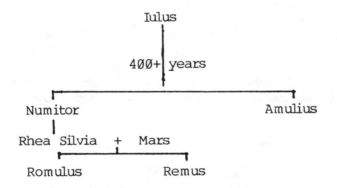

Twelve generations of kings ruled at Alba Longa in Latium. They were all descendants of Iulus, the son of Aeneas and the founder of the city. In the thirteenth generation King Numitor was deposed by his brother, Amulius. Fear of public reaction prevented Amulius from killing Numitor, and likewise kept him from murdering his niece, Rhea Silvia. He sent the former king into a closely guarded exile, and he forced Rhea Silvia to become a Vestal Virgin so that she would not produce children who might take action against him. However, the young vestal's beauty soon attracted the attention of Mars, the god of war, and their love affair produced twin sons: Romulus and Remus.

When Amulius discovered that Rhea Silvia had given birth despite his precautions, he ordered her to be killed for breaking the Vestal's vow, and he abandoned the infants in a basket which he set afloat on the Tiber River. The container, as so often happens in these stories, instead of drifting out to sea, came to shore near what would eventually become the center of Rome. The twins were discovered by a wolf who rather than devouring them, gave them nourishment instead. Indeed, this scene of the wolf and the infants became one of Rome's important visual symbols and is still in use today.

The children were soon found by a shepherd, Faustulus, who took them to his home and raised them as though they were his own sons. As the twins grew into young men, they became known for their courage and strength and assumed leadership of a large group of shepherds.

Since Faustulus had long suspected that the infants he had rescued might well be the missing grandsons of Numitor, he decided to present them secretly to the former king. There was immediate recognition, and all of them began to plot the overthrow of the tyrant, Amulius. With Romulus and Remus leading their band of shepherds, the rebellion was successful and the usurper was killed.

Numitor was restored as king of Alba Longa, and he readily granted the request of his grandsons to found a new city near the place where they had been saved by the wolf. The construction proceeded rapidly but was soon marred by a terrible tragedy. Each young man had his own band of followers, and an argument soon developed as to what the name of the city should be. Angry words led to blows, and blows to a brawl in which Romulus killed his brother. For those suckled by a wolf and fathered by the god of war, fratricide was perhaps inevitable.

The rape of the Sabine women

The new city, called Rome after Romulus' name, grew quickly in prosperity and strength. But its population was unbalanced on the side of males, since many fugitives and criminals had fled to Rome for protection. Despite Romulus' best efforts, he had little success in persuading the fathers in neighboring tribes to allow their daughters to marry Romans. Finally, in desperation, Romulus sponsored a large festival to which he invited many families from the nearby Sabine people. At a given sign, each Roman male seized a Sabine woman and ran off with her. The Sabine men, who had come to the celebration in all good will, were completely surprised at the treacherous abduction of their sisters and daughters. It meant war. They returned home to prepare and organize. When they came once more to Rome, this time for battle, they were again surprised: the women who had been abducted came between the battle lines and urged their fathers and brothers not to fight with their new husbands whom they had grown to love. The men considered the suggestion —neither side was eager for war, and first one, then another, and eventually all threw down their weapons. At Romulus' suggestion the Romans and Sabines were combined into a single state.

Tarpea

Tarpea was a Vestal Virgin who apparently resented the presence of the new Sabine women in the city. When the army of their fathers and brothers marched on Rome, Tarpea offered to show the Sabine king a secret path up a hill from which they could more easily make an attack on the Romans. As her price she asked for what they were wearing on their left arms, by which she meant their golden bracelets. When the Sabines had reached the top of the hill, the king turned to Tarpea and said: "Now you may have the reward you requested, and may it be a warning to all who betray their country!" And with that, the king and his followers crushed the woman to death with the shields which they wore on their left arms.

The death of Romulus

Romulus as the first king of Rome ruled for thirty-seven years and met his end in a mysterious way. As he was sitting on his throne in the Field of Mars observing army maneuvers, a sudden storm developed, and the area was covered by a heavy fog. When it lifted, Romulus was gone. The king's advisors said that he, a son of a god, had been taken up to be with the gods. From that time on, Romulus was worshipped as a divinity called Quirinus. The rumor persisted, however, that the king's enemies had used the fog as an opportunity to attack quickly and kill him.

The kings

The period of the kingdom: 753 B.C. - 509 B.C.

Romulus	753 B.C. - 717 B.C.
Numa Pompilius	715 B.C. - 673 B.C.
Tullus Hostilius	673 B.C. - 642 B.C.
Ancus Martius	642 B.C. - 617 B.C.
Tarquin the Elder	616 B.C. - 579 B.C.
Servius Tullius	578 B.C. - 535 B.C.
Tarquin the Proud	535 B.C. - 509 B.C.

There were in legend seven kings of Rome extending from the founding of the city in 753 B.C. until the overthrow of Tarquin the Proud and the establishment of the Republic in 509 B.C. Romulus as the founder of the city and the first king is the most famous of the seven. Numa Pompilius is usually listed as the next most significant since he established many legal and religious practices which lasted into historical times.

During the reign of the third king, Tullus Hostilius, a war began between Rome and Alba Longa. It was decided that, instead of the two armies battling each other, victory would be awarded on the basis of a fight between triplet brothers from each side: three Curiatians from Alba Longa, and three Horatians from Rome. The troops from both cities lined up as spectators and the deadly contest began.

As the struggle developed, two Horatians were killed, and the three Curiatians were each wounded. It was three to one; victory seemed certain for Alba Longa. Suddenly, Publius Horatius, the one Roman survivor, ran away! Unbelievable disgrace! He was pursued by the three Curiatians at various speeds because of their different injuries. Now, just as suddenly as he had turned to run, Horatius turned to attack, and, since his three opponents were separated, he was able to fight and defeat them one at a time. Horatius won the battle and the Romans won the war. The simple story reveals a military strategy basic to a people who were often outnumbered in the battles they fought: divide and conquer!

As Horatius marched back to Rome to the applause of his countrymen, he saw his sister sitting by the side of the road sobbing.
"You mourn for your dead brothers," he said.
"Yes," she answered, "and for the Curiatians too. I was engaged to one of them."
"What?" he shouted in disbelief. "Weep for an enemy of our country? Let this be a lesson to those who show grief for the opponents of Rome!" And he drew his sword and killed her.

The overthrow of the kings

The most infamous of the kings was the last: Tarquin the Proud. He had obtained the throne by killing the previous ruler, Servius Tullius, his father-in-law. The tyrant's power lasted for twenty-five years before he was overthrown in a revolt led by Lucius Junius Brutus.

The immediate cause of the rebellion was the rape of Lucretia, a virtuous Roman wife, by Tarquin the Younger, the son of the king, and a notorious womanizer. After her rape at sword-point, Lucretia summoned her husband, Collatinus, from a nearby seige, told him what had happened, made him vow to avenge her, and then, to the astonishment of all present, killed herself. Brutus, a friend of Collatinus, undertook the challenge, and many Romans, weary of the tyranny of the king, joined him. The civil war was successful; Tarquin the Younger was killed and his father exiled. Rome then became a republic and was ruled by various elected officials and a senate down to the time of Julius Caesar.

The Roman Republic: 509 B.C. - 27 B.C.

For various reasons the republic slowly collapsed, and the Romans returned to a form of autocratic rule.

The Roman Empire: 27 B.C. - A.D. 476

The year 476 is the traditional date chosen to represent the long process of the collapse of Rome and the disintegration of ancient civilization.

Roman gods

Latin literature developed much later than did that of the Greeks. By the time the Romans began to write about their own gods, the influence of Greek literature upon their culture was very strong. By about 200 B.C. most Roman gods and their myths had been identified with those of the Greeks.

The following were gods especially important to the Romans.

Roman	Greek	Function
Jupiter	Zeus	chief god
Juno	Hera	queen of gods, goddess of women
Minerva	Athena	goddess of war and intellect

The above three gods shared the temple of Jupiter on the Capitoline Hill in the center of Rome and were important in many civic and religious functions.

Vesta	Hestia	goddess of the hearth and home

The worship of Vesta by the Vestal Virgins was an ancient and respected religious devotion in Rome.

Mars	Ares	god of war
Venus	Aphrodite	goddess of love

Mars was the father of Romulus and Remus, the legendary founders of the city, and Venus was the mother of Aeneas who brought the Trojans gods to Italy and began the royal line which led to Romulus and Remus.

Following are some of the other Roman gods.

Roman	Greek	Function
Neptune	Poseidon	god of the sea
Ceres	Demeter	goddess of grain
Diana	Artemis	goddess of nature, of the moon
Vulcan	Hephaestus	god of fire, of craftsmen
Mercury	Hermes	god of commerce
Bacchus	Dionysus	god of wine
Cupid	Eros	god of love

Some Roman gods had no equivalent among the Greeks. Janus, for example, the Roman god of beginnings and endings (January), of gates and doorways, and of bridges, was not found in the Greek pantheon. He is portrayed as having two faces: one looking forward, and the other to the rear. His temple in the Forum was used to indicate whether Rome was at war or at peace. If the door of his temple was open, then somewhere in the vast empire Roman legions were fighting; if the door was closed, then tranquillity prevailed everywhere.

Some Greek gods had no equivalent among the Romans. Apollo, for example, was simply transferred into the Roman pantheon with his Greek name.

Sources

There are many sources for the early history of Rome and for their gods, but the most important are Livy, Plutarch, and Vergil. Other writers who are useful are: Ovid, Ennius, Varro, Lucan, Statius, Valerius Maximus, and Pliny the Elder.

Questions

1. List all of the dangers and violent actions which are present in the Roman foundation story. Why do you think these events are so prominent in the myth?

2. In what ways can the actions of the Sabine women be contrasted with those of Tarpea? What qualities does each story portray?

3. Show what Roman virtues the story of the three Horatians portrays. How can the second part of the story be explained?

4. Show how women play an important part both in the foundation story and in the overthrow of the kings.

5. Name the gods most important for the Greeks. Are they the same as for the Romans? Indicate similarities and differences.

Appendix I

CHRONOLOGY OF GREECE

The Greeks called their country Hellas and themselves Hellenes. We call the area Greece from the name which the Romans gave to the country (Graecia). Hellas is the chief center of Greek civilization. It is a peninsula located in the southeastern part of Europe which extends into the Mediterranean Sea. Hellas is about the size of the state of Maine with mountains covering about 80% of its area.

Paleolithic	:	Earliest times to 10000 B.C.
Mesolithic	:	10000 - 7000 B.C.
Neolithic	:	7000 - 3000 B.C.
Early Helladic	:	3000 - 2000 B.C.
Middle Helladic	:	2000 - 1600 B.C.
Late Helladic (Mycenaean)	:	1600 - 1100 B.C.
Sub-Mycenaean	:	1100 - 1000 B.C.
Dark Ages	:	1000 - 750 B.C.
Aristocratic rule	:	750 - 500 B.C.
Age of the tyrants	:	600 - 500 B.C.
Classical period	:	480 - 338 B.C.
Hellenistic period	:	338 - 133 B.C.
Roman conquest	:	133 B.C.

CHRONOLOGY OF ROME

Kingdom	:	753 B.C. - 509 B.C.
Republic	:	509 B.C. - 27 B.C.
Empire	:	27 B.C. - A.D. 476

Appendix II

SELECT BIBLIOGRAPHY

1. Primary sources

   A. Greek writers

Aeschylus: **The Plays.** 2 vols. Grene and Lattimore (editors). University of Chicago Press.

Apollonius: **The Voyage of the Argo.** Rieu (trans.). Penguin Books.

Euripides: **The Plays.** 5 vols. Grene and Lattimore (editors). University of Chicago Press.

Great Classical Myths. Godolphin (editor). Modern Library.

Hesiod: **The Theogony** and **The Works and Days.** Lattimore (trans.). The University of Michigan Press.

Homer: **The Iliad.** Fitzgerald (trans.). Anchor Books.

Homer: **The Odyssey.** Fitzgerald (trans.). Anchor Books.

The Homeric Hymns. Boer (trans.). Swallow Press.

Pindar: **The Odes.** Lattimore (trans.). University of Chicago Press.

Plutarch: **Lives of the Noble Greeks.** Dryden (trans.). Dell Books.

Plutarch: **Lives of the Noble Romans.** Dryden (trans.). Dell Books.

Sophocles: **The Plays.** Grene and Lattimore (editors). University of Chicago Press.

   B. Roman writers

Apuleius: **The Golden Ass.** Graves (trans.). Pocket Books.

Livy: **The Early History of Rome.** de Selincourt (trans.). Penguin Books.

Ovid: **Metamorphoses.** Humphries (trans.). Indiana University Press.

Seneca: **Four Tragedies.** Watling (trans.). Penguin Books.

Vergil: **The Aeneid.** Fitzgerald (trans.). Random House.

2. Secondary sources

Bowra, C.M.: **The Greek Experience.** Mentor Books.

Bulfinch, T.: **Mythology.** Modern Library.

Campbell, J.: **The Hero with a Thousand Faces.** Meridian Books.

Grant, M.: **Myths of the Greeks and Romans.** Mentor Books.

Graves, R.: **The Greek Myths.** 2 vols. Penguin Books.

Hamilton, E.: **Mythology.** Mentor Books.

Jung, C.: **Man and his Symbols.** Dell Books.

Kirk, G.: **Myth: Its Meaning and Functions.** University of California Press.

Kirk, G.: **The Nature of Greek Myths.** Penguin Books.

Kirkwood, G.: **A Short Guide to Classical Mythology.** Holt, Rinehart and Winston.

Mayerson, P.: **Classical Mythology in Literature, Art and Music.** Xerox College Publishing.

Morphord, M. and Lenardon, R.: **Classical Mythology.** Longman.

New Larousse Encyclopedia of Mythology. Hamlyn Publishing Group.

Reinhold, M.: **Past and Present: The Continuity of Classical Myth.** A. M. Hakkert Ltd.

Rose, H.: **A Handbook of Greek Mythology.** Methuen and Co.

Sebeok, T. (editor): **Myth, A Symposium.** Indiana University Press.

Tripp, E.: **The Meridian Handbook of Classical Mythology.** New American Library.

SELECTIVE INDEX OF NAMES

Achelous, 124,125

Achilles, 78,141,148,169,170, 178,180,183-192,194,195,197, 199,200,210

Acrisius, 104,105,108

Actaeon, 54,56,57,142

Admetus, 148,156,161,162

Aeetes, 146,147,150,151,155

Aegean Sea, 130, 137

Aegeus, 130-132,135,137,154

Aegisthus, 170,172,185,198-200

Aeneas, 78,84,102,178,179,208-212

Aeson, 146,147

Aethra, 130,131

Agamemnon, 170,172-174,182, 184-187,189,190,192,195-200, 207,210

Agave, 141,142

Ajax, 148,169,170,189-191,195, 197

Alcaeus, 115,116

Alcestis, 156,161,162

Alcinous, 153,205

Alcmene, 116,117

Aloads, 27,30,34,43,45,47

Althea, 156,158

Amazons, 72,110,112,113,122, 137,150,176

Amor, 38,76

Amphitrite, 45-47

Amphitryon, 116-118,127,139

Amycus, 146,149

Anchises, 75,77,102,208,210, 211

Androgeus, 134,135

Andromache, 177,178,196,210

Andromeda, 104,107,108,116

Antaeus, 43,46,47,123,132

Antigone, 140,143-145

Antiope, 137,138

Aphrodite, 38,39,54,72,74-78, 81,148,149,159,164,180,181, 198,208,217

Apollo, 31,34,36-38,48,54,55, 58-67,78,81,92,94-96,111, 118,119,122,125,130,140,142, 156,161,177,181,184,189,191, 195,199,209,218

Arachne, 68-70

Ares, 36,38,54,71,72,73,74,75,78, 140,141,147,150,156,217

Argo, 148-154,157,169,196

Argonauts, 124,141,146,148-153, 157,201,210

Argos, 83,99,104,108,144,196

Argus, 38,40-42,148

Ariadne, 89,93,95,134,136,138, 139,155

Arion, 45,47,51,53

Artemis, 36,38,54-58,75,78,120, 138,142,157,161,184,187,198, 218

Asclepius, 58,64-67,161

Asphodel, 83,85,86,88,96

Assaracus, 175,176,208

Astyanax, 177,195

Atalanta, 75,156-159

Athena, 34,36,38,43-47,54,68-70, 78,79,105,106,108,111,112,121, 128,129,140,141,148,176,180, 181,189,192,193,197,217

Athens, 45,51,68,70,95,99,117, 121,128-132,135,137,141

Atlantis, 134,166

Atlas, 27,32,39,81,104,107,123, 175

Atreus, 169,170,172,173,185,199, 200

Aulis, 180,182,184,185,187

Autonoe, 141,142

Bacchae, 90,91,94

Bacchus, 38,89,91,94,218

Baucis, 156,160

Bellerophon, 69,110-114,139,154, 155

Black Sea, 122,146,148-150,160, 167

Cadmus, 69,72,91,140-142,145,146, 151,175,180

Caenus, 156,162

Calchas, 184,189,193

Callisto, 54,56,57

Calydonian Boar, 156-158,169,174

Calypso, 102,201,204,207

Carthage, 208,210,211

Cassandra, 58,61,67,175,177-
179,181,186,195,198,199
Castalia, 58,59,62,67
Castor, 148,157,173-175
Cecrops, 128,129
Centaurs, 39,42,90,94,127,137
Centaurus, 41,42
Cephalus, 117,156,163
Cerberus, 21,26,83,85,88,96,
124,138
Ceres, 38,50,218
Chaos, 18,20
Charon, 83-85,88,96
Charybdis, 43,46,47,146,152,
201,204
Chimaera, 22,26,110-112
Chiron, 41,65,90,120,123,147,
183
Circe, 146,152,201,203,204,
206,207
Clytemnestra, 170,172-174,185,
198-200
Coeus, 19,36,54
Colchis, 99,141,146-148,150,
157
Corinth, 99,110-112,131,143,
146,154
Coronis, 65,67
Creon, 117,118,140,144,145,154
Crete, 24,85,93,99,121,130,
132-136,146,153,163,167,181,
182,196,197,208,209
Creusa, 144,154,175,178,208,
212
Cronus, 17,19,20,23-27,30,31,
33,43,48,50,54,59,74,83
Cumae, 61,208,211
Cupid, 38,72,74,76,77,82,218
Cyclopes, 18,19,25,46,208,210
Cyprus, 74,159,170,197
Cyzicus, 146,149

Daedalus, 134-137
Danae, 104,105,107,116
Danaids, 86,88
Daphne, 58,62,67
Dardanus, 175,208
Deianira, 124-126
Deiphobus, 175,178,198
Delos, 54,58,208,209

Delphi, 24,34,58-62,66,94,95,118,
125,127,130,135,137,138,140,
143,199
Demeter,24,33-35,38,43,45,50-54,
72,78,89,171,218
Deucalion, 29,160
Diana, 38,55,218
Dictys, 105,108
Dido, 210,211
Diomedes, 71,121,161,189,192,195,
196
Dionysus, 34,38,39,41,75,89-95,
97,136,141,142,218
Doliones, 146,149
Doris, 20,44

Echo, 156,163
Eileithyia, 36,55
Electra, 20,21,170,175,199
Electryon, 116,117
Eleusinian Mysteries, 50-53
Eleusis, 51,52,169
Elysium, 83,85-88,97,102,141
Endymion, 54,57
Eos, 22,26,163,175,176
Epidaurus, 65,67
Epigoni, 140,145,196
Epimetheus, 27-29
Erechtheus, 129,163
Eros, 18,25,38,72,74-77,218
Eteocles, 143,144
Europa, 134,140,153
Eurydice, 96-98
Eurynome, 33,35
Eurystheus, 116,118-120,124
Eurytus, 125,126

Fates, 35,37,156,158
Faunus, 39,82
Furies, 20,25,63,199

Ganymede, 175,176,178
Gea, 18-21,23-25,30,34,39,44,50,
59,128,129
Giants, 20,27,30,32,34,124
Gigantomachy, 30,32
Golden Fleece, 75,147,154,174
Gorgon(s),21,26,46,105,106
Graces, 35,37,38
Gray Ones, 21,26,104,106

Hades, 24,33,37,39,43,50,51,
    53,54,83-85,87,88,96,98,106,
    124,128
Harmonia, 72,141,180
Harpies, 20,21,26,150,208,210
Hebe, 36,38,126
Hecate, 55,57
Hector, 175,177-179,182,188,
    190,191,195,196,209,210
Hecuba, 175,177-179,182,188,
    190,191,195,196,209,210
Helen, 137,170,172-174,177,
    178,180-183,186,196,198-200
Helenus, 175,178,181,192,196,
    210
Helios, 22,26,50,62,63,72,78,
    122,134,146,203
Helle, 141, 146
Hellespont, 141,146,149,164
Hephaestus, 34,36-38,54,72-74,
    78,79,128,131,190,218
Hera, 24,33,36-43,55,71,78,86,
    91,92,94,115,117-119,122,
    126,127,141,145,147,151,152,
    163,169,180,181,209,217
Heracles, 21,22,29,30,41,46,
    69,71,102,108,115-127,131,
    132,136-139,146,148,149,155,
    156,161,162,169,176-179,184-
    186,192
Heraclidae, 115,126
Hermaphrodite, 74,80,81
Hermes, 38-42,54,63,74,80-84,
    87,106,160,171,181,218
Hermione, 170,199
Hero, 156,164,165
Hesione, 122,176,178,197
Hestia, 24,38,39,48,49,93,217
Hippodamia, 171,173
Hippolytus, 75,137-139,161
Hippomenes, 156,158,159
Hundred-handed Ones, 18,19,25
Hydra, 21,22,26,119
Hylas, 124,146,149
Hyllus, 125,126
Hyperion, 19,22,26,62,201,204

Iapetus, 19,27
Idomenus, 195-197
Ilus, 175,176,208

Ino, 92,141,146
Io, 38,40-42
Iobates, 111-113
Iolaus, 116,119
Iolcus, 146,147,153
Iole, 115,125,126
Iphicles, 116,117,119
Iphigenia, 170,185,198
Iris, 20,21,26,38
Ithaca, 168,201,203-206
Iulus, 208,209,212
Ixion, 38,41,42,86,88

Jason, 21,69,75,124,141,146-155,
    157,174,201
Jocasta, 142-144
Juno, 38,39,209,211,217
Jupiter, 33,38,71,217

Knossos, 133,135

Laius, 142,143
Laocoon, 192,193
Laomedon, 122,124,169,175-177,
    179,197
Lapiths, 137,162
Latium, 208,211
Leander, 156,164,165
Leda, 149,173
Lemnos, 75,148,186,196
Lethe, 87,88,97
Leto, 33,36,37,54,55,58,86,142
Lycia, 111,112

Maenads, 90,91,97
Maia, 39,81
Marathon, 121,132,138
Mars, 38,71,73,213,215,217
Marsyas, 58,64,67
Medea, 75,132,146,147,151-155
Medusa, 21,43,46,47,104-108,111
Megara, 118,129,135
Meleager, 124,148,156-158
Menelaus, 170,172,174,177,178,
    181,182,185,186,189,192,195,
    196,198-200
Mercury, 38,80,218
Metis, 33,34,37,68,70
Midas, 58,64,89,92,95
Minerva, 38,68,217

Minos, 85,93,121,130,134-139,
    146,163
Minotaur, 93,128,132,135,136
Mnemosyne, 19,33,35
Mt. Etna, 30,210
Mt. Olympus, 31-34,38,40,41,
    43,68,72,77,83,84,93,113,
    126,174,176
Mt. Parnassus, 36,59,64
Muses, 35-38,64,97
Mycenae,99,116-118,120,122,
    124,127,133,172,173,182,198,
    199
Myrmidons, 169,170,184
Myrtilus, 171-173
Mystery Religions, 50,52,53

Naiads, 38,44
Narcissus, 156,163
Naxos, 93,136
Nemean Lion, 22,119
Neoptolemus, 170,178,184,186,
    192,193,195,196,199,210
Neptune, 38,43,218
Nereids, 20,26,38,44,45,47,
    107,152,180
Nereus, 20,38,44,47,152
Nessus, 125,126
Nestor, 195,196
Niobe, 54,55,57,142,145
Nisus, 129,130,135

Oceanus, 19,20,22,27,34,35,38,
    44,47,74
Odysseus, 46,81,102,146,168,
    170,182-184,186,189,191-193,
    197,198,201-207,210,212
Oedipus, 22,102,140,142-145,
    196
Oenomaus, 171,173
Olympians, 32,33,38,39,42,50,
    54,124
Olympic Games, 62,121
Omphale, 126,137
Orestes, 58,63,67,170,196,199,
    200,210
Orion, 54,56,57
Orpheus, 96,97,102,148,152
Orphism, 96-98

Palamedes, 180,183
Pan, 39,58,64,67,80,82,92
Panathenaic Festival, 68,69
Pandion, 129,130
Pandora, 27-29,32
Paris, 75,175,177-182,186,191,
    192,198,209
Parthenon, 68-70
Pasiphae, 134,135,146
Patroclus, 184,188-191,194
Pegasus, 106,110-113
Peleus, 141,148,157,169,170,180,
    183
Pelias, 146,147,153-155
Peloponnesus, 119,130,153,157
Pelops, 170-173,178,192
Penelope, 183,201,204-206
Pentheus, 89,93,95,142
Persephone,34,35,37,39,50-53,72,
    84,85,96,124,138,171
Perseus, 69,104-108,113,116-118
Phaeacians, 153,205
Phaedra, 134,138,139
Phaethon, 62,63,67
Philemon, 156,160
Philoctetes, 178,180,185-187,192,
    195,196
Phineus, 107,146,150,210
Phoebe, 19,36,54,59
Phrixus, 141,146,147,150
Pirithous, 124,137,138,162
Pittheus, 130,137
Pleiades, 56,57
Pluto, 39,83
Pollux, 174,175
Polydectes, 105-108
Polydeuces, 148,149,157,173,174
Polydorus, 141,142
Polyneices, 143,144,196
Polyphemus, 43,46,47
Pontus, 18,20,38,44
Poseidon, 24,30,33,37,38,43-48,
    51,68,70,75,83,105,107,110,113,
    121-123,128-130,132,134,135,
    138,139,147,149,153,156,162,
    197,202,205,218
Priam, 169,175-179,181,182,186,
    190,191,193,195,196,199,209,
    210

Procris, 156,163
Prometheus, 27-29,32,34,78,
    120,123,180
Proserpina, 35,39,50
Proteus, 38,44,45,47,198
Psyche, 74,76,77
Pygmalion, 75,156,159,160
Pylos, 99,196
Pyramus, 156,165
Pyrrha, 29,160
Pythia, 59,60,66,126
Pythian Games, 58,62,64,67

Remus, 71,213,214,217
Rhea, 19,23,24,26,36,39,43,
    48,50,59,83
Rome, 49,66,71,73,75,123,152,
    211,213-218
Romulus, 71,102,213-215,217

Salamis, 169,170,197
Satyrs, 39,90,94
Scorpio, 56,57
Scylla, 43,46,47,130,139,146,
    152,201,204
Scyros, 138,183,184,192
Seasons, 34,37,38
Selene, 22,26,55,57
Semele, 91,92,94,141
Seriphus, 105,107,108
Sibyl, 58,60,61,66,84
Sibylline Books, 61,66
Sileni, 90,94
Silenus, 90,92,94
Sinon, 192-194
Sirens, 146,152,201,204,207
Sisyphus, 86,88,110
Solymi, 110,112
Sparta, 99,137,172,173,177,
    181,182,198,199
Sphinx, 22,26,143
Styx, 83-85,87,96,183
Sunium, 43,46,137
Symplegades, 146,150

Talos, 146,153
Tantalus, 86,142,170-172
Tarquin, 61,215,216
Tartarus, 18,21,25,30,41,43,
    83,85-88,96

Telamon, 148,157,169,170,176,197
Telemachus, 183,201,204-206
Teucer, 169,170,176,195,197
Thanatos, 83,84,87,88
Thebes, 56,72,89,91,93,99,116-
    118,127,140-146,151,178,196,203
Themis, 19,33,34,37,59
Thera, 133,134
Theseus, 93,121,124,128,130-132,
    134-139,141,144,154,155,157,
    161,174
Thetis, 141,152,170,180,183,186,
    187,190,196
Thisbe, 156,165
Thyestes, 170,172,173
Tiresias, 140,144,145,203
Tiryns, 99,108,111,125,127
Titanomachy, 17,25-27,30,33,43,
    44
Titans, 18,19,23,25,27,34,35,44,
    86
Tithonus, 175,176,179
Tityus, 54,57,86,88
Triptolemus, 52,53
Triton, 38,45,47,82,153
Troezen, 130,132
Trojan War, 71,75,81,148,167-
    169,173,177,212
Tros, 175,176,179
Troy, 61,75,99,122,148,166-169,
    172,175-178,180-186,188,191-
    201,203,208,209,211
Tyndareus, 169,173,174,182,183,
    186
Typhon, 21,27,30,32,34

Underworld, 41,50,54,80,83-88,
    97,102,110,124,134,138,144,171,
    174,211
Uranus, 17-20,23,25,30,31,34,39,
    44,74

Venus, 38,74,77,208,209,217
Vesta, 38,43,48,49,217
Vestal Virgins, 48,49,217
Vulcan, 38,78,123,218

Zeus, 23-45,50,51,53,54,56-59,
68,70,71,74,77-81,83,86,91,
92,104,105,107,111,113,116,
117,120,123-125,134,141,142,
145,147,149-151,153,154,160,
161,163,169,171,173-176,180,
182,185,195,209,217